THE UNGRATEFUL REFUGEE

This Large Print Book carries the
Seal of Approval of N.A.V.H.

THE UNGRATEFUL REFUGEE

WHAT IMMIGRANTS NEVER TELL YOU

DINA NAYERI

THORNDIKE PRESS
A part of Gale, a Cengage Company

LIBRARY OF CONGRESS CIP DATA ON FILE.
CATALOGUING IN PUBLICATION FOR THIS BOOK
IS AVAILABLE FROM THE LIBRARY OF CONGRESS

ISBN-13: 978-1-4328-7316-5 (hardcover alk. paper)

Published in 2020 by arrangement with Catapult, LLC

Printed in Mexico
Print Number: 01   Print Year: 2020

For Sam and Elena.
You make every country home.

Why did you lie to me?
I always thought I told the truth.
Why did you lie to me?
Because the truth lies like nothing else
and I love the truth.
— MARK STRAND,
"Elegy for My Father"

No way. You will not make the Netherlands home.

— GEERT WILDERS,
message to refugees, 2015

To make someone wait: the constant prerogative of all power, "age-old pastime of humanity."

— ROLAND BARTHES

■ ■ ■ ■

PART ONE:
ESCAPE

■ ■ ■ ■

(on good faith, credible risk,
and opportunism)

I

We became refugees. Somehow it felt more settled than what we had been for the past ten months, hiding out in the United Arab Emirates. There, we were illegal: all the same dizzying displacement, uncertainty, and need, but we had to find our own shelter. Without a state to say, "Yes, we will be responsible for you," we were so unmoored it was hard to fathom a next step. Maybe that's why every move had been last minute, someone's kindness or a stroke of luck. Miracles. And so, when we landed in Rome in winter 1989, I bubbled with love for Italy and every Italian; it was unlike anything I had felt for Dubai or Sharjah. This airport was so European, so brimming with leisure; I wanted to run to every kiosk and smell the Western chocolate and touch the expensive fabrics. But a man in a black suit held a sign with Maman's name, and

11

we were led away to a car.

My mother, younger brother, and I bundled in the backseat, cold, and dirty from the long flight. I tried to stay awake for the ride through the Italian countryside. Finally, after an hour, we spotted a house on a hill, breaking up the rolling valleys in the distance. We had been told that we'd be taken to "a good refugee camp," a temporary safe space for transients seeking asylum outside Italy. It was called Barba, and it had once been a hotel. The Italian government had leased this building to house the likes of us, political and religious asylum seekers and passers-through with particular need: elderly family, children. It was exciting to watch Barba appear, and to know that, even though our clothes and bedding and daily routines would be those of refugees, though we would be confined there, our house would be on a hilltop, in the husk of a pretty hotel.

We pulled up a winding hill road after dinnertime. Our room was small, perhaps even smaller than the cockroach hostel in Sharjah, and we had no fridge or hot plate this time. Only a bathroom and a bed. We sat on our bed and wondered where we'd get money, if we'd find friends among our neighbors. Would we meet Farsi speakers?

How long would we stay? Which country would finally take us? We wondered about that night's meal.

We considered walking to a store in Mentana. Then someone knocked. An Italian woman, young, with a punkish haircut gestured to us that we had missed the dinner call. That night, for the first time, I saw the canteen, a glass circle overlooking all that lush valley. Now empty and dark, in the morning it would fill up with displaced families like us, Iranians, Afghans, Russians, Romanians. It would buzz with many languages, many kinds of prayers. There would be children, mothers, grandmothers. But for now, the room was silent. We ate bowls of leftover pasta in semidark and heavy silence, and thanked God that meals were provided here.

Despite its grand skeleton, Hotel Barba was a refugee camp and we had to stay put, as we had no status in Italy. We were served soup, pasta, coffee, bread at precise times each day, and we sat in the winter chill, praying that by summer we'd be gone from there. Every day when the postman arrived, we would swell outside the mail cubbies, jostling for a good view. We wanted to know, "Who got his letter today?" When someone did, the crowd would hush as he opened the envelope, fingers trembling, eyes scanning, then either wept quietly into his palm, muttering curses, or loudly on his knees, thanking his god. Everyone was frantic for a letter from America or England or Australia or Canada (roomy anglophone countries). A letter would mean the wait was over; our lives could now begin.

In the absence of work or school, all we did was dream, a maddening state, and battle loneliness. We ate with people from our own countries; we prayed in our own ways, some before eating (sitting, heads bowed), and some after (standing, holding hands). On cool days, the children snuck into a neighboring orchard to steal unripe peaches and plums, because our tongues were itching for something sour, and there was nothing else to soothe the craving. I tried to teach some English words to a handful of burly Russian men, skipping around the yard in my pink skirt and pointing to a tree, a fence, a chador, a babushka (the men indulged me by taking notes).

We fought boredom in increasingly desperate ways: an Afghan grandmother collected bricks from a nearby construction site and carried them back to her room under her chador. Her daughter read our fortunes from the leftover sludge in mugs of

14

instant coffee. A young Iranian soldier with his face half-bleached from a wartime chemical burn taught us how to play soccer. Despite his new kind of whiteness, he was as interesting to me as princes in my storybooks. Perhaps I sensed that he was attracted to Maman. And wasn't she just *me,* in another body? Here was a man who wanted *us,* who wanted to play games with me, to make me laugh, and then to look out of the corner of his eye to see if Maman was watching.

We had left Baba behind in Isfahan. I began to understand, bit by bit, over years, that I would never live with my father again. I was beginning to understand other things, too, to peek out from inside my own skin. I spent time with loving grandmothers from many countries. I joined Maman for tea and oranges in the rooms of Russian Christians. I read English books and played hopscotch and became obsessed with having a home again, with ending the wander days, rooting, and with the mysteries of adulthood. I craved everyone's stories — I was becoming some later version of myself.

In a refugee camp, stories are everything. Everyone has one, having just slipped out from the grip of a nightmare. Everyone is idle, without permission to work or run away, reckoning now with a new place in the world. Everyone is a stranger, in need of introduction. And tea is cheap (at Barba, we all came from tea-drinking countries). What better conditions than these to brew a pot, sit on pillows around a low table, and talk? At Barba, I learned to listen, and to savor startling details, byproducts of a strange confluence that may never recur: a grandmother hiding bricks in her chador, a splash of cream across a handsome face, a stampede for jam.

It wasn't just a pastime. Our stories were drumming with power. Other people's memories transported us out of our places of exile, to rich, vibrant lands, and to home. They reminded us of the long, unknowable road. We couldn't see yet, fresh from our escape, but *other* sharp turns lay ahead. We had created our life's great story; next would come the waiting time, camp, where we would tell it. Then struggle for asylum, when we would craft it. Then assimilation into new lives, when we would perform it for the entertainment of the native-born, and finally, maybe in our old age, we would return to it, face it without frenzy: a repatriation.

For two decades, our escape defined me. It dominated my personality and compelled

16

my every decision. By college, half my life had led up to our escape and the other half was spent reliving it, in churches and retreats where my mother made it a hagiographic journey, on college applications where it was a plea, at sleepovers where it was entertainment, and in discussion groups after public viewings of xenophobic melodramas like *China Cry* and *Not Without My Daughter,* films about Christian women facing death and escaping to America. Our story was a sacred thread woven into my identity. Sometimes people asked, *But don't a lot of Christians live there?* or *Couldn't your mother just say she was Muslim?* It would take me a long time to get over those kinds of questions. They felt like a bad grade, like a criticism of my face and body, an unraveling of that sacred thread: *I am rescued cargo; therefore, I am enchanted. I have purpose. With every good work, I repay the universe.* If I didn't have that, then I would be faceless, an ordinary person toiling for what? Soulless middle-class trifles?

Once in an Oklahoma church, a woman said, "Well, I sure do get it. You came for a better life." I thought I'd pass out — a better life? In Isfahan, we had yellow spray roses, a pool. A glass enclosure shot up

17

through our living room, and inside that was a tree. I had *a tree* inside my house; I had the papery hands of Morvarid, my friend and nanny, a ninety-year-old village woman; I had my grandmother's fruit leather and Hotel Koorosh schnitzels and sour cherries and orchards and a farm — life in Iran was a fairytale. In Oklahoma, we lived in an apartment complex for the destitute and disenfranchised. Life was a big gray parking lot with cigarette butts baking in oil puddles, slick children idling in the beating sun, teachers who couldn't do math. I dedicated my youth and every ounce of my magic to get out of there. A better life? The words lodged in my ear like grit.

Gradually, all those retellings felt like pandering. The skeptics drew their conclusions based on details that I had provided them: my childhood dreams of Kit Kats and flawless bananas. My academic ambitions. I thought of how my first retelling was in an asylum office in Italy: how merciless that with the sweat and dust of escape still on our brows, we had to turn our ordeal into a good, persuasive story or risk being sent back. Then, after asylum was secured, we had to relive that story again and again, to earn our place, to calm casual skeptics.

18

Every day of her new life, the refugee is asked to differentiate herself from the opportunist, the *economic* migrant.

Like most refugees, after a life-threatening escape, my family and I were compliant, ecstatic, grateful. But we had sustained damage. If the rational mind is a clean road, ours had potholes, pockets of paranoia and fear. Yes, I could summon joy and logic and change. But a single triggering word could trip me up for a day, a week, make me doubt my worth, my new place in this world. Am I a *real* refugee? The implication burned.

Why do the native-born perpetuate this distinction? Why harm the vulnerable with the threat of this stigma? It took me decades to know: the instinct to protect against competition from a talented horde. To draw a line around a birthright, a privilege. Unlike economic migrants, refugees have no agency; they are no threat. Often, they are so broken, they beg to be remade into the image of the native. As recipients of magnanimity, they can be pitied. I was a palatable immigrant because I programmed myself with chants: *I am rescued cargo. I will prove, repay, transform.* But if you are born in the Third World, and you dare to make a move before you are shattered, your dreams are suspicious. You are a carpetbagger, an opportunist, a thief. You are reaching above your station.

There's something unnatural and sinister going on here.

My mother didn't think to question people's hardwired distinctions. Were we really refugees? She fended off that question by telling our story: she was almost murdered by the regime, so she shouldn't have to deal with people's prejudices. She fumed at stories of religious asylum seekers who had lied, and she asked new arrivals about the Bible and their underground church — but unlike the native-born around us, she never asked anyone to prove their fear. A tortured mind, terror of a wasted future, is what enables you to abandon home; it's a prerequisite for stepping into a dinghy, for braving militarized mountains. No one who has lived under a dictatorship, who has scooped up their children and run to a bomb shelter, doubts the fear. To my mother, Christianity is too sacred to lie about, and it's hard to accept that a rigid, illogical system leaves some no other choice, but, at the same time, she knows that the reasons for escape are complex and muddled. They always include a fear *and* a tangible hope. It's a reinvention that grows out of your nightmares, but also your drive and agency. And so, the

20

bureaucratic parsing of dangers from opportunity is grating and absurd. Where is the humility? The compassion?

And what is a credible danger in a country that hangs apostates and homosexuals and adulterers, and where a hateful finger in your direction is enough to make you one? A country so corrupt that one mullah's whim can send you to the firing squad or the crane, your gallows, and the sunrise after challenging a *pasdar* can find you framed for drugs? A country where record keeping is a farce, where in whispers the land's riches are divided among a few, where young men languish without work, where young women wither with unspent ambition and desire, where the enchanting whisper of opium is always in your ear, and despair fills your lungs so thickly that your best chance is to be your own executioner?

What is escape in such circumstances, and what is just opportunistic migration? Who is a true refugee? It makes me chuckle, this notion that "refugee" is a sacred category, a people hallowed by evading hell. Thus, they can't acknowledge a shred of joy left behind or they risk becoming migrants again. Modern Iran is a country of refugees making do with small joys, exiled from the prerevolutionary paradise we knew. With the

Iraq war over, their plight is often considered insufficient. Syria is hell. Afghanistan, South Sudan, Eritrea are hell. Iraq is . . . a bit less so? And Iran? What is hell enough for the West to feel responsible, not just as perpetrators of much of the madness, but as primary beneficiaries of the planet's bounty, who sit behind screens watching, suspicious and limp-fisted, as strangers suffer?

Meanwhile, we assign our least talented, most cynical bureaucrats to be the arbiters of complicated truth, not instructing them to save lives, or search out the weary and the hopeless, but to root out lies, to protect our fat entitlements, our space, at any moral cost — it is a failure of duty. More infuriating is the word "opportunism," a lie created by the privileged to shame suffering strangers who crave a small taste of a decent life. The same hopes in their own children would be labeled "motivation" and "drive."

And while we grumble over what we are owed and how much we get to keep, the displaced wait at the door. They are painters and surgeons and craftsmen and students. Children. Mothers. The neighbor who made the good sauce. The funny girl from science class. The boy who can really dance. The great-uncle who always turns down the wrong street. They endure painful transformation, rising from death, discarding their faces and bodies, their identities, without guarantee of new ones.

A Dutch officer asks an Iranian refugee, "Do you fear for your safety?"

He says, "Yes, my two friends and I were arrested as communists twenty years ago. Each week we check into the local police headquarters. Last week, both my friends disappeared after their check. I ran."

"Have you become involved with underground communists again?"

"No," says the petitioner. He isn't a dissident. But he *is* hunted.

"Then you're safe," says the officer. "It seems your friends resumed their political activities. But you didn't, so you have no reason to fear."

The assumption of the office isn't just thoroughness and justice on the part of the Iranian government (laughable), but also infallibility. How is one to honestly navigate such a dishonest, self-serving system? The savvy ones who have asked around know not to explain how the Islamic Republic works, how often innocent people disappear. They simply say, "Yes, I got involved again," so that the officer can check a box.

Escape marks the first day of a refugee's

life. On the day we left home, I was told that I could live however I wished, that my gender would no longer limit my potential. And this was true. I was born out of Maman's Three Miracles. But already a limit had been imposed. Until now, the world waited for me to define myself. Would I be artistic or analytical? Shy or bold? Religious or secular? But now, my first category had been assigned: refugee, not native-born. I didn't realize it then, because escape is euphoric. It is a plunge into fog, a burning of an old life, a murder of a previous self.

Escape creates a chameleon, an alert creature always in disguise. What does that first blush feel like? An itch. For me, it was a daily, unrelenting discomfort in my mind and skin. It inflamed my OCD. I developed a tic in my neck. Changing color soothed those pains for a time.

Now, thirty years have passed; I have so much to say. The world no longer speaks of refugees as it did in my time. The talk has grown hostile, even unhinged, and I have a hard time spotting, amid the angry hordes, the kind souls we knew, the Americans and the English and the Italians who helped us, who held our hands. I know they're still out there.

What has changed in three decades? A reframing is in order. I want to make sense of the world's reaction to us, of a political and historical crisis that our misfortunes have caused. I feel a duty: I've lived as an American for years, read Western books. I've been both Muslim and Christian. There are secrets I can show the native-born that new arrivals don't dare reveal. I've wished to say them for thirty years and found it terrifying till now.

In 2016, I began a journey to understand my own chaotic past. I was a new mother and confused about my purpose. I had changed my face and hair, my friends, my education, my country and job, so often that my skin felt raw. My memories had grown foggy, and I had combed them ragged for fiction. I had prided myself on being a chameleon, as many immigrant children do, but now I felt muddied by it — I felt like a liar.

I spent months traveling. I went to refugee camps in Greece, to communities of undocumented Dutch. I visited immigration lawyers and homes of new arrivals. I drank tea with refugees and asylum seekers and naturalized citizens. I spoke with mothers, lone travelers, schoolchildren. I was looking for stories, for whispers of stories hidden by shame or trauma, and for lies too. I searched for people from my own refugee hostel, Hotel Barba. I spoke to my parents, who reminded me of the many complications of point of view. During my travels, I came across dozens of stories; I have chosen a few to follow in these pages, tales all the more harrowing because they are commonplace now and, in the asylum office, often disbelieved.

And so, I've left out the story of the Syrian man I met in Berlin who floated with a child for seven hours then found himself cleaning a slave ship, or the jailed scholars or activists who are hit with public fatwas — even your everyday Trumpian admits that those guys deserve rescue. I'm interested in doubt, in the feared "swarms." These are stories of uprooting and transformation without guarantees, of remaking the face and the body, those first murderous refugee steps — the annihilation of the self, then an ascent from the grave. Though their first lives were starkly different, these men and women were tossed onto the same road and judged together. Some of their stories are far from over, but they have already repeated them so often, practiced and recited them so much, that these dramatic few months (or years) have become their entire identity. Nothing else matters to their liteners, and all suffering seems petty after the miracle of escape. But did the miracle happen? Now their struggle isn't to hang on to life, but to preserve their history, to rescue that life from the fiction pile.

Though the truth of these stories struck me hard, I know that I, a writer, was peeking in different corners than the authorities. I wasn't looking for discrepancies. I abhor cynical traps that favor better translators and catch out trauma victims for their memory lapses. I don't have accent-verifying software. I saw the truth of these stories in corroborating scars, in distinct lenses on a single event, one seeing the back as vividly as another sees the front — no flat cutouts. I saw truth in grieving, fearful eyes, in shaking hands, in the anxiety of children and the sorrow of the elderly.

And yet, to re-create these stories, I was forced to invent scenes and dialogue, like retouching a faded photograph. Writers and refugees often find themselves imagining their way to the truth. What choice is there? A reader, like an interviewer, wants specific itches scratched. You will see.

In the meantime, where is the lie? Every crisis of history begins with one story, the first drop in a gushing river. Consume these lives as entertainment, or education, or threats to your person. It is your choice how to hear their voices. Use all that you know to spot every false stroke of the brush. Be the asylum officer. Or, if you prefer, read as you would a box of letters from a ruin, dispatches from another time that we dust off and readily believe, because the dead want nothing from us.

II / DARIUS

Darius took a last drag from his cigarette and stamped it out on the tiles outside the tea shop. "Has she texted today?" his friend asked.

"No," said Darius. They were standing under Isfahan's famous Thirty-Three Arches after an evening coffee and water pipe. "Let's hope this means . . ."

"Yes," said his friend. "A shame though. Such a piece."

Darius chuckled and said goodbye. On the way home, his pocket vibrated. Nowadays, each text sent an icy rivulet down his back. He glanced at his phone. It was her. *Dariuuuuuus. What's going on?*

He stopped in the road to reply — quick disavowals. No games. *Please, Miss, stop texting. I've had so much trouble.*

She wrote again: It's fine. I just want to say hello.

Please delete my number. You'll get me killed.

He switched off his cell phone and quickened his pace. It was already past ten. He was three streets from his house, crossing a narrow alley, when they came. "Hey, Seamstress!" a voice called. Darius was a tailor, a good one. He didn't care that they found it low. He was tall and handsome, and he knew how to make clothes that fit. One day he would have a chain of shops. One day he would make beautiful Western suits. Before he could turn, someone had punched him in the side of the neck. Then a baton bludgeoned his leg and he was down, holding his side to stay their kicks.

In the chaos, every detail detached from reality. The world narrowed to a series of sensations, and his aching brain could only make room for snippets: That they were Basijis, the pitiless volunteer militia. That they were four or five young men. That he was so close to home that his parents could probably hear his screams. That one of them said, "Leave Iran or die."

He slept in the alley for an hour after they left. The last thing he heard was a distant echo down the alley, "Don't let us see you again."

Then he went home. The next day, the

doctors stitched his face, arms, and legs. His mother cried in her room. "What a world these young people have inherited," she wailed to his father. "Twenty-three and our boy has known no other life. Remember the days before the revolution? Remember 1978?" Darius was born in 1992. The paradise of old Iran gave him no nostalgia, only curiosity and some pride. Still, he wished for a chance. To make a business, a life, a family. He wanted to tell that girl that he liked her company, though he rejected her two or three times a week. He wanted to take her for coffee, to see the wind tangle her hair, to watch her laugh in a movie theater. Maybe they would fall in love. Maybe they wouldn't. They'd never know, because her parents, both Sepâh, both militant and revolutionary with jobs in the ministry, had found out and decided to kill him.

They had no interest in questioning their daughter, telling her their plans for him, or hearing that she was the aggressor.

In a year, they returned for him. Darius's wounds had healed, but he had scars on his arms and face. He hadn't spoken to the girl again, though she tried. Now he sat at his mother's *sofreh* cloth, eating dinner with his parents. They knocked hard and his father answered. They tore into the house, knocking a vase over and stepping on the *sofreh* with their shoes.

"Have you texted with the young lady again?" one of them barked.

"I swear, only to beg her not to text. I swear. You can look." Darius tried to tell them that she didn't understand; that she felt safe because of her parents and so she thought he was safe too.

"So now it's the young lady's fault?" said the most senior Sepâh. They lifted him off his feet by his shirt and dragged him to their headquarters. He waited for hours. The Sepâh opened the door. He didn't ask questions, just lobbed accusations and waited for a reaction. Darius kept his gaze on the table. "You have disgraced the daughter of Mr. Mahmoodi."

"No, sir. I didn't," he said to the table.

"You are a communist operative."

"No, sir, I'm a tailor. I make shirts."

"You have been drinking."

"No, sir." He was so tired. It didn't matter what he said. A guard entered, whispered with the Sepâh about drug trafficking. They intended for Darius to hear. He wanted to weep — they would never let him go. He would die on a crane, or facing a firing squad, before he turned thirty.

"You've been drinking and you attacked Basiji officers in the street," said the guard. When he shook his head, the Sepâh knocked him in the temple with the butt of a huge rifle. Darius toppled off his chair. He gripped the table leg and pulled his legs into his stomach, like a newborn. Before he lost consciousness, he felt another two blows to his head, then one to his back, just behind his heart. They were striking to kill.

He woke in the hospital with his parents standing over him. His body felt light, his mouth dry. He had been in a coma for three months.

"You can't stay in Iran," said his father. "They'll kill you."

His mother had explained that they had visited the house almost weekly. "Your son is antiregime. He has problems with Islam. He's a drug dealer. An apostate. And underground operative. His blood is halal for us."

It seemed that was all they wanted — to establish that Darius's blood was halal. When his parents went to complain of harassment, every officer said that Darius had attacked Basijis in the street. "If they get you in the street again," said his father, "you'll be dead. Please, I have some money. Take it and get out and live some kind of life. You can make home anywhere if you

32

try. Find happiness away from here."

Darius spent two weeks letting his siblings feed him as he recovered some of the thirty pounds he had lost. He took his pills. Pockets of black formed in his memory. His body was covered in scars now — his arms, face, neck, legs. Every morning his parents begged him to leave.

When asked to describe his journey, Darius forgets things. He recalls details out of order. His head pounds. Once in a halfway house, all his muscles clenched and a tic twisted up half his body for hours. He is a single man; he looks fit and isn't yet so jaded that he can't laugh now and then. But he stumbles into dark patches; he loses details as a liar would. He is rarely believed. "Economic migrant," they call him, seeing only his youth and potential. In newspapers and on his iPhone, Europeans are always debating how much refugees will contribute; they claim to *want* the economically beneficial kind, the "good" immigrants. And yet, they welcome only those with a foot in the grave. Show any agency or savvy or industry *before* you left your home, and you're done. People begin imagining you scheming to get out just to get rich off an idea (or a surgery or an atelier). They consider the surgery or atelier that doesn't yet exist as property stolen from *them.* The minute you arrive, though, even if you *did* have a foot in the grave, god help you if you need social services for a while.

Darius drove to Urmia, an Iranian city near the border with Turkey. From there, with the help of a smuggler, he crossed the mountain on foot. He wore running shoes, and the mountain crossing took him forty-five minutes. Every few steps he thought he felt the gunshot in his leg or back. If he fell, he knew, the smuggler would leave him. "Now you're in Turkey," said the smuggler somewhere on the mountain. "I turn back here. Good luck."

In the Turkish village, he was driven to a mud hut and taken for twice the agreed fee. "Call your family and ask for more," they said. "The journey was more treacherous than expected." He recalled no hardship that hadn't been explained before the trip, but single young men from Iran rarely stir up sympathy — economic migrants, exploiters, opportunists. He paid. He sat in the hut for four days, awaiting the next step, though this one was already disappearing into the dark patches, the spoiled, battered parts of his brain.

The first airboat was too full. Sixty, including many exhausted children watching

Darius with shy eyes. A few meters in, it toppled, releasing its occupants into the Aegean. All luggage washed away. The strong swam back, not daring to imagine what had become of the others, those tired children. Darius ran into the woods, where Turkish officers picked him up and took him to jail.

He wasted away in a Turkish jail cell for two months. He had no papers, gave a false name, and spent his days in a delirium. Trapped in a fever dream, he remembers little — it is so easy to doubt him. He spent that time with his eyes closed. They released him when his brain medicines ran out. Too much trouble. "Get out of Turkey," they said, and he tried to oblige.

On his next try, Darius's boat made it to Lesbos. As joyful men jumped out and began pulling the boat ashore, a voice nearby whispered, "Don't celebrate too soon. This is where the hardship really starts."

"We're in Europe," said Darius, to the dark. "We're on free soil."

"But we're not going into Europe. We're going to Moria."

III

I was born in 1979, a year of revolution, and grew up in wartime. The itch in my brain arrived as war was leaking into our everyday — sirens, rations, adults huddled around radios. It announced itself one lazy afternoon in our house in Isfahan, between the yellow spray roses and the empty swimming pool, whispering that I might take a moment to count my pencils. Then, that night, it grew bolder, suggesting that the weight of the blanket be distributed evenly along my arms. The itch became a part of me, like the freckle above my lip. It wasn't the side effect of *this* blistering morning at the Abu Dhabi United Nations office or *that* aimless month in an Italian resettlement camp. Those days simply made it unbearable.

Even in Ardestoon, my father's village, where I tiptoed with my cousins along a riverbank, picked green plums in leafy orchards, and hiked in mountains, the itch endured. It made me tuck my grandmother's chestnut hair into her chador with the edges of my hands, circling her face and squeezing her cheeks until I was satisfied. It took up space in my personality, as the freckle did above my lip, so that now and then I tried to straighten the papery skin of my ninety-year-old nanny, Morvarid, pressing my palms across her forehead as one would an old letter. I picked everyone's scabs. Zippers had to be forced past the end of the line. Sometimes when furious, the itch showed up as a tic in my neck. At other times, it helped me be better. It made me color inside the lines. It made my animals sit in a row. I didn't miss any part of a story, because I triple-checked page numbers.

Now and then Maman joked that I was becoming fussy like Maman Masi and Morvarid, that I was becoming a tiny old lady. This was fine with me — I loved their floral chadors that smelled of henna, their ample laps and looping, gossipy stories, their dirty jokes. As a toddler, I marched around in an old flowery chador that Morvarid had sewn for me. I wore it so much it started to make my hair fall out. In a fit of anger, Maman tore it to pieces.

At school, my scarf was lopsided and my handwriting a disaster, but my math was perfect. The teachers in my Islamic Republic girls' school were witchy creatures who glistened in brutal black chadors. They didn't lean down and tuck in your stray hairs. They billowed past. They struck rulers against soft palms. They shouted surnames at six-year-old girls. *Nayeri. Ardestani. Khalili. Shirinpour.* The minute you turned your headscarf inside out to cool your damp neck, they appeared, swaddling your bare skin again with their own hot breath. The school was stifling, and militant women were empowered to steer girls away from Western values — this made them cruel. If they didn't like your work, they tore it to shreds as you sat humiliated, picking splinters off your unsanded desk. They taped weekly class rankings to the gray cement wall outside the classroom window. Every week twenty girls rushed that wall. The schoolyard was a concrete block. Opposite the classrooms was a putrid cave of water fountains and dirty squat toilets, the ground a mess of wet Kleenexes and cherry pits and empty tamarind packets that oozed brown goo into the drain. I liked to keep my back to it. But that meant facing the rankings, and if you turned another way, you had the nightmarish Khomeini mural, and on the fourth wall, the enormous bloody martyr fist (and rose). The only way to have a safe place to look was to be number one on the rankings.

One morning, Khadijeh, whose name routinely appeared at the bottom of the list, released a quiet river of pee at her desk. She never moved. She sat still as her gray uniform slowly darkened below the waist, as drops of sweat released her bangs from her scarf, and she wept without a sound.

She had fallen three sentences behind in the *dictée* and given up, not just on the test, but on the whole business of civilization. What a quick, uncomplicated solution, to go feral: to sit there, leaking, waiting to be dragged out by a murder of Islamic Republic schoolteachers, listening for the snap and swish of the principal's chador down the hall.

On the day of Khadijeh's quiet surrender, I was number one on the list, so I had a place to look.

At day's end, I took the short way home, down alleyways lined with drainage gutters where live fish traveled the old city. I ran to my room and thought of Khadijeh, how she had just let go. I pitied and envied her. I knelt to examine my pencil tips, then checked the bookshelf for the seven books I had recently bought, and the four I had bought before that. It wouldn't be right to count to eleven — I had to count the seven books, then the four. And the next time I bought books, say three of them, I would count the three, the seven, and if I still remembered them, the four, each time I left my room. When I was finished, I breathed deeply until the thing floating too high in my chest (I imagined a metal bar) had moved back down, away from my throat.

Years later, when I heard the story of Sisy-phus, I said, "Like pushing down the bar," and tapped my chest; my teacher frowned.

The following week, during silent reading time, a present arrived for me. This was custom. If you ranked high, your parents could send a gift to be presented to you in front of the class. Ms. Yadolai, my first-grade teacher, an old woman I loved and whose name is the only one I remember, brought in the gift to my third-grade classroom. She was Baba's dental patient, so he must have delivered the package to her. Baba never bothered with details; he entrusted every-thing to friends. It was a book of constella-tions. Everyone clapped. I lifted the lid of my desk and slipped the book inside next to my pencils and the tamarind packet I had squeezed from a corner and rolled shut, like toothpaste.

Khadijeh never came back.

I was instructed to work on my handwrit-ing. I sat with Baba on the living room carpet, an elaborate red Nain knotted on Maman Masi's own loom, and we ate sour cherries with salt and we practiced. I asked Baba about Khadijeh. He said that every-one was made for a certain kind of work, and maybe Khadijeh had realized early that school wasn't for her. This is why I had to

40

earn twenties in every subject, to distinguish myself from the Khadijehs of the world and to reach my great potential. "You are the smartest," said Baba. "You can be a doctor or engineer or diplomat. You won't have to do housework. You'll marry another doctor. You'll have your PhD." His voice contained no doubt or worry. It was just how things were destined to be. "Your mother came in seventeenth for the Konkour. Not seventeenth percentile. Seventeenth person in the country." If I had to make a list of mantras from my childhood, it would certainly include *not seventeenth percentile, seventeenth person.* My mother's national university entrance exam result was legend. I came from test-taking stock.

We did such good work, Baba and I. He emptied his pockets of pistachio and chocolate and sour cherry, and we sat together on the floor, cross-legged and knee to knee, whispering secrets and jokes as we drew bold, stout-hearted Ks and Gs. I clicked our finished pages into my rawhide messenger bag and, the next day, I took them to show my teacher, a woman whom we called only by the honorific *khanom.*

Khanom scanned my pages as I straightened up in my chair, my hands tucked beneath my haunches. She frowned and exhaled heavily through her nose. Then she glanced at the girls watching us from the edges of their scarves, tapped the pages straight against my desktop, and tore them in half. She reached for my practice notebook and tore the used pages in that too, taking care not to destroy any unused ones. This was to show me that my work was worth less than those unfilled pages.

Tears burned in my nose. I imagined a metal storm-door shutting over my eyeballs, so that nothing could get out. I reminded myself of Khadijeh, her watery surrender. I imagined that under her chador, Khanom's skin was dry and scaly and she needed girl- ish tears to soften her, as she couldn't af- ford black-market Nivea Creme. I tried to pity her for that.

A few years before first grade, my family had spent three months in London. There, my mother had converted to Christianity. Since our return, teachers had been prob- ing me for information. Maman and Baba were respected in Isfahan. They had medi- cal offices and friends and degrees from Tehran University. Maman had round, melancholy eyes and Diana haircuts in jet- black. She wore elegant dresses and a stethoscope. Her briefcase was shiny pol- ished leather. No schoolgirl rawhide and click-buckle for her. But Maman was an apostate now, handing out tracts to her patients, a huge cross dangling in her windshield. Baba may have remained respected and generous and Muslim, but that wasn't enough to protect me from abuse when I declared myself Maman's ally.

"What is your religion?" the teachers would ask, every day during recess. They would pull me aside, to a bench between the toilet cave and the nightmarish Khomeini mural, and they would ask this again and again.

"I'm Christian," I would say. In those days, I thought *Muslim* literally meant "a bad person," and no individual or event helped dispel that notion — not even Baba, or his mother, Maman Masi, who was devout. We lived under constant threat of Iraqi bombs. We endured random arrests, executions, morality police roving the streets for sinful women (*Gashte-Ershad* or "Guidance Patrol," they now call it). Though they were picked off and dragged to gruesome fates, the underground Christians we had befriended seemed consumed with kindness. Meanwhile, my teachers pecked hungrily at us all day, looking for a chance to humiliate.

Later in life, far from Isfahan, I would

meet kindhearted Muslims and learn that I had been shown half a picture: that all villainy starts on native soil, where rotten people can safely be rotten, where government exists for their protection. It is only among the outsiders — the rebels, foreigners, and dissidents — that welcome is easily found. Since our return from London, we had lost our native rights; we were exiles in our own city, eyes suddenly open to the magic and promise of the West, and to the villains we had been.

In 1985, when I was nearly six and hadn't yet attended my Islamic girls' school, we visited my beloved Maman Moti — Maman's mother — in London. Years before, Maman Moti had run away to England, leaving all but one daughter behind. That spring, we went to watch my aunt Sepideh, Maman's youngest sister, marry an Englishman. Our stay was temporary, a visit followed by a half-hearted stab at emigration. It only lasted a few months, but I was enrolled in school for the first time. I spoke only Farsi.

In the airport, the guards tore through our things. Baba seemed unbothered as he unzipped his suitcases and buttered up the guards. "*Ei Vai,* did I leave an open pack of

Lucky Strikes with my shirts? Agha, you have them. The smell will ruin the fabric . . . I smoke Mehrs, but people give the strangest things to their dentist."

We were surrounded by so much clamor and haste. A guard picked up Babaeejoon, a beloved stuffed sheep, and turned him over in his hand. He took out a knife and ripped open its belly, pulling out its stuffing while my brother, Khosrou, cried on Maman's shoulder. "Be brave, Khosrou *joon*," Baba said. "They have to check so bad people don't smuggle things." Though Babaeejoon had been my gift after tonsil surgery, his death became my brother's trauma, because at the time of his disembowelment, Babaeejoon was Khosrou's sheep. I soothed myself by reciting everyone's ages: Aunt Sepi was nineteen. Maman was twenty-eight. Maman Moti was forty-four. I was five, Khosrou two. The airline served saffron rice pudding.

That night, I slept beside Maman Moti, whom I called my city grandmother. With her rolled hair and silky blouses, she was the opposite of Maman Masi, whose henna hair I had never seen below her temples. I heard a noise. Maman Moti was praying. "Can I pray too?" I asked. She told me about Jesus and love and freedom, and I believed. Soon, Maman became a Christian

45

too. Everything was a miracle after that. Maman's metal allergy? Gone. Because of Jesus she could wear bangles again. Every night, I heard Baba shouting through the wall. What was this insanity? Didn't she have enough sense to know that all religions were manipulative and irrational? Hadn't she just watched her own country fall into religious madness?

My parents had a terrible marriage, screaming-throwing fights that lasted into the early hours. He was addicted to an unnamable demon something. She would stage detoxes for him, and he sat shaking for a day or two, until some animal part of him burst out and chased her for the keys. At first, these were medical rages. Later, they were rages of coming loss. I heard stories of their courtship when Baba used to hide raw almonds around the house and write clues in verse for her to decipher, because he knew she loved riddles. He was as addicted to poetry and riverside picnics as he was to his pipe. At family meals or parties, eyes flitted to the door until he arrived. And yet, I was afraid of him. When I was two he had pulled out my front teeth because the tonsil surgeon had broken them on his way into my mouth.

In London, Baba sensed a looming danger

in Maman's new calling. Devotion to a faraway god, too, can be a powerful addiction.

For many nights, Maman sat up with her distant mother, a woman young enough to be her peer and whose elusive love had been Maman's lifelong grail. They drank tea and discussed purpose and belief. My mother, Sima, was Moti's second daughter: she wasn't the infallible, beautiful eldest, Soheila, after whom Moti pined most, or her only son, or the precious youngest she had scooped up on the day she ran away to England, the only person she hadn't left behind, and in whom she had invested all her English hopes. Maman was only the dutiful second. The one who read her medical books and cooked for her broken family. The one who obeyed. No one had taught her that this is how you get overlooked. She married young and found herself tricked: he was an addict. Maman hated being a doctor. Seventeenth on the Konkour meant the family gave her no choice but medicine. If she had confessed that sometimes she dreamed of owning a farm, they would've laughed — her father was a mayor. She went to medical school, married Baba. She found kindness with Baba's Maman Masi, a sweet farm woman with turmeric-stained fingers

47

who hugged and kissed, fed and praised. Maman Masi was old enough to be a mother to grown-ups.

By the time we arrived in London, Maman was strung out and ready for life to start meaning something fast. Trapped in the Islamic Republic, she craved rebellion, freedom. Too conservative for feminism, she reached for the next best thing: Jesus. Now she shared something more vital with her mother than Soheila ever had. Now she stood for an ideal that even the Islamic Republic couldn't take away, because she was willing to die for it.

Maman Moti boasted that she had the gift of prophecy. She had dreamed that, one day, her four children would gather around her in the West, and they would all be true believers. Having fulfilled her duty, Maman smiled and started on dinner.

What does it mean to believe *truly*? I don't know anymore, though I did then. Maman believed in Jesus more than I had seen her believe in anything, and that made him real. Every night, we both spoke to him, either alone or together, with more passion than we'd spoken to anyone.

We celebrated my sixth birthday with strawberry cake in the park in Golders Green. We let ice cream drip onto our fingers. We saw ginger hair, platinum hair, dark coffee skin, and we bought bananas and wandered the city, without fear of bomb sirens or morality police. Maman and Maman Moti let their over-brushed curls fall onto their shoulders. I learned to write from the left side of the page and bought three new toys: a ballerina that danced on a podium, a Barbie doll, and a row of penguins that climbed some steps and slid down a curly slide. Baba had paid a tailor to sew and pad tins of Iranian caviar into the lining of his suitcase. He passed them out one night at a pre-wedding celebration.

When the suitcases were stashed away, I began to imagine a free life in England. I believed that we had moved to be with my dear, elegant Maman Moti and Gigi, her pompous cat. I was going to school. I would learn English. They let me believe this.

The children were welcoming at first, teaching me English words using toys and pictures, helping me figure out the cubbies and milk line. But after a few days, a group of boys began to meet me in the yard and, pretending to play, pummel me in the stomach. Each morning it seemed a little less like play. They followed me in the playground and shouted gibberish, laughing at my dumbfounded looks. Maman Moti told me to pray and imagine God protecting me.

One day, I was playing with some girls, pretending the door handle to the art studio was an ice cream dispenser. The art studio was a freestanding room (like a shed) in the middle of the blacktop, and we often ran in and out of it during playtime. As I pulled on the handle, a boy grabbed my hand and shoved it into the doorjamb. Another boy slammed it shut, and I heard a sickening crunch.

At first it didn't hurt — just a prick at the base of my pinky nail and a numbness spreading up through my hand. But then there was blood — a lot of it — seeping out of the hinge and creeping down the doorframe. The teachers ran across the playground, shouting foreign sounds. I felt my breath changing and climbing to the top of my throat where it grew quick and shallow. When I pulled my hand away, a piece of my pinky dangled by a shred of skin and fell to the ground. The boy looked ill, all pasty and slack-jawed. He didn't run away. I was sticky with blood up to my elbow, the red smears covering the front of my shirt and now my face, too. I had wiped at my tears without thinking. That's when the fire sparked in the place of my missing nail and shot up my arm and down the side of my torso.

I howled.

If I had been seven, maybe I would have handled it better. Maybe I would have collected enough English words by then to keep that gang of blond boys from tormenting me every day, from punching me in the stomach, from grabbing my ponytail at lunch. Maybe if I was seven, I could understand the words the teachers were shouting at me now.

I soaked through the first napkin, then a second, until the springy blacktop under my feet was covered in red blossoms. Amid the chaos, one of the adults picked up the tiny piece of my finger. She wrapped it in another paper napkin and gave it to me, and that made sense. It was a piece of my body. I should keep it. I held my finger-bundle tightly against my chest as I was rushed to the hospital.

No one asked me about it, until it was my turn to be with the doctor, a broad-shouldered man my parents' age. More blond hair, this time over a kind face. I held the napkin out to him. He examined the nub, and he smiled at me. I didn't understand what he said, but my mother was there, and she said that it was very clever of me to save it. I closed my eyes as he sewed the tip of my finger back on. "The nail won't grow back," the doctor said to my mother, and I saw the grief in her face when she told me instead that it might not grow as fast as the others.

We drove home through the foggy streets, the same streets I had seen in cartoons and picture books back in Isfahan, with bananas sprouting from fruit stands, bunches of helium balloons, and ice cream with two sticks of chocolate Flake. What miracles England had offered me in just a month. Despite the ache in my hand, I still loved these streets. I wanted to walk up and down my grandmother's road in West Hendon, looking for change so I could buy Maltesers and real Kit Kats (with the logo in the chocolate) and Hula-Hoops. I wanted to go to the park in Golders Green and visit the incredible Mothercare shop and the adjoining McDonald's in Brent Cross. I wanted to keep collecting English words so I could ask my classmates all the questions I was storing up for the day my tongue adjusted and we could be friends.

Did you know it takes a week to eat through a pack of tamarind?

What is at the bottom of shepherd's pie, and why does it resist so nicely when I put my fork in it?

Who is Wee Willie Winkie? Am I the only one who finds him sinister?

Where are your hammams? Why do you bathe next to the toilet?

How can you bring yourself to sit . . . on a toilet?

I love your yellow hair, your red freckles, your chocolate brown skin.

Do you want to come to Maman Moti's and meet Gigi, her snooty cat?

But I didn't do or ask any of those things. I didn't know the words.

That night Maman Moti told me to pray. "Thank God he could sew it back on," she said. I dreamed Jesus was sitting by my bed. Again, I believed.

In the chatter of grown-ups from my grandmother's church and in my parents' soothing whispers, I heard a steady refrain about gratefulness and my lucky finger. God had protected me. It was my moment to shine! But I was furious. *Why isn't anyone angry? Someone should punish that boy.*

I never went back to that school. I kept wondering why those boys were so nice to me that first day, before they began stalking me in the yard. Years later, I figured that must have been how long it took them to tell their parents about the Iranian girl.

A few weeks later, we were back in Isfahan. I was sent to an Islamic school for girls and told that no cruel British boys would follow me. Here at home, I was safe. The school issued me a headscarf that obscured my neck and hair. They draped my body in a shapeless gray *manteau.* Nothing was simple or practical; nothing was as I liked. And so, one day in the first grade, I started counting things on my lucky fingers.

We returned altered. Now we were converts in the Islamic Republic, illegal Christians in an underground church. We endured three nightmare years before the day of our escape — three years of arrests and threats, of armed revolutionary guards (*pasdars* or Sepâh) slipping into the backseat of our car at traffic stops, bursting into Maman's medical office. Three years of daily terrors and Maman's excuses about faith and higher callings.

It was a daily whiplash. The idyllic village life of my father on Fridays, sitting in my sweet grandmother's lap, kissing her henna hair, listening to her reedy voice, eating her plum chicken or barberry rice, then traveling back to the city, to another phase of Saddam Hussein's War of the Cities (a series of missiles that killed thousands in

1987 alone) that waited at our doorstep. Every few days, sirens blared. We taped our windows and ran to basements, where we chatted in the dark with our neighbors.

That Maman chose this moment to become a religious activist out of her medical office baffled Baba — they fought night after night. Making a life after the revolution had been hard work. Baba had learned which patients to prioritize, which palms to grease, which tailor altered suitcases, who to smoke with in relative safety. But now Maman hurried down unsafe streets pulling two children along, her scarf falling back as she slipped into strange doors to meet Christians. She broadcast her story over an illegal Christian radio station, tucked brochures into women's chadors under the nose of the morality police, and did everything a person could do to draw attention to her apostasy. *Maybe she feels guilty,* Baba thought. She had once been a devout Muslim, and though she was never political, preferring to make her strict, conservative father happy, Maman *had* joined other medical students in the streets to protest the Shah, willingly covering her hair.

Teachers began to pull me away at recess. When I tried to opt out of weekly Islam classes, they held me in the schoolyard and told me that Maman would be jailed, beaten, maybe killed.

When I told Baba that Khanom had torn our proud, far-reaching Ks and Gs, his eyes flashed. My Baba was known for his pleasure-seeking ways: his riotous humor, his sumptuous feasting, his devotion to poetry. We were kindred spirits in our secret excesses. His vices, though, weren't all bright and merry. He loved the poppy, and it made him rage. His anger was slow to ignite, but God help you if you were the one to light him up.

The next day in the schoolyard, we lined up by grade and performed our required chants, straining our small lungs. An older girl, a fourth or fifth grader, pressed her lips to a bullhorn and led us in muffled pledges we didn't understand: *I am the daughter of the revolution. I am the flower of my country. Death to America. Death to Israel.*

Then Baba stormed through the metal gate, striding in his Western shirt and tie past the Khomeini mural. In seconds the principal and two teachers were surrounding him, nodding, lifting and lowering hands. I could only hear snippets. "Yes, Dr. Nayeri . . ." ". . . I'll speak with her . . ." ". . . Sir, we're in the middle . . ." When old Ms. Yadolai arrived, he calmed, because she

56

was sweet and harmless, like Maman Masi, his mother.

Then Khanom stepped out from in front of our line and started toward him. Suddenly she looked small, like one of us. Was she twenty? Twenty-five? She was trying to look strong, professional, but Baba was on a crusade. He wanted her heart. "She's just a child!" he shouted across the blacktop as he approached her at twice her pace. "You're a grown woman. She isn't responsible . . . She's not your enemy." Khanom began muttering that this was only about the handwriting. Baba railed on. "She worked hard, and I checked the work. How dare you! Where did you go to university?"

I noted that the last question was germane to the proceedings. That it affected her credibility, her allotment of power against my father. Baba was no sexist. If she had lifted her shoulders, bellowed out "Tehran University," and defended her actions, if she had said, "Dina is chatty, fussy, and odd. She has an itch in the brain and bad handwriting and one of her eyes is too small," he would have shown *some* respect for her methods. I know this because Baba — though he smoked opium and beat my mother and was incapable of lifting a finger for himself — instructed me never to cower to men. If you flinch, they will hit harder. Show your fangs, not your throat. But this was 1987 Isfahan and most Babas didn't teach their daughters these things. The poor woman didn't have the training.

She cried. She leaked before a man who shook his head at her and walked away, stopping to wave to his daughter who stood spellbound in a row of muppety gray heads, quietly growing a coarse new skin.

That night we walked along the Thirty-Three Arches and Baba took us to Hotel Koorosh, my favorite restaurant, where Baba and other local doctors had a membership. We ate schnitzel and crème caramel on white tablecloths. We drank yogurt soda with three sprigs of mint. I knew now that my teacher wasn't scaly or witchy or a demoness, and that it was important not to bend. And I knew that I was capable of rooting for someone who wasn't totally on the right side of a thing. In war, villainy and good change hands all the time, like a football.

A few days later, Maman was stopped in the streets by the *Gashte-Ershad.* We were at a traffic stop and my younger brother, Khosrou, opened the back door and jumped out into the madness of Isfahani morning traffic. I was in the front seat beside Maman, so I didn't see him do it. All I saw was Maman throwing the car into park and hurling her body out of the car, dashing across three lanes, and snatching him up. In the process, her scarf slipped back a few inches, revealing half a head of loose hair. Then we heard the shouting; a *pasdar* was pointing and ranting at Maman. "Watch your *hijab*, woman!" As he crossed the asphalt, his shouting grew louder, angrier. He began to curse, calling her vile names.

"My son ran into traffic," she said. She had already fixed her *hijab* so that every strand was tucked away. But he towered over her, threatening, spitting. They stood by the open driver's side door. If he had leaned in, he would have seen the huge cross hanging on her rearview mirror. Maybe he would have made an issue of it. He shouted a few more times, gave Maman a warning, and returned to the other officers watching us from their car.

When he was gone, Maman's cheeks glistened with rage. I wonder if she imagined herself in a country where men are punished for such things, where women can defend themselves. I wonder if she ever fantasized about slapping some fool hard across the face. Khosrou and I sat in that car, conjuring violent scenes. My brother glared silently at the car roof. Later he told Maman stories of how he would protect her, build her a castle in a mountain far away, fill it with Smarties.

Maman dropped me off at Baba's dental office while she ran errands with Khosrou — my chronic motion sickness made me a terrible passenger. I slipped into the surgery, sat in the nurse's chair to watch Baba fill a tooth. Long reddish hair fell over the back of the chair. I leaned to get a better look. The patient wore a silky blouse and jeans. Her chador hung on a rack near my face — in Baba's office, women could cover as they pleased if the door was closed. "Aren't you going to say hello, Dina *joon*?" said Baba.

I mumbled hello. Baba frowned. "Since when are you shy?"

I glanced at the woman's red lips and made-up eyes. She was a stranger. And anyway, who can recognize a face with the mouth pried open? But then Baba leaned back and she sat up and spit. "Hello, Dina *joon*," she said. I knew that voice — it was my first-grade teacher, Ms. Yadolai. Old Ms. Yadolai, restored, it seemed, to twenty-five or thirty by some witch's spell. "I saw you in the waiting room, telling everyone to *shush*," she said. "Where did you get that

60

sweet nurse's costume?" She meant my photo hanging across an entire wall of Baba's waiting room, my finger to my lips.

I shrugged. I was too transfixed by the miracle I was witnessing.

"Dina, don't be rude," said Baba.

"I'm sorry," I said. "Ms. Yadolai, what red hair you have."

Little Red Riding Hood was one of few storybooks not banned by the clerics; that joke was well-worn. She laughed, thanked Baba, and gathered her things. "See you in school," she said, whipping her black chador around her body, tucking at the temples. Despite makeup, she gained twenty years in one swing of her arm. A good scrub would cost her another twenty, and all her power, returning her by morning to old Ms. Yadolai.

Now, finally, I understood the function of *hijab.*

I started to believe that Christianity was feminism. Years later, my mother told me that when she had been a Muslim she was simply searching, and Islam fit only *some* of what she held sacred. In Christianity, she found her beliefs in their purest form. I now know that I was searching for feminism, and along the way, I shed every doctrine and institution that failed to live up to it. Islam went first. Later, all religion would follow.

Our church wasn't underground; it was behind gates and thick curtains. A rotating schedule in the homes of Assyrians and Armenians, who, if they could prove their ancestry and refrained from proselytizing, were theoretically left alone. Only apostates and pied pipers risked arrest and death. By allowing us into their homes, the Christian-born who hosted us tied their fates to ours, and this bonded us beyond friendship.

News of pastors, even Armenian ones, being shot or disappearing into the notorious Evin Prison wasn't rare. Political prisoners were routinely tortured and killed in Evin. We focused our attention elsewhere. Once we slipped past the front gate, headscarves came off and we sang songs, and planned Christmas celebrations, and heard funny sermons from our portly, heavily bearded Assyrian pastor, Brother Yusuf. The year we returned from England, Maman explained Christmas to us. She told us about Father Christmas and stockings by our beds, and it struck me that this character sounded like an older Brother Yusuf.

"If he visits all the children in the world," I asked, "why didn't he come to us before?" Maman told me that he only visited Christian children, and now we were Christians, wasn't that exciting? "But I didn't know about Jesus before," I said. "You said Christianity is fair. If I didn't know, why would he skip me? What about kids who are too young to have a religion? Does Father Christmas only visit houses with Christian *parents*?"

Maman blinked a few times. "Dina, it's for *fun*. Maybe it's Father Christmas. Maybe it's Brother Yusuf in a costume. Do you want a stocking, or do you want to sit in protest for all the ones you didn't get?"

"Yes, I want one," I said, and immediately suspended disbelief.

"Good," she said, then added (as she often did), "Keep asking these kinds of questions. You can think for yourself now; no more reciting."

For a while I did this. I read my Bible, found inconsistencies, and presented them to Brother Yusuf. I often asked my questions over meals at our *sofreh,* or his *sofreh,* with several families sitting around a feast on the floor. Brother Yusuf was the slowest eater I had met. He delighted in every bite, relishing and savoring and licking his lips, his big bearded cheeks bouncing as he chewed, nodded slowly, and complimented the chef. He treated my questions as he would an adult's, as if I were part of an important theological conversation. Though, he didn't always solve my problem. Most contradictions were dispatched with one of two answers: "The rules were different under the Old Testament," or "That reads differently in the original Hebrew." It didn't matter. The important thing was that he was impressed, that he called me clever.

When Brother Yusuf and the Christians visited, Baba disappeared to Ardestoon or stayed in his office — he despised Brother Yusuf, called him "that dirty Assyrian" or "that bearded charlatan."

Sometime in 1987, while the war raged on, sirens shrieked, and the days thrummed endlessly with news of executions, Maman was arrested. I didn't know the details, only that her office had been stormed, the patients sent home, and she had been questioned for hours. She had been given a choice: spy against the underground church or face arrest and execution.

Maman and Baba fought. Baba threatened to take Khosrou and me away. One night, Maman took us to a hotel, but they wouldn't accept a woman alone with two children.

Having found her purpose, Maman intensified her efforts. She kept stacks of Christian brochures under a thin blanket in her backseat, passing them out to patients and acquaintances. She started studying braille and sign language, so she could reach out to the deaf and the blind.

Maman was arrested again, her office ransacked, her records stolen. She grew rigorous in her domesticity, sewing complicated, lifelike stuffed squirrels and cats. She found thin mattress foam and made a stuffed car for Khosrou. As the gaze of the morality police grew hotter and more unbearable, she leaned heavier on the church, and on Brother Yusuf. Sometimes when I spied on them talking in his home office, I detected an intimacy that felt like a betrayal to Baba — their talk was too playful. It was a strange habit of new Christians, these overly loving exchanges that were supposed to mimic brotherly or sisterly love. "My dear sweet" this or that. Each time Maman met with the pastor, his office door remained wide open.

One afternoon, a car screeched to a stop behind the high wall separating the street from Brother Yusuf's front gate. His wife rushed out of the kitchen, scooping up her baby girl, Rhoda. His son, Yoonatan, and I stopped playing cards. Maman and Brother Yusuf stashed their Bibles away. Maman fixed her *hijab*. A hard knock shook the metal gate outside. "I'll break it down!" a man shouted. And though his voice was angry, almost violent, all my fear dissolved. I knew that voice, and no matter how much he shouted and whom he threatened to hurt, it brought me only joy.

Khosrou was terrified, though. He screamed and jumped into Maman's arms. He cried for a while, then his brow furrowed as if he were accepting new orders, a new role. "Don't worry, Maman. I'll protect you!"

Brother Yusuf had hardly opened the gate before Baba rushed in and grabbed him by the throat. He shouted terrible things. "You dirty Assyrian," he spat into the man's face as he hovered over him, his shirt collar still in his fists. "Don't you have your own wife to corrupt? Do you know what trouble you've caused?" Why had Baba come today? Maybe he had been smoking, or had a visit from the moral police. Baba didn't harm Brother Yusuf. He released his anger and, when the women managed to calm him, turned back toward the door, leaving Maman to apologize again and again.

The war made everything seem like the last of its kind. Every lazy afternoon, every family dinner, every drink of water. Some days at school, only a third of the students were present, the classroom eerily quiet and breezy, because parents had heard of a coming bomb raid.

My teachers reached in deep and planted gruesome images. They told me just enough to make me ask around and fill in the gaps. 1987 was a brutal year. For some, 1988 would be worse. Thousands of intellectuals, leftists, and political dissidents disappeared that year, massacred by firing squad and hung from cranes, dying slowly. Sliced feet and skinned backs, hot irons to the thighs, their deaths covered up — it was a purge unprecedented in Iranian history. These images competed in my nightmares with scenes from the Book of Revelation and movies about the rapture: horsemen and plagues and the Antichrist. Which was the worse fate? Did most eight-year-old girls have such choices?

I decided to talk to my teacher, to make peace. One day after class, I waited for the room to empty, straightened my scarf, checked my area, and meandered to her desk. "Khanom," I said. She didn't look up from her papers. "I've been practicing my handwriting."

"Good," she said, her head still down so that all I saw was the gray fabric lump of her head. "That's why we're here."

"I didn't tell Baba," I said, trying not to let my dignity leak away. "He looks at my notebooks. I didn't . . ."

Now she looked up with her stony eyes, folding her arms over her papers in a rehearsed, wooden sort of way. "Miss Nayeri, the world is brutal for women. It's a thousand times harder than for men. Whatever our private conflicts, we don't betray each other to men. Do you understand?"

I shook my head. "Baba isn't one of *those* men. He was just angry . . ."

She rolled her eyes, capped her pen, and sat back. "Who's your biggest rival in the class? Who do you hate more than me?"

"I don't hate you, Khanom," I said. What a terrible mess this was.

She waited. I didn't want to answer, because Pooneh was also my best friend and a distant cousin. I loved her and craved to beat her so much that sometimes when we kissed hello, on both cheeks as our parents had taught us, I squeezed her face hard to calm my itching teeth. It was a painful, confused affection, like a Mafia boss kissing a rival brother goodbye.

Now Khanom smiled. Even though I came in first twice as often as Pooneh did, I was the one always chasing, because I was the one who publicly cared, while she shrugged and smiled and puffed her porcelain cheeks. That I would have to suffer another twenty years of sprinting alongside Pooneh exhausted and thrilled me. "Whatever you do to each other to win," she said, "the minute you run to a man, you're a traitor."

Then she went back to her work. "I'm sorry," I said, though I felt that the story had been unfairly rewritten. "I'll do the work over. I *do* love you."

She gave me a strange look. I had said the wrong thing. You don't tell teachers you love them. Why had I said it?

For a moment, we both stood our ground, Khanom determined to ignore me, as I remained planted in her line of vision. I shifted onto my other foot, moved my messenger bag to my back.

She glanced up again, smiling kindly now. "It's OK, Miss Nayeri," she said. "I'm OK. I'm stronger than you think." She made muscle arms under her chador, and we both laughed. "How would you like to do a very special job that only the top students can do?"

My fingertips went cold — I knew my school's rituals and rewards, and yet I wanted so much to please her. She lifted herself off the chair with a weary sigh and opened the book cabinet behind her. She pulled out a piece of paper tucked beneath the red bullhorn. When I didn't move, she waved it at me until I reached up and took it from her.

"You can lead tomorrow's morning exercises," she said. "Don't be sad." She leaned down to my height and touched my cheek. "We're friends again." Then she hugged me and muttered encouraging words in my ear. She smelled like my mother's soap, and I wrapped my arm around her neck. Under her chador, a familiar lump comforted me; a ponytail, bound low, hanging down to the top of her shoulders. It made me trust her: yes, my teacher was a person. Her body wasn't covered in scales. She had real hair tied up in a girlish ponytail. I didn't want to stop touching it, but a moment later she pulled away.

I slogged home in cement shoes, feeling the breath of the four horsemen on my neck. Was there any way to escape hell if I led a schoolyard full of girls in chanting death to Israel, God's own people? I might as well drive the nails into Jesus' hands and feet. I pictured Rhoda and Yoonatan, Brother Yusuf savoring my mother's Salad Olivieh and strapping on his Father Christmas belly. I would be betraying them all.

Alone in my bedroom, I agonized. I took off my uniform and dropped it in the laundry basket. I sat at my desk, tried to do math through tears. How would I survive tomorrow? Aside from damning myself to hell, it would be humiliating. I had been so brazen and boastful about my new faith. A few hours later, Maman burst in. "What is this?" she said. She was holding my *manteau* in one hand, the scrap of paper with the chants in the other. "Why is this garbage in your pocket?"

The metal bar was so far up my throat now that I could hardly take a breath. I confessed everything. "You cannot do it, Dina," she said, then she went on to repeat the story of Peter denying Jesus three times, and Judas, and every other betrayer in the Bible and in history. "When the class lines up for chants, what do you normally do?"

"I don't say them. I ask Jesus for strength, like you told me to."

"You tell your teacher that your mother forbids you. Tell her that in our faith we don't recite things. Don't argue with her about the text. Then get back in the line and do as you always do, OK?" I nodded.

The next day, I dragged myself to school. I separated from my body with each step, and by the time I passed through the school gate, crossed the blacktop, and climbed the podium, I was numb and limp, hovering

71

outside myself. I was already in Baba's car speeding toward Ardestoon, toward my Morvarid's withered henna arms. The stage was only inches from the ground. I read the words into the red bullhorn, barely waiting for the back chant. I conjured up the blond London boys who had punched me and severed my finger, and I thought, maybe viciousness is genetic; maybe some people, like British boys and Persian girls, are bred for it.

When my volume dropped, a teacher straightened my back and the bullhorn so that it touched my lips and I tasted plastic and metal. I said the final words, and started back down the podium to join my class, stopping as I passed to return the paper to Khanom. The moment the last syllable dropped like phlegm from my mouth, I began praying for forgiveness; I prayed all day. I never told Maman what I had done. Maybe she knew. It took months to escape the nausea of that morning, and even then, I was marked: long after the Islamic Republic, the war, and the refugee years had receded and I had become an ordinary American, I would still be someone who once stood on a podium in an Isfahani schoolyard and shouted "Death to America" into a bullhorn.

■ ■ ■ ■

For a few weeks in the spring of 1988, everything was on apocalyptic pause — that's how it felt when sirens warned of bombs already on the way. A pause as we looked up to the sky, waiting for word that our daily labors were worth continuing, that in an hour we would still have homes and schools. Or bodies. The television blared out insanity — was it propaganda, or had the producers succumbed to madness? I shiver at the memory of a drama in which two boys with shaved heads and long white robes, good Muslim boys from less sophisticated cities, walked through the bombed-out rubble of their neighborhood looking for the bodies of their parents. They passed a weeping man carrying his son's limp body — their friend. When they stumbled upon a wreckage that had been their roof, they sat atop it and cried, caressing the ground, now a family gravesite, with the sacred touch of new orphans. This drama played at 3 p.m., during children's hour.

I couldn't breathe. I didn't deserve to breathe. Nothing was mine to keep. "Maman," I ran to her and cried into her skirt. "Tell me a riddle."

73

School was a ghostly place, nearly empty now. The teachers didn't bother with lessons. We sat in lonely silence and wrote. During breaks, we wandered the hallway and the blacktop one by one. No groups remained. Pooneh didn't come. I missed her. I needed her to make me try my best.

"A worthy rival is a precious thing," said Baba.

"You shouldn't compete with anyone but yourself," said Maman.

Had there been a day when these two agreed on one single thing?

Isfahan grew quiet and sad. People tiptoed, exchanging ration coupons for basics and rushing home, taking their tea to the bomb shelter. The New Year slowed things down. It brought smoked fish and spray roses and tiny pink buds, but little hope. We cocooned in the church and listened to news of our murdered brothers and sisters, and we prayed for rescue.

Meanwhile, in the Ministry of Intelligence, one man was making Maman's case his pet project. She was arrested a third time in her office, thrown in jail for the night. Next time, the man said, if she didn't agree to disclose church secrets, she would be executed. Baba paid them to release her into house arrest. As she was leaving, the man promised Maman that tomorrow she would have her final chance to accept his offer, or she wouldn't return home again. That night, police cars surrounded our house.

Maman didn't sleep. She packed. "We are leaving. I know we are. This is the moment when Jesus will perform miracles."

Khosrou grew tense, his little brow always furrowed. It seemed he would have to act fast, if he were to build Maman that castle in time.

"Your Jesus is going to save you?" Baba bellowed. "At least admit that the person performing the miracles will be me. I've lost my family because of this lying, grifting, pied piper man. Please be sure to thank him for me."

The arrival of this day struck Baba like a rock hurtling down a mountain; he had tried so hard to keep that boulder moving upward. But now Maman was taking his children, abandoning him, her country, her life.

Baba spent the night on the phone. Maman in prayer.

The next morning, to allay suspicion, Baba went to his office as usual, and I walked to school. A handful of teachers and girls in half-hearted *hijab* roamed the halls. In class, we read silently, and I left early. At

75

home, I packed my things. The itch pawed and suffocated me. I stared at my animals and books all lined up, my solar system and the Victorian doll with folds in her dress for hiding secrets. I couldn't bring the squirrel with its furry white belly, or my cat, elephant, or duckling. They would be safer here, Maman had told me. Remember Babaeejoon?

I clenched my fist around some dried sour cherries, warming and loosening there, staining my palm bright red. I stared into a drawer of dried berries and fruit leathers. I ate the hot cherries in my hand.

Despite everything, I was excited to go: beyond our borders lay every kind of possibility. If I could just pull myself away from my things . . .

We waited in the kitchen for my uncle Reza — my father's younger brother. Baba had sent him to fetch us in a borrowed car. A few months before, we had moved from the house with the pool and the spray roses. Now we lived in a third-floor flat, and the plan must have been to climb down the fire escape and leave from the back.

Reza was thirteen when I was born. Now twenty-one, he had soft chestnut hair and a lazy smile, faded jeans, the kind of youth and freedom that Iran granted only to some men, and only briefly. I couldn't imagine a more heroic person. On Fridays in Ardestoon, Reza would put me on the back of his motorcycle, and we would whiz through the countryside, past rivers with ducks and orchards full of sour cherries, mulberries, almonds, and green plums, to a mountain where sheep grazed. The back of that motorcycle was peace for me, a place of no worry. It was freedom, my hair flying as I clutched his stomach and screamed into his shoulder. How would I live without those afternoons? Who would be my new Uncle Reza? What if it took him years to follow us? What if he never did?

At the kitchen table, Maman underlined her Bible in a third or fourth color (one for each year). I began to panic about leaving. I had two months left of the third grade. I'd have to learn English. How long would that take? How could I be number one in school if I didn't speak English?

"Maman," I said. She continued to read.

"Maman!" She looked up. "What is it?"

"How do you say the word 'write' in English?"

She told me, then frowned and said, "Why?"

"Because," I said, "math will be the same, but during *dictée,* the teacher always says, write this, write that. So if I just listen for 'write' and sound out what comes after . . ."

After three years of Iranian *dictée,* after Khadijeh, I divided tests into two kinds: the easy kind, and the kind with a *chadori* teacher breathing down your neck, shouting sentences that must be written verbatim in calligraphy, with a fountain pen.

Maman laughed. "English spelling isn't like that. You'll see."

Reza arrived just as sirens began screaming. We watched the surveillance cars from the kitchen window; they hesitated, then scattered. "Let's go," said Reza. A lucky crack had opened in Maman's house arrest; I held my favorite uncle's hand for the last time, and we ran through it.

We scrambled into the back of the car with our suitcases. The street was deserted, just a long sun-streaked hollow where I played with the neighborhood children. Blurred by rain and tires and shoeprints, our chalk hopscotch ladders still colored the street from top to bottom. We weren't going far on this leg of the journey. We would fly to Tehran, then drive to Karaj, where we could hide in the home of Maman's elderly grandmother (Moti's mother). She had pillows lining a wall beside a small television, a bedridden husband, and cherry trees that would be blossoming now.

Earlier that morning, before he left for work, I had asked Baba, "When are you coming?"

"Soon," he said. "I'll come to Karaj."

Uncle Reza drove us past Baba's building; his office was on the third floor, his operating room facing the street.

"Wave goodbye to your Baba," he said, his voice too quiet and low.

I squinted at the man in the window and waved. I knew the window, the big chair beyond, the desk with our photos scattered under glass. I couldn't see his face. We were in a moving car, and he was three stories up.

In the front passenger seat, Maman stared at the streets with grieving eyes, taking in every shop sign and utility pole. Waving to Baba had unnerved me. Maman *always* told me the truth. She told me about her arrests, the death of church leaders. But now I understood that we were sealing a door even tighter than I liked, that I'd never again see this life from inside. I may never sit beside my cousins, glance for my name above Pooneh's, or tuck in Maman Masi's hair. Morvarid would die without me.

I made promises to myself. If we made it to the United States or England, I would work twenty times harder to avoid Khadijeh's fate. I would learn English and become exceptional. In the West, the criminals wouldn't be in charge. Teachers would be kind. Worthy rivals would abound.

From his office, Baba was making calls. I don't know when they found the solution for sneaking out of Isfahan. I only know that it happened at the eleventh hour, because when we got in the car and headed to the airport, we had no tickets and no hope. Every flight was canceled because of the bomb alert. Somehow, though, either before we left or as we drove, Baba's phone connected to a friend: maybe a village classmate, or a fellow prisoner, or a guest at his hookah, or, most likely, a patient relieved of pain.

A mile or two outside the terminal, our car broke down. The road to the airport was sandy and flat, like desert, and there was no traffic now that the airport was shut. Then Reza spotted a far-off Jeep. As it approached, the olive of a police vehicle stained the horizon and Maman began to pray.

Did Reza grow up with a booming personality like my father or brother? I remember him as a quiet person with a silent laugh, and I never saw him after that day. I have a photo of us at my eighth birthday party, running around the last of the musical chairs, my hair flying, Reza grinning. He was no showman like Baba, but at twenty-one, he was charming enough to befriend a police officer who hadn't bothered to speak to any central authority that morning. The name on his ID matched my mother's. His hair was tinted red like mine. Maybe the officer was bad at birthday math (Reza was far too young to be my father), or maybe he just didn't bother. He gave us a jump and escorted us to the airport.

Minutes later, Baba's friend (or classmate or patient), now an airport security agent, snuck us onto a cargo plane that had stopped only to refuel. We sat beside the merchandise, and we flew to Tehran undetected. For decades, I believed our escape was divined. In Karaj, we hid in the house of my great-grandmother, Aziz. There, Maman and Baba rushed to get us out of the country, and Maman's Three Miracles, the foundation of our escape story and therefore our future identities, came to pass.

A few nights before we left the country, a man called Baba's office at midnight, expecting to get an answering machine. He was in agony over an abscessed tooth. Baba was slumped behind his desk, puffing smoke into the darkness, thinking of how to get us out without exit visas or passports, in a country where even plane tickets took months to secure. In the midst of this fog, and for no apparent reason, he answered the telephone. The man begged for help, but Baba got calls like this all the time. He was one of the best dental surgeons in Isfahan. "I know Dr. Nayeri," people would say. "He grew up in Ardestoon and he drives an American car. He must be good."

Just before hanging up, Baba asked, "Where do you work, Agha?"

The man said he worked at the passport office. Baba laughed. Surely, this was a joke. But no, the man gave his credentials. Within hours, Baba had sobered up and was bent over the man's mouth, performing a free root canal. The next morning, my mother, brother, and I had our passports.

We decided to try for Dubai. Baba had friends there. And the route through Turkey seemed more dangerous, more the fugitive's way. We needed a visa and plane tickets, which were sold out for months. Back then, Iranians booked flights in advance and paid a fluctuating rate on departure day. One morning as we broke fast with bread, cheese, and sweet tea with Aziz, the radio announced that due to pressure from inflation, Iran Air was changing its pricing model. Many bookings were canceled in the transition. Maman clapped her hands and reached to the sky. "Another miracle!" When she said this to Baba, he raged. "Again . . . it was *me.* Not God. I'm God."

Days later, Baba's distant relative in Dubai, a stranger named Jahangir, agreed to sponsor us for tourist visas. His reasons are a mystery to me; Baba knows. Jahangir wasn't privy to Maman's troubles or her plan to stay past our visas and make us refugees, to throw us at the mercy of the United Nations. Within days, in spring 1988, we were on a plane out of Iran.

IV / KAWEH AND KAMBIZ

Lately, I have become enraptured by a pair of stories. I came across each man in a newspaper article, years apart, and chased both stories last year. Sometime in the early 2000s, two promising young men left Iran through Kurdistan. They were strangers to each other, though they could be brothers. Their faces, their names, are eerily alike. Fate, though, spit them out at two ends of a long spectrum, two extremes so distant that one wonders how civilized societies allow a single hour, or day, to carry such consequences (where is our humility?). Both men ran from danger while harboring big dreams; one was labeled an opportunist, the other a survivor.

Kaweh and Kambiz each left Iran in early adulthood. Earnest and hardworking, they set off without family, money, or a change of clothes. I am drawn to the place where their stories diverge, the vital hinge where one man is believed and the other is not, this weighing station of human worth operated for profit by winners of a great lottery of birth.

Like many Iranian boys, Kaweh spent his mornings in a strict Islamic classroom, his afternoons kicking soccer balls and paddling Ping-Pong balls for the pride of his village, and his evenings reading all the Western books he could get his hands on. His older brother was studying math in university and brought him Jules Verne: *Twenty Thousand Leagues Under the Sea. Around the World in Eighty Days. Journey to the Center of the Earth.* At night, Kaweh raced through the books, inviting Verne to show him the vastness of the world. His three older siblings, clustered at around a decade older than Kaweh, and his baby sister, six years younger, shared bedrooms. Kaweh camped in the living room. Like an only child, he slept, did his work, and walked to school alone. He developed a rich inner life, his solitude interrupted only by his strict, military father — a man with few words and no desire to hike mountains or explore rivers — coming in to watch *Poirot.*

Born in 1981 in lush mountainous Kurdistan, the neck of "the cat" (the shape of modern Iran on a map), Kaweh had never known his country before the 1979 Revolution. Every day, his teachers checked the boys' homework. If it wasn't done, they cut tree branches and whipped the soft of the children's hands. In winter, they made the boys bury their hands in snow until all feeling was lost. They squeezed pencils between tiny fingers.

Paveh was a relatively poor and tight-knit Kurdish town. Everyone knew one another, and the children competed for academic and athletic honors. And yet, the law required them to speak only in Farsi in school, at the bank, and at other places of business. "I don't understand," Kaweh told his mother one day as they picked eggplant and tomatoes from their garden. "Hozan can't even speak proper Farsi. In town we speak in Kurdish, but when I go to the post office to give him a letter, I have to tell him in Farsi and hope he does it right? If I say a word in Kurdish he gets scared."

"It's the law," said his mother, kicking a fallen walnut and stretching her back. "He doesn't want trouble."

When they had filled two baskets of ripe apples and autumn vegetables, Kaweh asked, "Daye, can I have some money?"

"What for?" she said, already reaching into her skirt pocket.

"There's a new thing people are drinking in the square. It makes them burp and say *that's delicious.*"

"Disgusting, Kaweh." She laughed and gave him the money.

That afternoon Kaweh tasted his first Coca-Cola, a brief joy since most of it came out of his nose a few seconds later. "It's like needles," he said.

That was the year the family got their television and discovered *Poirot* and other dubbed shows on two channels. Every night, villagers knocked on their door to congratulate the family on their acquisition. The congratulations were heartier when there was a soccer match on. Soon the first washing machine came to the village, and fridges began to pop up through the town. The family acquired these things slowly and faithfully, and life became more varied and enjoyable. There was time for river hikes and snowy mountain games in their four-season village, and Kaweh began to travel to competitions for table tennis and soccer.

The prohibition on Kurdish continued to baffle him. He wanted to read the magazines his brothers read. He didn't want to speak to his teachers in Farsi. Every morning he woke to his father listening to the BBC and Voice of America for the news. That's how he learned of the Kurdistan Democratic Party of Iran (KDPI), the progressive rebels operating just outside Iran, beyond the Iraqi border, who fought for Kurdish rights and self-rule, and whose leaders were regularly hanged in town squares. He had seen preparations of the crane and the gallows, the public announcement: "We have arrested so-and-so, a traitor. He will be executed today." The regime had declared holy war on KDPI, and thousands were slaughtered. Once, a local man was hanged, his feet tied with a rope and his body dragged by a car through the town, as a warning against joining the party.

When Kaweh was eleven, KDPI leader Sadegh Sharafkandi was famously assassinated by Iranian operatives in the Mykonos Restaurant in Berlin. Sharafkandi's predecessor, Abdul Rahman Ghassemlou, a hero for Kurdish autonomy, had been murdered in

1989 in Vienna. Both men were buried at Père Lachaise in Paris. This second assassination created much noise in Paveh and greater Kurdistan. Did the Iranian authorities carry it out? For years, the story sat heavily on Kurdish hearts until in 1997 a German court issued an international arrest warrant for the Iranian intelligence minister responsible.

By the time Kaweh was seventeen, his private anger at the treatment of the Kurds had peaked, and he found inspiration and purpose in the stories of his political heroes. One day, Kaweh's cousin, Sattar, a studious boy his age and a known prodigy in math, physics, and the Koran, suggested that they run away to join the party and fight for Kurdish rights. "Let's present ourselves. If we're good, they will send us to Europe to study. We can fight for something good." Kaweh agreed. At home, tensions were high. He told his parents he was going away for a week to compete in table tennis, and his cousin was going for an academic competition.

"Where is the competition?" his mother asked at dinner. The boys had agreed that they couldn't cross into Iraq from Paveh, since everyone knew them there. They chose another border town.

"Marivan," said Kaweh, thinking of how little he could carry in an overnight bag and what he'd have to leave behind. "I'll be gone for a week."

Kambiz lived in a northern Iranian province close to Kaweh's. If Kaweh was in the front part of a west-facing cat's neck, then Kambiz was on its back, due east, in Shomal, where people came to hike and ski the Alborz, or swim and eat fish from the Caspian Sea. His mother had spent her life competing with her sister-in-law. Every time that sister's children brought home an honor or a good grade or a sports win, Kambiz's mother said, "Kambiz jan, you must get into university and make your mother proud. Show us some talent. Don't shame me in front of my sister-in-law."

Kambiz thought maybe he'd become an electrical engineer. He sat in his room and tinkered with gadgets, old phones and radios. He was decent at math, physics. But his mother's daily pleas exhausted him. Sometimes, he stared at his mother's spices and thought, Why is it so low a calling to create pleasure out of chicken thighs and a basketful of ground-up roots?

At the border, a man told Kaweh and Sattar where to go, what Iraqi village to aim for, and where to find the KDPI (they were headquartered in Koy Sanjaq). "If you cross tomorrow," he said, "I can meet you on the other side, in Penjwen."

But later that day at the border, guards stopped and questioned them. Sattar told them that they were visiting family for a day. When they asked for "a sweet" to wave them through, Sattar pulled out their money. "We have to forget about our bags and cross now," he whispered to Kaweh. "People on day visits don't bring bags."

They crossed into Penjwen. They had only enough to pay for one boy's travel permits. Since Kaweh looked young, they bought one for Sattar. At the first stop their bus was boarded by Peshmerga officers, and Kaweh was arrested. Vowing to find each other, Sattar continued on to Koy Sanjaq. Kaweh spent the next hour convincing the officers that he was just a boy visiting his uncle. He had nothing with him, no money, no clothes. A young Peshmerga said, "Come on, he's a poor kid going to see his family for Nowruz."

Hours later, Kaweh arrived at the head-quarters. "I'm here to join the party," he said. Just as he was asking if Sattar had arrived, a car pulled up and out came his cousin. The boys rushed at each other, laughing and hugging. And the man in front said, "You are very welcome here."

Their early days were spent in screenings and interviews — were these boys sent by Iranian intelligence? Had they thought this decision through? The party members were surprised by Kaweh's knowledge of Kurdish literature and history, despite his near illiteracy in Kurdish. When the party members were satisfied, the boys spent a month in Acceptance, a room of beds for forty men waiting to enter a two-month course.

One day, during the waiting period, their mothers arrived and were given ten minutes in a visitor's room with their sons. They wore black chadors, their faces tear-streaked and flushed. They kissed both boys and listened as two young party members, accustomed to the arrival of frantic mothers, gave instructions and sat in the corner of the room. "We are only present to ensure no party information is exchanged," they said — but the boys could decide for themselves. No one was forcing them to leave or stay.

"We looked in all the hospitals in Iran," said Kaweh's mother, wiping her face with her chador. "Someone saw you at the border and told us you had probably done this. Just tell them you're going home."

Kaweh shook his head. "I'm not going home."

Hands shaking, she pinched his leg, squeezing so hard, he bruised. No one spoke for a while; they listened as Kaweh's mother cried, as Sattar's mother made rational speeches about the good they could do for the party if they had university degrees. After ten minutes, the mothers were escorted out. They telephoned again, demanding to speak to the boys since they were underage. When Sattar took a long call from his father, Kaweh knew his cousin's resolve was weakening, but he couldn't go with him. He had political dreams, a drive to be part of something important.

Sattar returned with the family, crying all the way home. He was accepted for physics at Kermanshah University. He finished his degree, began his master's, then gave up science to start a chicken factory. He blamed the rigor, claimed he couldn't keep up, but rumors spread that he had been frightened by assassinations of top scientists working on Iran's nuclear program. Iranian physicists were targets for Israeli assassins and Iranian intelligence; how long would a top scientist with a history of joining a dissident group last? In the end, Sattar chose peace, safety, and family.

Kambiz met a woman. He met her for tea and thought, maybe some good will come of this. He had no desire to compete with his cousins. He would start a business, have a family, make his own happiness. He hated the war and the excesses of the revolution. He wrote two articles under an assumed name, both for small local publications. His mother kept digging in about his cousins' accomplishments, asking about Kambiz's plans. The only way to quiet her was distraction. "Maman, will you teach me to cook ghorme sabzi?" "Why should you need that?" she'd say. "You'll marry and your wife will cook for you." "But till then . . ." Slowly Kambiz found he had a delicious hand. He learned all the best recipes — lamb and fenugreek. Eggplant and whey. Walnut and pomegranate with chicken. One day as he cooked, plainclothes Basijis arrived at his door, accusing him of adultery.

After a year as errand-boy, Kaweh became a party teacher. His Kurdish improving, he wrote for a newspaper. His first publication, a Chekov story, was a translation from Farsi to Kurdish. Then he was assigned to a big project, the immortalization of the people's hero, KDPI founder Abdul Rahman Ghassemlou. He was to collect every speech, article, and transcript written or recorded by the great man into an archive. Kaweh was transported — how visionary and good-hearted Ghassemlou was. How hard he fought for democracy, rule of law, and self-determination for Kurdistan, growing a tiny opposition party into a true political threat to the establishment. Those hours with Ghassemlou ushered Kaweh into adulthood, teaching him how to speak and to reason and to persuade.

It didn't take long for the Iranian authorities to find Kaweh and to discover that he worked within party archives. They visited his family, making strange threats and promises: "We can cut your pension. You must see the futility of his cause. He has only two choices: return or provide information. If he works with us, we can send him to Europe to study."

One day, an older cousin called to invite Kaweh to lunch at a restaurant in nearby Arbil. He sounded nervous. "I'm visiting a friend," he said. When Kaweh arrived, two men were waiting with his cousin. They claimed to be friends from Halabja, but they spoke with Kermanshah accents. "These friends want to help you," said the cousin,

"They want you to go to Europe and study. You're so bright."

"You bloody are not from Halabja," said Kaweh. "I have ears."

His cousin took Kaweh's hand. Finally he said, "These are Iranian intelligence officers. They just want to have a friendly talk with you."

"We could have killed you on a number of occasions," said one of the men, "if that's what we wanted. Your father worked for the revolutionary army. Your brothers are civil servants. You belong to the revolution, and we want to help you." The men went on to explain the kinds of information they wanted, how Kaweh could get it to them. One of them took out two hundred American dollars, more than three years of salary from the party.

Kaweh took it, thinking, *The Islamic Republic has given me nothing.* He recalled Ghassemlou's calmness under pressure, his resolve. Kaweh wanted to be like him. "You can't expect me to make this decision now."

"How about a month?" said one of the men. As he put his wallet away, Kaweh glimpsed a gun in a holster. "Is that good enough?"

Kaweh agreed, refused a ride back, and left the restaurant.

A month later, they called. "Have you thought about it?" Kaweh said he had decided against it. The conversation took less than thirty seconds.

The pressure increased. Now and then they threw his mother in a car and dropped her off outside the compound. "Go get your son," they'd say, and they'd abandon her in the street like a living symbol. Someone would let her in and arrange for her to be taken back. How she had aged, Kaweh thought.

In 2002, with the pressure peaking and America's war with Iraq inevitable, Kaweh decided to confess to the party and escape. He returned his card, shook the leaders' hands, and set off. He walked to Turkey with a fellow defector. It took them seven days through mountains, past rivers, from the Iraqi border to reach Turkey. Some days they walked fifteen hours. Some days they had a guide. They carried packs and slept in the mountains. Smugglers brought food — tea for breakfast, a cucumber for lunch, a piece of bread and cheese for dinner.

The mountain was a dangerous route. PKK fighters (the Kurdish workers' party based in Turkey) were stationed there, along with the Iranian army and south Iraqi Peshmerga. It was entirely possible to be shot

96

dead in the night. And yet, staying in Iraq was riskier.

Once in Turkey, they walked to a city called Van and claimed asylum. Kaweh had collected his writings, legal papers, photos, and letters from his years at KDPI. He was granted refugee status by UNHCR, who believed that, while Iraqi Kurdistan was safe, Iranian authorities wanted Kaweh. But the Turkish authority refused to recognize him or to honor UNHCR's decision. So, when UNHCR arranged an interview at the Finnish embassy, Kaweh had no permits to pass the checkpoints to Ankara and he missed his chance.

Then one day, the Iranian authorities called him in Turkey. "We know where you are," they said. He began to fear kidnapping, or deportation. Police often arrested asylum seekers on the streets and handed them to Iranian authorities, or they left them on the mountain at the mercy of smugglers, stray bullets, and the elements. Waiting to be captured or freed was torture on the mind. Kaweh ate only twice a day, and he tried to sleep away the days. After two years of agonizing limbo, teaching himself Turkish in a mud hut, Kaweh packed his letter from UNHCR and left.

Days later, he found himself in a smuggler's boat to Greece. Before setting foot on the boat, he thought, *This is like admitting I've decided to die.* But the boat looked efficient and new and the smugglers made such lofty promises. They pointed to the horizon and said, "You see that light? That's Greece. You'll be there in half an hour in this modern boat. It was so expensive. Have trust." One smuggler controlled the main boat and the other followed in a dilapidated dinghy, promising to follow the fifteen refugees (including two children) the entire way as a safety measure.

Halfway to the island, the boat stopped. "Something is wrong with it," said the driver. He made a half-hearted attempt to check the controls. Then he said, "Everybody in the other boat. Hurry, we don't want to get caught." The rest was so efficient, it was obviously rehearsed. The refugees were loaded into the old dinghy and shown the controls; then both smugglers jumped into the nice boat (now working again) and sped back to Turkey.

Alone on the waters, the refugees tried to head for Greece. It was dark and heavy rains were looming. It didn't take long for the old boat to sway and fill with water. If the Turkish police hadn't come to arrest them, they would have died. And yet, it felt like no blessing at the time. The officers took their money, their phones, anything of value. They drove Kaweh to the border and left him there. But Kaweh had clung tightly to his UNHCR letter, the paper verifying that a respected humanitarian watchman believed his story. Now he entrusted it and his other papers to a friend; he would send for it after the journey. He knew that his greatest challenge wasn't the mountain or the sea or corrupt smugglers or hours of tedium and worry. It was the likelihood that the gatekeepers to safety wouldn't believe.

The next smuggler said, "I don't send people to die at sea. I use trucks. You won't know the driver's destination, maybe Bulgaria, maybe Greece, or Italy. Then I'll call my local contact to do the next leg. You will advance into Europe. For you, I want England." England, of course, was more expensive. Kaweh didn't care. He would request asylum as soon as his foot hit European soil. Whether he became a Bulgarian or Italian or French, he would learn the language and find his way into public service; he would be a scholar and activist for ordinary people, like his hero Ghassemlou.

Kambiz ran. His studies would wait. One day,

maybe he'd be an electrical engineer. He was good with his hands, and this wouldn't change in a year or two. But for now, he'd be damned if he let them hang him from a crane to soothe a vengeful husband. In the early 2000s, crossing into Turkey was simple enough. A few nights in the mountains, or, if you're lucky, a tourist visa. You didn't take your life truly in your hands until you made that second choice: enter Europe by land or sea?

At night, the smuggler packed twenty-one adults into the first truck. The driver gave them instructions for the road: "Remain silent. At stops, don't breathe unless I open the door to give you food." Toilet stops were thirty seconds on the side of the road every ten or twelve hours. Nights passed in silence. Now and then, when they were on a quiet stretch of highway, they could hear the driver talking on the phone with a smuggler.

They slept for two nights in a destroyed factory, a big, musty ramshackle space. A smuggler brought food enough to survive, and new refugees. After two days, the original group walked to a caravan. They rode for a long time, twenty-one squeezing in, filling every foot-space and armrest with their bodies. It was risky riding in a van, and they had no idea where they were now — but they were on a quiet road and had no other option. By the next stop, they had been traveling for six days. They hadn't bathed or changed their clothes, and they had only been outside at nighttime. They had no papers, and they still had no idea where they were.

Another truck unloaded them on a road in a wooded area behind a gas station. They hid among tall, thin trees that would have given them away in daytime, and they waited for the smuggler to call them. They were Iranians, Afghans, Kurds, Pakistanis, even African refugees. Kaweh heard the chatter of other drivers going in and out of the station, saw the signs and the advertisements, and decided they were in France or Belgium. Before this stop, the smuggler had always spoken to the driver, and the driver always offered his own instructions. "You must be silent," he would say. "If you say anything, we could be discovered." But this time, the smugglers were watching the station from a distance, sneaking between vehicles and waiting for the drivers to leave their trucks. They signaled each other from the truck stop and the trees, but neither entered the station. Now Kaweh realized that they would attempt this final leg of the journey without the knowledge of the drivers. A single word could give them away.

A smuggler called seven names (all Kurdish), including Kaweh's and a child's. None had traveled with him so far. In two or three minutes, they were swept into the back of a truck, the doors were shut, and silence and dark swallowed them. Kaweh worried about the child. Could he keep silent? Could he hold in his tears long enough for them to reach England?

At one or two in the morning, everyone sat shivering and red-eyed. The truck was reinforced in metal, a frightening shiny gray space. The passengers remained watchful and listened, though none dared to look out the small window in a high corner. "When do we make ourselves known to the driver?" whispered one man. "Or should we go with him to the end?"

"We'll sense the ferry to England," said another. "After that."

"Long after that," said another. "It's risky to get out near the border."

"And we can't wait till the final stop either, when they unload the cargo. If we make ourselves known somewhere remote, the driver will let us go. He won't want hassles, and then we have a few hours to think before we present ourselves." It turned out that some had families in England that they wanted to telephone before being arrested. So, it was agreed. They spent the night interpreting the motions of the truck.

These long nights in trucks didn't bother Kaweh — they were physically brutal but they would end. He relished the forward motion, the assurance that nobody knew his whereabouts. Every minute spent in a rest stop or in that hut in Turkey, waiting to be kidnapped, killed, or rescued, was like five hours in the truck. There is nothing worse than waiting for someone else to act. Tonight, though, they were only vulnerable when the truck stopped. As long as it was moving, they were safe.

Still, the metal box took its toll on the mind. "What if the traffickers try to kill us," whispered a younger man, choking on his anxiety.

"We'll overtake him," a man said, as he shivered inside his thin jacket.

The ferry was easy to recognize — locked wheels, the roll of the water. An hour after the wheels began moving again, someone stood up and peeked from the window. "The cars are driving on the left."

Tiny gasps rang out inside the metal box like musical notes. Every lip was quivering, everyone smiling madly. Tears were shed, hands squeezed.

"We're here," whispered someone's hoarse voice.

Kaweh arrived in England on November 24, 2004, with epic dreams. He had been traveling for over a week. He was unshaven and dirty; his body itched. He was freezing and hungry — without a complicit driver the final leg included no food. His mouth tasted like iron. *I'll be English then,* he thought. How comforting finally to know into what life he had been reborn, to glimpse the version of himself that waited down the road. *What is the people's party here? How long will it take to perfect this language?* Briefly he wondered at his own gall, and yet, why should he shy away? Why should anything be impossible? The intelligence service of a brutal dictatorship, one of the most brutal in the world, wanted him. He must have some value. *I have talent,* he thought. *I have ideas. They can call it what they want — opportunism or undeserved ambition — but I will make something good of it. I will go to university. I will help them be better.*

Six hours after Dover, they began knocking and shouting. After days of devoted silence, they thought the smallest noise would give them away. But their cries were muffled by the reinforced walls, and it took an hour for the driver to hear them. Then the truck slowed and pulled onto a quiet road. The driver flung open a street-side door and said, "Just get out."

It was daytime now and they could see a town in the distance. They set off toward it on foot, arriving in the city center twenty minutes later. Some went to call their families, asking passersby, "Hello, telephone please?" Within minutes someone called the police, and they were arrested.

Kaweh exhaled as an officer approached him. He spoke almost no English, but he knew the words for this moment: "I am refugee," he said.

Kambiz crossed Bulgaria, Serbia, Hungary, Austria, Germany, and Belgium, but his truck didn't head west toward Calais as Kaweh's did. It took him north to Holland. On the journey, a kind Iranian gave him the name of a man in Almere who had work for any Iranian with a skill, papers or not. All his tinkering meant he could do basic electrical work. He tucked the number into his pocket. He would need Iranian friends, a community.

Once safely off the truck, he broke from the group. He cleaned his body with a bottle of water in a hidden patch of wood. He had a little money. He bought a ticket and rode a train to Amsterdam. There, he wandered past flower-lined canals. He stared at the ancient gabled homes, like cookie houses in a storybook, and at the happy blondes on bicycles, and he thought, I'm here. Iran is over and the journey is over and I'm in Europe — only good things lie ahead. I'm young. I have talent and a good mind. I will make it here. I'll find my family. I'll find my work.

He went to asylum offices in the village of Ter Apel, to which all asylum seekers are required to report, and said, "I am a refugee."

■ ■ ■ ■

Part Two:
Camp

■ ■ ■ ■

(on waiting and in-between places)

I

On the plane out of Iran, all we did was marvel in whispers about what we had just done. I kept verifying it with Maman. "Is it over now? They won't follow us? How do we know those things were miracles?"

For years Maman's Three Miracles became our identity, the story of our resettlement and therefore the story of our lives. Long after I shed that narrative, my mother held on; she still defines her life by it.

"Because they were very unlikely," Maman said.

"Will there be Smarties there?" Khosrou asked. For three years since London, my brother had held on to the promise of more Smarties, and also *Divist-jib,* or "Two hundred pockets," which was how his toddler ears had heard "Digestives." I imagined a portly Briton with a chef hat and a small fork tapping exactly two hundred dents onto the chocolate side of each cookie.

"*How* unlikely?" I asked — I wanted to know the numbers. How often did stories like ours end badly? I knew I shouldn't doubt, that doubting would show the frailty of my belief and dry up my future blessings. And I *did* believe. But I was also a mathematical kid and I had questions that, for lack of a statistical vocabulary, I couldn't articulate then. Instead I asked about my toys and books again. "You promise no one will go in my room?"

Miraculous or not, the manner of our escape meant that we didn't land in the United Arab Emirates as refugees. We had a three-month sponsored visa courtesy of Baba's wealthy relative, Mr. Jahangir, miracle number three, the man who had surfaced during our weeks in hiding. But Maman knew that soon we *would* become refugees. Or worse, illegal immigrants. We had no intention of returning to Iran when our visas expired. The day after we landed, Maman requested European asylum from the United Nations office in Abu Dhabi and hoped for a response before our visas ran out and the Emirati immigration authorities found out we had blown through our welcome. We told Mr. Jahangir nothing of our plans.

"It smells," I moaned into Maman's lap in the hot, sweaty car ride to Sharjah, the city outside Dubai where we were to settle. "I can't breathe with this smell." She held my head in her long denim skirt as she had done hundreds of times before, on desert trips to our village house in Ardestoon, through a fussy, motion-sick, chafe of a childhood. Unfamiliar smells made me crazy, but I was learning how to alter them with pleasant mental associations, an early hint of how much I *could* change, if I really focused, inside my faulty, itchy mind, which Maman playfully compared to Morvarid and other grumbling old village women I had loved. Smells of other humans, though — never. They made me want to scratch off my skin.

Maman rented a single room in a hostel populated by other runaways who didn't qualify as refugees. I hated our building, a smoky industrial stack of studio apartments with paper-thin walls, a lobby encased in glass like a holding cell, where the manager, a Korean student, sat watching television all day. We paid by the month from Maman's life-and-death satchel (the cash, the passports), shared one bed, and tried to ignore the cockroaches and mice. The night I saw the first cockroach I jumped on the bed and

111

held my arms and legs and rocked until I stopped imagining it crawling all over my body. Maman jumped onto the bed too, and the three of us held each other, until it became a game. Now we were in a boat. Now the seas were churning and sloshing. "Keep your legs in!" Maman warned, and we squealed, delighting in the fear. "Don't let the sharks get your toes! Here comes a big wave!"

"Oh no! Shark!" I shrieked and burrowed under my mother's arms and torso. "It's under the boat! We're going to die! We're dead!"

"Who's the strongest rower?" said Maman, as Khosrou jumped up and down, panting and puffing out his chest. "Don't overturn the boat!"

"We may have to sacrifice one of us to the shark," I said, eyeing my baby brother and his juicy limbs.

"Dina!" said Maman. She pulled us close to her, under the covers, so that soon we were breathing in her soft powdery daffodil smell and we quieted down. We were finally alone, Khosrou, Maman, and I. We had a small bathroom, a mini fridge, a hot plate, and bare walls; and we were safe.

"What do you think Baba is doing now?" I asked, burying my face in the soft spot under her arm. I imagined my playful *baba* with no one to play with, or sneak ice cream with, or read poetry to. Baba had no sense of proportion or appropriateness or any of the parental senses at all. When I was two, he would routinely wake me from my bed at midnight to eat ice cream with him. When we were alone, he would ask me things I couldn't fathom, like "Where's the olive oil?" or "Was there mail today?" I was three.

"I don't know," said Maman. "Maybe he's pulling a tooth or doing a root canal? Maybe he's gone to Ardestoon and is having some nice *ghorme sabzi* right now . . . Ouch, don't do that!" I had picked a scab off her arm.

"It was ready!" I said as Maman rubbed the raw skinless flesh I had exposed. I nuzzled back under her arm again. "I want *ghorme sabzi.*"

"I want Smarties," said Khosrou from under Maman's other arm. "And chicken schnitzel!" We pronounced it *sheh-nee-sell.*

"We'll never eat chicken schnitzel again," I said, "Only Hotel Koorosh makes that, and Hotel Koorosh is in Isfahan." I thought of our special-occasion dish, so tasty with its lemony skin separating from the slim chop.

"They have chicken schnitzel in other

113

places," said Maman.

"No, they don't," I said. "Only Hotel Koorosh has schnitzel. Everyone knows that. I miss Hotel Koorosh. Do you think Baba is there tonight?"

"I miss Babaeejoon," said Khosrou — years later he still mourned that toy sheep, disemboweled by airport guards looking for contraband.

"Tomorrow," said Maman, "maybe we'll find Smarties and schnitzel and you can write Baba a letter." She yawned, and we fell asleep in each other's arms, where we would sleep every night for sixteen months.

The UAE was a strange country where Middle Eastern unrest collided with Western decadence. The Persian Gulf beaches were dotted with fancy resorts, but if you dared wade past their beachside pools into the waters of the gulf, crude oil stuck like black tar to your legs, suggesting some nearby oil spill, or a bombed-down plane. In Dubai, an entire mall was devoted only to gold, and secular and religious alike spent obscene sums on trinkets. Burkas, chadors, and headscarves glided up and down streets, while Western women sat bareheaded in cafés beside Arab millionaires in crisp white robes that added bridal grace to their movements.

Maman and I threw away our headscarves like so much dirty tissue paper. I wore my hair in ponytails or loose, even in the streets, and she cycled through a tiny wardrobe of Western staples. After three years sweating and itching under Islamic school uniforms and the extra-tight academic *hijab,* the Emirati heat was nothing — I had never felt so free.

And yet, for the first time, the management of money became urgent and visible for us. We didn't have much, and Dubai was expensive. Any Iranian we might find there would be obscenely wealthy. Iranian refugees rarely go through Dubai; Turkey requires no visa, and they can get there in the back of a truck. But Maman had, more or less, panicked into Dubai, and we would soon know if straying from the herd was foolish or wise.

Most mornings we sat inside our gray boxy room to avoid the suffocating heat (you could cook an egg on the sidewalk) and tried to utter the new sounds and syllables Maman remembered from university English classes. We found a beachside public pool, but evening admission prices were too high; everyone wanted to swim at night. During the day, the water was near bubbling, but the prices were low and the pool

115

was entirely ours. Maman wore tights under her one-piece suit, out of modesty and as protection against the relentless sun, and taught us how to float.

One day we wandered away from the pool, toward the gulf — it was only a few steps away. And Maman didn't say no. Despite her conservatism and piety, she liked to instigate adventures with us — she had only just turned thirty-two and escaped a bad marriage, and she wanted to live. We ran in heedlessly, stupidly, considering the beach was deserted and mottled by something black and gluey. In the water, our toes sank in and we wriggled them and laughed. When we emerged, our legs and feet were streaked with sticky black tar. Our toes were stuck together. We peeled and scrubbed, but the stuff refused to come off. The pool staff scowled and pointed to the gas station, where the attendant showed us how to wash our legs and feet with gasoline. That night we slept in a fog of gasoline fumes.

On evenings and cooler days, we explored Dubai. We window-shopped, imagining the items we might buy once we had our new home, wherever that might be. I would buy a My Little Pony bedspread. Khosrou wanted a set of Transformers. Dubai was alluring in its Westernness, and I still associate certain items with those first fugitive days. Playgrounds featured giant exotic fruit — banana slides, pineapple swing sets, seesaws like a pair of cherries. I liked the alligator slide, the way you emerged from its open jaws, uneaten. Rotisserie chickens turned behind foggy glass doors, the birds on the top rows red and juicy, dripping onto the paler ones below. Maltesers and bananas constantly beckoned. Dubai had supermarkets with long aisles, shopping carts on wheels, mountains of Western snacks. Nilla Wafers. Cornettos. The deceitful promises of a tin of Spam. Kentucky Fried Chicken with salty, minty yogurt soda (a magic pairing). And Corn Flakes: in a city that drew out your sweat within minutes of waking, crushed corn soaked in ice-cold milk was a revelation. It cooled your mouth like a summer dip in the Caspian. And yet, it wasn't sweet enough to satisfy us.

Then, we found Frosted Flakes and were busy for weeks — eating it, waiting to eat it, walking around remembering the taste of it.

"Why don't they crumble in the milk?" I asked one day, randomly, as we walked. "Why do cookies crumble and not Frosted Flakes?"

"Don't talk about food all the time, Dina," Maman said. She wiped her brow. "Do you want people to think you're some *nadid-badid*?" This was a primary concern, it seemed, after the loss of one's entire life: to be recognized as someone who has seen, done, eaten as much as the next person. Nonchalance in the face of displacement — that was our strategy.

Those first days in the hostel thrilled us because we were alone in a wonderland. Nothing seemed real here; we were only passing through, or acting in a play, and for a while, we let the days slip away. Briefly, life narrowed to three in a bed (or a capsizing boat, a desert island, an enchanted castle), on the run, having broken free. However briefly, we lived in a land of Smarties and real Kit Kats and Big Macs. We had no school. Maman never had to leave for work. We walked a lot, trying to tag each day with a marker for future memories. The days blurred anyway.

Then we had an invitation from Mr. Jahangir, our sponsor. We took care with our hair and clothes. "It's impossible to stay clean in this heat!" Maman said as she dressed us. "You step out looking like doctors' children and by the time you arrive, you look like you've crossed the Sahara."

"We can take our clothes and change there," said Khosrou, big sincere eyes on

118

Maman. He lived to protect her, and his plans were always serious.

"We'll just change in their front yard," I teased. "No problem."

Maman tossed her head back and laughed — a triumph for me every time. "Excuse me, Sir," she said, "if you just give us a minute with our plastic bags, you'll see we're very respectable people, not *dehati* at all."

"May we just use your shower please?" I said, giggling.

"Can we play your Nintendo?" said Khosrou, jumping up and down.

"You can ask that," said Maman, stroking his cheek. "That one's OK."

We played this game all the way to the Jahangirs' house.

Mr. Jahangir lived in a huge house with his beautiful wife and a preteen son and daughter who I assumed were twins. When we arrived, they eyed us like defective merchandise. The girl's sleepy, heavy-lidded eyes gave the impression of simultaneous boredom and a kind of patient, blueprinted treachery. They were beautiful people, all four of them. And the first time we stood in their foyer, waiting to be invited in, Khosrou and I shuffled around, speechless, graceless, like children of the help.

Outside their enormous door, the jokes we had made mortified me.

The twins spoke three languages, listened to Michael Jackson, and drank Pepsi. Each had a bedroom draped in music posters. The girl wore rock star pins on her jean jackets and a tight Speedo racing suit. She knotted her T-shirt at the waist and undid it theatrically as she prepared to dive into their private pool. Then she swam laps as her father kept time. We paid them a handful of visits over ten months; each time the girl eyed me with a disdain I had associated, until then, only with the British. *How did she learn to make that face,* I wondered, *when she isn't even blonde?*

"Your swimsuit doesn't fit," she said one day, pointing to the folds in my straps and the creases just below my belly. Nothing ever fit back then. I had no hips, and my underwear routinely fell to my ankles when I ran fast.

It took two months away from my girls' school in Isfahan, where my grades had earned me respect, to realize that I was nothing special. This family was better than us. They knew how to seem British, or American.

One morning, after a visit to the Jahangirs, I woke to find Maman at the folding table by the hot plate, picking at her lips. Her eyebrows were gathered tight and low, like she had decided something. "We're not going to sit here and wait," she said. "As long as we're here, we can get two things done: you can learn swimming and good English." I understood that those were the skills that separated us from the Jahangirs. Educated, respected people spoke English. And they swam.

Maman found a local grammar school for us to visit — maybe they could help. The principal, a kind, slim woman with a long braid and a sari, greeted us. She explained that the semester was long underway, that they charged tuition, that we weren't the usual candidates. She seemed resolved that we wouldn't enroll there, and I don't think Maman had hoped for that; it was almost May. The bell rang and the halls filled with children in uniform — the principal explained that the school was English-Hindi, and so even the language courses wouldn't do us much good. She offered us some used workbooks, free of charge (those too were populated by South Asian school children and their grown-ups), and Maman happily accepted.

Back in our room, Maman erased the answers in our workbooks, making sure she left no trace to cheat by. We weren't getting school credit for this; we would be judged by each syllable that came out of our mouths. Would we sound refined in our next life, or would we fall into the uneducated class? This seemed of vital importance, now that we had nothing. The thought of a fall in station frightened me. In my three years in my girls' school in Isfahan, I had learned that only two things made me special: my place at the top of the class, and my parents' medical degrees from Tehran. How shameful to lose that, to sound like a villager in front of the other children, and to have the most ordinary of them pity my luck.

I wrote my name inside my freshly rubbed-out English vocabulary book and got to work.

A few mornings later, shortly after another brutal Jahangir visit, when Khosrou was still five and I was just about to turn nine, we woke to find Maman already up, reading her Bible, underlining it in a fourth or fifth color. "Good morning!" she beamed. I sensed a scheme.

She got up and turned on the faucet in the bathroom. "Come on, you two, let's wash up and go out." Then she stopped, hesitated only briefly as she pulled out underpants and T-shirts for us. Something was happening; I knew it in that second before she spoke. "Dina," she said, "Daniel, come now, get dressed. Let's go to the park."

Who the hell was Daniel?

Khosrou's coin-shaped eyes grew rounder. He was a chubby kid, and prone to masculine posturing — especially when it came to Maman and the business of her daily protection. Every day, he held her hand in his (not the other way around) and pretended he knew just what was going on, that he was in charge of it.

Now he looked up at me for an answer, and I was still working it out.

"Dina, Daniel," Maman repeated. "Come on. We have work to do."

"Who's Daniel?" I asked, tentative, but also feeling the excitement. I loved it when Maman got up to stuff. I thought she was a warrior. And I was starting to catch on: this was no petty betrayal; it was a strategy. Maman wasn't going to let us be any less dignified than the stupid Jahangirs.

She smiled. I don't remember if she explained: *This will be your brother's name from now on because Westerners can't pronounce Khosrou.* She said this later, many times. But did she say it in that moment? I remember a rushed morning, and a dedication to the game — she had to see it through, like sleep training a baby or finishing a bottle of antibiotics. When the realization hit him, my brother's eyes welled up. It was time for sweet Khosrou to bid us farewell, to make room for Daniel, his American counterpart. He was five. Until around that year, each time he felt the sting of welling tears he would roll his eyes back into his head, stare at the ceiling, and wait for the feeling to pass. He thought if he couldn't see anyone, then no one could see him. He could hide in the cracks of the ceiling and return to us strong and brave, never having cried at all. But, though I disappeared from his sight each time his gaze drifted upward, I was still standing there. I saw his quivering chin and his wobbling cheeks, his angry eyebrows, all those very private things.

The fact that Maman held strong meant something to us — she adored Khosrou; his tears turned her to putty. Not this time, though. She helped us dress and gather our things. She promised a day of fun, maybe a rotisserie chicken for dinner. My brother was confused for a few days, burst into tears now and then, but eventually he accepted it. And by the third morning, Daniel was Daniel just as easily as I was Dina. (And it has felt strange writing his name as Khosrou until now. I'm glad to be past it.)

Soon long hazy days of solitude inside our trio came to an end. Baba sent money through a messenger. He also sent his friend, a man he had known during a prison stint for opium. (Once, I visited him there. The memory is unshakeable: being lifted onto the back of a motorcycle by a prison guard in the terrifying olive *pasdar* uniform, Maman behind me in a long, black chador, the courtyard outside Baba's cell appearing. A thin man waving. His shaved head and white pajamas. His eager smile.)

The prison friend had moved to Sharjah with his wife and four children and owned two Iranian restaurants. Now, we ate at Isfahan Restaurant free of charge at least once a week, Daniel and I running around their shimmery tiled fountain with the younger children as the owner's wife took orders. Who knows if Baba was later sent the bill. I would be surprised if he was. Iran runs on favors, and everywhere he went, Baba collected them. They saved us more than once. Now and then for many years, in our lowest moments, a man would appear at our door with an envelope of cash. Or someone would call and invite us to a meal.

Though this family, too, had money, we were far more comfortable with them. They were villagers, like Baba, but with far less education — this made the arrangement feel more equal and dignified for us all. They fed us, and we showed them interesting things we had read in books. Their naked respect for our Baba dulled the shame of receiving charity. The father had a fat black shoeshine-brush of a mustache. Their home was decorated as in Isfahan, with old Persian rugs and gaudy gold-backed chairs, nougat in silver bowls, nothing Western. Over his restaurant, a sign read, "All Kinds of Special." In May, they bought me a ninth birthday cake and their younger daughter blew out the candle with me. She brushed out my braids. She had never heard of Michael Jackson, never swum a lap in her life.

And how would we have learned in Iran, anyway? Girls had to be covered from head to toe, and almost every public pool was for men only.

One morning the younger daughter and I walked into the restaurant with ice creams. We sat around the fountain and giggled and schemed. That night Maman said, tentatively, as if she had been considering something all day. "Dina *joon,* you're nine now. Don't lick ice cream in public again."

I was confused for a long time, until a decade later when, after years of screaming fights about the length of my skirts and the right to shave my legs, I realized that something dark would forever separate me and my mother. She had been brought to adulthood believing that every disgusting male thing was her fault, and the fault of her daughter.

I could see Maman wishing she could make all the men in Sharjah blind until we could escape to Europe. And she thought she could hurry it along by working harder, at anything. She read books, taught us English words, quizzed us on our multiplication tables, and, every morning and night, she underlined her Bible in new colors.

One morning, a few months after we arrived, we were shopping in an open bazaar in Dubai when Maman noticed a man in Arab dress. He was watching us. The man was tall and thin with a short, modern beard and warm eyes. When he saw that he had been spotted, he walked over.

"You're from Iran," he said in perfect Farsi, then told a joke about the gaudiness of the market, its fabrics, its gold, the women with enormous cell phones. Maman laughed. He told another joke. Soon he was guiding us through the bazaar. A book caught my eye. It was a photo-book of English words divided into categories: fruits, modes of transport, types of houses. The page called "family" was a diagram of the Windsors. The man bought the book for me, and I spent the day staring at the English royal family. The princes seemed more educated and refined than even the Jahangirs.

Maman and the handsome man became friends. He took us on outings. I imagined they spoke of Isfahan and Dubai, of Persian food and their warring gods. I tried to notice only his face, which was striking, though he wore the long white robes of the enemy. By then, I had my categories of men, and I knew that the ones in white robes wanted to rob my strength. Still, I liked this stranger. He was funny and kind and provided hours of fun. It was easier walking around Dubai in his company. People seemed to know and respect him. My mother never covered her hair or otherwise betrayed herself because of their friendship. And it made people look at us, and, after months as a displaced person, an invisible girl without even a school where I could distinguish myself, I loved being looked at.

The next day Maman's handsome new friend revealed that he was a minor prince. I was stunned, though he said that it was nothing — the Arab world has many. Still,

128

with one syllable, this man was imbued with all the stuff of my girlish imagination. Then, one day, when he said to Maman, "Your daughter is very clever," I forgot my objections. He was my friend.

It wouldn't last. One day, he invited us to dinner in his home, the only meal we ate there. We hadn't brought dinner clothes to Dubai, but we did our best, draping ourselves and fluffing our hair. A woman greeted us at the door. She didn't speak much, just led us into a lavish sitting room, with enough pillows arranged for a feast of twenty, and left us alone there. We waited an hour, then two. No other guests arrived. Daniel began to whine of hunger, so we ate, morsels at first, then we filled our plates. As the minutes ticked on, we began to notice other details. Movement behind a screen door. His wives and children had been watching us. I imagined that they whispered about my mother's defiant eyes and petite figure, my healthy hair and chatty mouth, Daniel's chubby cheeks. After dinner, we were escorted out, having spoken to no one but each other. We were confused, and I can't imagine that Maman slept much that night.

The next day, our new friend asked Maman to become one of his wives. Worse, he asked to marry me to his oldest son. Maman was livid, but she couldn't have been as angry as I was. How dare he make me a footnote in someone else's marriage proposal! He had said I was clever! Didn't he understand that I was meant to study at university and to be someone in the West? Didn't he want to help me do *that*? We never saw him again.

That strange dinner in the minor prince's home is my most vivid memory of Dubai, though I learned English and swimming there, tasted Corn Flakes and bologna for the first time, peeled tar off my legs, and saw a man in Arab clothing play vigorous tennis with a woman in white shorts, her wild yellow hair brushing her shoulders as she dashed across the court.

The asylum process involved many interviews, forms, letters, trips to Abu Dhabi. I dreaded those days when we had to sit in a hot, nauseating car for hours, all the way to the United Nations office, then in a sweaty, stinking room with plastic chairs for hours more, only to turn around and drive back.

In May 1988, we were called to the United Nations office in Abu Dhabi for an interview or some such errand. Daniel and I tumbled out of the car, sick and exhausted, and started whining for food and water. My bangs stuck to my forehead in sticky clumps. I hated Abu Dhabi so much.

We found a convenience store. Maman pulled on the door. It was closed. So was the next one. The streets were emptier than usual. Where was everyone? Then Maman remembered: it was Ramadan; the Muslim world was enduring a month of prayer and daytime fasting. Living in our own timeless fog, our world reduced to a room and a restaurant and a public pool, we had forgotten the Muslim calendar altogether.

We walked for a long time before Maman found something: a small hot-food vendor idling in front of his counter. Maman tried to order.

"It's Ramadan," he said. "Not until sundown."

"We're traveling from Dubai," she said. "They're children. Please."

When he refused again, she pressed on. Then he paused. "Eat in there," he said, pointing to the utility closet. "And only the children."

We ate fast in the musty dark and made our way to the address tucked in Maman's Bible. A sign read "United Nations Development Program (UNDP)." Maybe it helped that we arrived for our interview disheveled and glassy-eyed over a single meal. Maybe it helped that Maman's stride was wearier than her age and that Daniel and I were covered in so much sweat and ketchup and pantry dirt. Their answer would take months, and who could guess what Westerners needed to witness in order to believe a story.

A few weeks later our visa expired. We were now illegal immigrants.

Was it before or after our change in station that we met the Sadeghis? The days blur together, but soon, our world expanded. Another Persian family arrived in the hostel. They, too, had left Iran on a tourist visa. They, too, would become illegal, or had already done so — we didn't ask.

Mozhgan Sadeghi was my age, taller, with thick black eyebrows and hair. She spoke Farsi; no more having to mutter broken English to strange girls in playgrounds. She knew all my games and songs. To have a friend here, in this waiting place, was a miracle, an event so unlikely (I now understood) that it causes pain, a brief distortion, and panic that it might not have happened, though you didn't know a moment ago that it would.

Mozhgan and I played every day in front of the hostel. We walked down the street and went to the pool in the daytime. Daniel too now had a friend, because Mozhgan had a younger brother, though Maman was cautious about allowing us to swim with him. He had bald patches in his cropped black hair that Maman suspected were caused by a fungus.

One day, the second or third time we played together, Mozhgan was showing me a doll her mother had sewn, chattering on about its dress and hair. Suddenly she stopped. Her eyes grew wild, then emptied, and both arms shot out in front. Her head fell between her extended arms, her ears grazing her biceps. She reached out far, muscles taut, like a rower in a boat. The doll dangled from the fingers of one hand. She wriggled her fingers for several seconds, as if playing a fast tune on an invisible piano, then grew still and dropped her arms, panting as she recovered from the spasm. She glanced around, eyes shy, and tucked the doll under her arm. "I'm sorry," she said. "That happens to me. Was that very long?" she felt her forehead, which was dry. "It wasn't long. You shouldn't be scared."

I shrugged. That night, I told Maman what had happened. "Poor girl," she said, "she has seizures. That was a special kind of seizure. Not everyone falls to the ground like in movies. Don't worry. You just play and be kind and try not to stand directly in front of her."

"What if she kicks me or bites or something?"

"Dina!" said Maman. "She's not rabid. It's just the arms." I understood more than Maman knew. She had the urge to extend her arms, to feel her muscles tighten as far as they would go, like a person exercising, or the way I craved to feel my chin against my neck or breathe in so deep that the metal bar would move back down into place.

I understood the illness, and yet (perhaps because I felt only a sliver of difference between us) I ran away soon after each attack. Daniel and I were afraid of Mozhgan for as long as we knew her. But there was never any question of not playing together. Mozhgan and her brother were our friends, the only ones in our same situation. Mozhgan could sit on a stoop and talk about missing our old rooms, or a teacher, or a best friend. She could lay about for hours and imagine where we would both end up, what our homes would be like, and what books we'd replace first. We each had a backpack, and I had lately begun to pour all of my obsessive habits into mine: counting the change, the hair bands, the Smarties in the baggie. With Mozhgan I didn't have to pretend I didn't crave the bag in my lap, just so I wouldn't seem strange. I could obsess over a dull pencil point that had been sharp that morning, digging into the bottom of my bag for the missing lead tip, and she would wait for me to finish. And if she felt a seizure coming (she didn't always), she inched away and I knew to wait quietly for her to finish. Sometimes she had an object in her hand and I marveled that she never dropped it. One finger was always alert, hooked securely to her toy or sweater or bag of chips. Her body's practicality impressed me.

We were allies in our strangeness. And yet, I knew that I was luckier, because my thing could be overcome, given time and some breathing room. Mozhgan didn't study or go to school. And this, too, felt unlucky for her. Maman let me play with her only when I had finished my lessons. I never objected. Maman's rules made studying feel more official, like real school.

One evening in late summer, after Mozhgan and I waved goodbye and ran to our respective doors, I saw Maman reading a letter. Her face was clouded and tense. When I asked what was wrong, she said, "We're moving."

"Why?" I asked.

"They're turning the building into dorms. We all have to move out this week." She seemed confused and muttered about the rent we had paid. We were just a few days into the month. "I'll talk to Sanjagh in the morning," she teased, but I couldn't laugh. *Sanjagh,* Farsi for "hairclip," was our mispronunciation of the Korean super's name: Sung-Jin. We had a hundred of these mispronunciations that we kept up for laughs.

I had never liked living in that building, but I had also never been evicted, or lived in the kind of place that made eviction a possibility. I had always had roots. My grandparents' village home had been theirs for decades, maybe a century — it had an old-world *tanoor* oven and a cave of a kitchen. My parents had owned every home we lived in. Each chair and couch and table seemed welded to its place, and there was a small tree growing through a glass enclosure in the living room. But here, someone had decided to build dorms, and, with a snap of a capitalist finger, we were out. Until that moment, I had been too busy to feel my displacement. I missed home and Baba and my big family, but I was never afraid. We were having an adventure. Now, though, I felt like we were lost in a strange country, and that we weren't fastened to anything at all.

The next day, Maman rushed into the room and told us there had been another miracle. The hostel had no leases, only a handful of month-by-month tenants. The owner, with his vast oil sums and his capitalist plans and his rush to repurpose the building before the new academic year, announced that he would move the paid-up tenants to a hotel down the street for the rest of the month. Only one hotel had enough capacity for the thirty or forty displaced residents: a tourist hotel with a lifeguarded pool and tennis courts, color televisions in every room, soft comfortable sheets, plush towels, and Western toilets. We wouldn't be able to eat at the hotel, or touch anything reserved for the tourists. We'd have to be light-footed and invisible. But we could sleep there.

All I heard was the thing about Western toilets. I couldn't use them. My body refused to adjust. I was accustomed to a porcelain hole in the ground with striated foot rests, like a radiator panel, my strong thighs holding me up in squat position as I relieved myself. To sit while taking a shit was unheard of, barbaric, like doing it on the couch. "Dina, stop this *vasvas,*" said

137

Maman. (The Persian word for OCD is quaint enough for parents to throw around. I hated it, though. My habits were *normal,* and I liked them treated as such.) "We'll figure out the toilet in the two weeks we have there," said Maman. "And you'll learn breaststroke and freestyle."

Arriving at the hotel felt like emerging from icy water into sun, or walking into a schoolhouse after the last stifling day of summer. The Sadeghis were there too, and Mozhgan and I whispered as our mothers checked us in. We were shown our rooms — thirty years later, I remember the sensation of stepping inside: we were offered two rooms, each with a large bed, connected by a double door. Mozhgan came with me to our part of the hotel. When she saw our space, she squeezed my hand and rushed to find her family, who were settling in.

An hour later, a hotel manager knocked on our door. "I'm so sorry, madam," he said. "But we have to lock the door between the two rooms. You only have one, not both. I'm sorry for the confusion."

Maman and Daniel didn't mind. We had spent months sharing a bed, and now we would share a much nicer one. I was angry though. I had looked forward to privacy, to breathing room and clean walls.

"It's strange," said Maman, after we realized that the adjoining room would remain empty. The real estate developer had paid for a block of rooms. It was hard to imagine him bothering with petty negotiations about room size. Why did they make a point of taking away some of our space? Maman went downstairs to investigate. She returned shaking her head, her eyes darkened by disappointment and anger. "Mrs. Sadeghi complained that we had the same amount of space as them, even though they're five and we're three. Can you believe it?"

"Mozhgan's *maman* told the hotel to take our room?" I asked. "Why?"

"I think she got greedy," said Maman. "She thought they'd give her a third room. Instead they took ours away."

"Can't she ask to change it back?" I said, feeling hopeful.

Maman shook her head. "You are never to mention it to them, Dina. They won't fix it. Because it was probably jealousy, too. They're villagers who saw a woman doctor alone with two children, calling herself a Christian out in the open, no scarf, and they wanted to punish us. Next time you see Mozhgan, you make sure to say how happy you are here. And teach her some of your English words, OK?" I giggled. I loved this

Maman; yes, this was petty, but she was always vigilant, making sure Daniel and I didn't lose an ounce of our dignity, that we never suffered from shame. Over the decades, as I grew into a Western woman, and as a gulf of culture and taste opened up between us, we fought over this Iranian habit more than any other: the value she placed on dignity and face, the way she guarded against bad faith and jealous eyes. And yet, I know that if she hadn't warned me against the Sadeghi's bitter intentions, or the Jahangirs' brutal class markers, I would have grown up unable to change myself. I would be bound to a single safe habitat, without the confidence or boldness to live like a chameleon, free to make my home in any corner of the world.

Those windfall weeks flew by. I swam so much my skin turned from olive to dark brown. One afternoon, Maman jumped into a cab. "Take me to a church," she said. The driver wore a turban and a long beard. He turned and eyed her. Then he pulled onto the road. Had this been a mistake? she wondered. *Will he take me to some alley, or worse, the Iranian embassy?* He drove for a long time, through unfamiliar streets and a patch of desert, and pulled up in front of an unmarked building with a typed sheet on the door. "What is this?" she said. "Go," he said, "this is the church for converts like us." Maman grinned. For her, exile was one astounding kindness after another, which she called miracles, forgetting that she was a young mother with a wan, girlish face, in a world run by guilt-eaten men.

The paper listed denominations and languages, each with a timeslot. She checked her watch. The anglophone Protestants were about to meet. There she met Jim and Barbara, an Australian missionary couple with a son, Nathan, exactly my age. They gave her VHS tapes for us, a Christian cartoon called *The Flying House.* On her way in, she gave it to the hotel manager and asked if he would play it on the video system (a VCR in the manager's office feeding to a channel shared by all hotel guests). He agreed, happy to make up for the business with the Sadeghis.

A few days before we were to leave the fancy hotel, Baba visited from Isfahan, to bring our clothes, and to see me and my brother. The authorities had questioned him for weeks after our escape, and after a period of palm greasing and low lying, he convinced them that he had nothing to do with Maman's new religion, her proselytizing, or her escape. And, we would soon discover, he had another reason not to fear suspicion on our account.

We opened the door and fell into his arms, our jolly, happy Baba with his red hair and pockets full of chocolate and sour cherry. "Dina! Khosrou! I missed you," he said, and we hugged him and asked what he had brought us.

Maman flitted about, rearranging suitcases. She made tea. Once or twice she called Daniel by his new name. Baba raised an eyebrow. Then he asked my brother, "Are you Daniel now?"

"Yes," he said.

"Sima, what are you doing? Khosrou is my great-uncle's name! He named Dina. You can't change our son's name."

She shrugged. "He's going to live in an English country. They can't make the sounds; you know this."

They fought. Over the name, and over where we would live, and over money (there was never any for us), and over his opium, and over her troublesome Christianity. But most of all, they fought over her clothes.

"These don't fit," she said, standing in front of the mirror in a skirt so stretched out it wouldn't stay over her hips.

"You've lost weight," said Baba.

142

"Someone much bigger has worn this," said Maman.

"You're imagining things again. Everyone is against you, aren't they, Miss Born Again?"

"Don't pretend like I'm crazy," said Maman, holding a ruined dress against her body. "You know you've let some woman go through my house and wear my clothes." Maman had looked forward to being reunited with some of her wardrobe. Almost everything we had brought had worn out, and we were beginning to look a little more refugee-like every day — it doesn't happen all at once, I now knew, and we had to break free of this waiting place quickly or we would be one of the indistinguishable Eastern hordes. Who would take us in looking like so much riffraff?

"*Some* woman?" Baba shot back. "A kind, motherly woman who at least knows how to live instead of hiding behind god all the time," he muttered. His Cheshire smile was gone. Now he chewed his tongue, and the cat-like tip of it protruded from his mouth, his eyes full of the same feline fury. In Isfahan, he looked like this just before he blew up and slapped Maman across the room. It was the one thing I didn't miss about home.

"Throw them away if you don't want

143

them," he said. Then he dug his cigarettes out of his shirt pocket and left, slamming the door.

"Maman, why is there another woman in our house?" asked Daniel, when we were alone. He sat beside her and held her hand like a little man.

"It's OK," she said. "It's normal. It's because Baba is a man. He can't cook or clean, and every man needs a woman to do . . . woman things."

Daniel thought for a moment. "But who will do your man things?" he asked, eyes wide, as if they had just opened to the ugliness of the world.

Maman burst into tears. Baba left the next day, or the day after that. This was why he didn't worry about visiting us. Maman had been naive not to guess it: he had married again — his right, under Sharia law, as husband to only one woman. And as far as the authorities were concerned, he had renounced his unmanageable first wife to her fate. He was free to live unbothered in Iran, as is any straight, married man with money and open doors, a gentle, necessary profession, and a decorative Koran.

That night, the manager paid us another visit. "I can no longer play those videos, madam, I'm sorry."

"Why not?" asked my mother as she took the VHS tapes from him.

"You know why," he said, his voice no longer kind. "I thought they were just cartoons."

We moved into Jim and Barbara's house the next day. There, we learned the rhythms of the Australian household, thinking maybe they would be similar to English or American ones. We ate dinners of cold meats and sliced vegetables at five o'clock, an absurd hour. We buttered our bread with something made of oil. We sat on Western toilets and showered in the morning instead of mid-afternoon. Maman enrolled us in Nathan's English school. Somehow Barbara got our fees waived. The school taught an Arabic and British curriculum. It had uniforms and a motto I liked because it wasn't bombastic but practical and easy to achieve: *Be Thorough.* I was assigned to the third grade, the grade I had nearly finished last year in Isfahan. I put on my uniform and endured the shame.

The children on the playground explained to me that two types of people lived in Dubai: the Arabs and the English. You could tell them apart by their clothing, but it was trickier with fair-skinned girls in school uniforms, like me. They knew I was from

Iran because of my broken English. I hadn't realized until then that my English was all that broken. Every night, I read Nathan's old children's books — *Babar* and Richard Scarry hardbacks about animals with service jobs, and Roald Dahl. But, each morning before the first bell, I made a dozen new mistakes. I didn't realize that we were divided, not only by grade, but by *houses.* I was in Dougherty House. Though Dougherty had done nothing for me, offered no true refuge or identity, and though I had no ties to it, I had to find some hidden stores of loyalty for my house. If I received good marks or points for good behavior, my house would benefit.

"You're closer to an Arab," the playground girls would say. "You're not an Arab, but not far from it." I never played with these girls. I only watched them. Nathan had a crush on a girl named Naomi, a waifish blonde thing who never finished her lunch. When I finished mine, she called me greedy. Still, I found her fascinating. She sang in choir and always smelled like daisies. One day, our grade filed by a high school classroom with its curtains drawn. Flashing lights and music seeped through an opening in the curtain. I peeked in. The older kids were dancing, boys and girls together, as a disco ball made their faces glow in many colors. "What's that?" I asked.

"It's just a dance," said Naomi, as if it were nothing.

"At school?" I said. "With the teacher standing there?" I thought these were things you did in secret when you were twenty, your parents old and asleep in their bed, and if you got caught you might be lashed. Naomi shrugged. I kept peering in. One of the teenagers, who seemed not to be reveling so much as completing a task, frowned at me through her breathy exertions, and the teacher pulled the curtain shut.

I decided to enter a swim race in breaststroke. The event was public and, when I came in third (out of four), Maman ran to the edge of the pool and pulled me out. "I'm proud of you," she said. "These girls have been swimming since they were babies. You learned to float two months ago in boiling water. Nobody would know that watching this race." *That,* Maman knew, had been my only goal: that no one should guess who I had been before I turned nine, a girl who couldn't even float. I hadn't come in first, but I had passed for one of them; I had won something better than a medal.

For some crazy English reason, Dougherty House got my points.

Everyone knew that any day, or month, I might leave, and so there was no permanent place for me in clubs or teams or in friendships: I was too mired in uncertainty. Even my uniform was borrowed, and too big. I was offered a role in a play, but Maman mentioned to my teacher her hopes after our latest Abu Dhabi trip, and my role was pulled for fear that I wouldn't be in Dubai on opening night.

I began to fret again, to count everything, to hold my chin too long against my neck. I decided to fast, thinking maybe God would see how serious I was and take us away from there, to someplace I could stay, get comfortable, make real friends, buy fresh workbooks. I wanted to go home — *anywhere.* When my teachers saw that I wasn't eating, they scolded me for dieting and made me eat; they thought the pressures of a coed environment were getting to me. Dougherty lost points. But Maman believed me when I explained that this wasn't about looking like Naomi.

In February, Maman began to look distracted. She prayed and prayed. She traveled to Abu Dhabi without us. Something was happening again.

I found out later that, as she had done in Isfahan, she had begun passing out Christian tracts in Muslim communities, a dangerous and reckless thing. She was desperate for something to do, a way to make the gears move faster. Whether it was the tracts or something else, the United Arab Emirates now knew that we had overstayed, that our visa had expired months before. Mr. Jahangir was called. A court was convened.

"Madam," said the judge, "you are in violation of several laws here. You must pay a fine of twenty thousand dollars and leave the UAE in two weeks, or you will be put in jail with your children. Do you understand?"

Maman just stared. The color fled from Jahangir's face; he put a hand over his mouth, shaking his head.

"Do you understand that you must leave?" asked the judge.

"Yes, your honor," she said, her voice weary.

The judge paused, looked at his papers, as if considering the case again. He said, "I will forgive the fine. But leave in two weeks or risk jail." Jahangir made a small noise (who else would have been saddled with the fine but the sponsor?). Maman thanked the judge. "See that you pay the court fees on your way out," he continued, "and, madam, do not pass out any more of your tracts in this country." Maman nodded.

"What will you do now?" asked Jahangir, his relief from the fee pardon gone after a moment's thought about the deadline. "Nothing gets done in two weeks, Sima. All three of you in jail? How? How will this work?"

If you ask Maman now, she will tell you that she did nothing but pray. That she asked the entire church to pray. And I believe that to be true. I also believe that either Barbara or Jim or Jahangir or someone at the church called UNHCR. Perhaps that's the purpose of prayer: that it reaches *human* ears. Maman disagrees. She says that our application had been in the works for months; maybe it was already in the final stages. Whatever the case, thirteen days after the court date, we received a call that Italy had said yes. They weren't offering us asylum, but they would be our next passthrough state, a safe haven as we petitioned other countries. We needn't worry about the judge's deadline, as Emirati immigration authorities had been contacted and were satisfied. Regardless, we should pack immediately.

The next day, in February 1989, we were flown to Rome, then driven to Mentana, a village outside the city, to a home for refugees on their way elsewhere. We hardly had time to say goodbye to those we had known.

II

We drove up the winding path to Hotel Barba. It was winter. We ate hot pasta in the glass room. We drank tea in the courtyard, listened to stories in one another's rooms. An old lady collected bricks. We gossiped.

Maman didn't partake in the human drama of the place. People grumbled. They complained. They fought. But she kept to herself. When it became obvious that we would be staying at Hotel Barba for a while, she made it her job to continue our education as before. She refused to languish in the hotel like the other exiles.

Now and then, workers from churches and charities drove up the hill and dumped huge piles of donated clothing in the courtyard. The residents would rush to dig through the piles, scattering the clothes. For hours or days, unwanted items were strewn around the yard. The workers would hand out coupons that the residents could redeem for tins of snacks if they visited the church. Maman never bothered with either offering, not because we didn't need these things, but because you can only accept so much charity before you lose sight of who you once were. "It won't happen any faster if we sit and wait," Maman said. "People pay a fortune to visit this country. Let's be tourists." She stuffed our backpacks, and we rode buses to Pisa, Venice, and Rome. She was still thirty-two, braving public buses alone with little money, no Italian, and two whiny children.

In Venice we discovered that traveling isn't cheap. We could barely afford a slice of pizza or an arancini rice ball, let alone hotel rooms. Maman negotiated her way around cities: if we arrive at midnight and leave at 5 a.m., if we sleep in the service room, can we stay for next to nothing?

Some Barba kids had enrolled in local Italian schools, but Maman insisted on English. Living in a remote village with no car limited our options, but she found an American homeschool that met inside a Roman church. It was over an hour away by bus. More importantly, we would miss lunch at Barba. So, Maman devised a plan that would enable us to join the homeschoolers but still get all three meals from Hotel Barba. She enlisted the help of the punkish staffer, who would give our lunches to the Afghan grandmother, who in turn would wrap them up and save them for us to eat at night. We would save our fresher dinners to take with us for lunch the next day. No matter what was served for dinner, Maman would put it inside a sandwich (hard, crusty rosetta rolls came with every meal) and hang the sandwiches in plastic bags over the balcony where they might cool and survive the morning bus ride to Rome. I still remember the singularly satisfying texture of a rosetta made with pot roast and a layer of green peas, the roll finally soft enough after soaking in gravy overnight.

And yet, the act itself was embarrassing, and so very visible. The bringing in of the lunches, now cold, to the canteen at dinnertime, the packing away of the fresher dinners. We filled the bread rolls with strange things: mashed potatoes, pasta, chicken, slices of meat under carrot. To this day, whatever their quality, leftover sandwiches evoke survival for me.

Because we joined the homeschoolers in spring, we didn't have workbooks, and we had fallen far behind our grade. Again, Maman spent days erasing hundreds of used pages, making sure she removed every marking so we could do our own work without the temptation of old answers peeking through. As the weather grew warm, we spent our mornings and afternoons in the courtyard, Maman erasing her fingers raw, while Daniel and I raced through the grades we had missed: fourth for me, first for him. It cut the tedium, and soon our boredom died down.

Then, one day, a drama erupted among the adults that captured the attention of every refugee in Mentana. A Romanian wife fled into the arms of a young friend, the only other Romanian living at Hotel Barba aside from her husband. I was captivated by their love affair. Why was this woman so unhappy with her husband? Why was she willing to risk her asylum, a life of every possibility, for a handful of sad, runaway days with her friend?

Probably the couple had befriended their compatriot, a student with a guitar and a spasm of curly brown hair, before their sentence at Hotel Barba began. Maybe they met on the journey. Day after shapeless day, the three sat in that Italian courtyard, smoking and suffering quietly together, awaiting their release from this house of political outcasts. I imagined that they spoke of home. Mostly they watched the children play.

She wasn't beautiful. Her face was flat, her eyes sleepy — but she had a sly smile, the look of a secret always on her mouth. She was tall with dark hair, wide hips, and painted-on jeans. The couple had no children. The husband was clean-cut with sad eyes and a kind smile. He worshipped his wife. A few days after their arrival, though he was college educated, he found a cash job as a gardener so he could buy dresses for her. "So she doesn't feel like a refugee," he said. Residents of Barba didn't have jobs, though it wouldn't have been unheard of to help the local builder lay some brick, or hold down a bleating lamb for the butcher, or deliver a few newspapers in the early morning. But this man labored with purpose, every day, and it seemed that he craved to diminish himself to show her his love. What then — the adults wondered aloud — did she want?

In the evenings, the husband returned from a day in the gardens, looking worn. He drank a beer on his balcony, too sated with work to engage in theater. His wife pined and slinked. She whispered with her lover behind the hotel. One day in the sunny courtyard, with the husband just there, the student looked at her with a hunger so intense that I recoiled.

Every night the three shared dinner. At mealtimes, we sat with our own tribe, slipped into our native tongue, complained in our own way. As a community, the residents of Barba had only a handful of rituals: gatherings around the mail cubbies; displays of affection for the boy who ladled the soup course with a sing-song *"Zuppa!"*; morning stampedes for the strawberry jam and collective contempt for the grape which seemed to multiply and became a symbol of our many deprivations. And, of course, we gossiped. The women whispered about the Romanian wife, "She's so foolish, so cruel." Once, in an attempt to teach me about reputation, wisdom, and gravitas, Maman said, "Do you know how many strangers from all over the world got to know her only as *that stupid woman*?"

Like Maman, I believed she was stupid. Soon, her husband was spending most daylight hours away from Hotel Barba, sweating outdoors despite the chill, to make extra money for her. He would return after dark and give her small gifts and kiss her and they would smoke together. But she spent her days flirting with her friend and talking to a Polish woman who became a repository for her breathless confessions.

Maman told me that in Hotel Barba, no one really knew anybody else's situation. Maybe the shabby old man at the breakfast table was a brilliant professor. Maybe the red-clad woman humming in the yard was an heiress or a housemaid or a doctor with nimble fingers. Maybe she had escaped political or religious persecution. All we knew was that everyone was bored, watching each other, and why would you want to be their clown only to find out later that the squinting eyes fixed on you belonged to a president or a poet or a judge?

For months, I watched the Romanians and tried to guess their story. As with all Barba guests, something frightening had happened and they had fled. Their rooms were on the same hallway as ours. An agile person could climb from balcony to balcony. Once I climbed to the couple's room and knocked on the window, and the husband gave me a sip of beer.

Another time I wandered into the empty dining room. I found the wife alone with her friend, their heads almost touching. She looked up abruptly and offered me hot milk and sugar with a few drops of coffee. Later, in the courtyard, her husband held her hand and they watched me in that amused, longing way lonely couples look at other people's children. I thought, "She loves both men, but she's already married so it's too late." I didn't attach any heartache to the too-lateness of it.

A few months into our stay news spread

that the young woman had abandoned her husband and fled with the young friend to the Swiss border on foot, hoping to cross over illegally. She was tired of waiting for asylum, tired of the boredom, tired of her husband. She was withering. The rumors flared up again. The lovers had vacated Hotel Barba, becoming fugitives in Italy. I'm not sure if we were allowed simply to leave Hotel Barba. Yes, we left every day for school, but could a person just pick up their bags and move out? We were, after all, carrying flimsy documentation and were largely unemployable, un-house-able, and without options. We were social cripples, and Barba was our temporary guardian. What would the lovers do alone in the inhospitable bowels of a foreign country with nothing but their passion and his guitar? "They're just bored," the older women would mutter. "The days are so long here." I'm sure that these words were whispered in Barba's many languages, though my gossipmonger of choice was the Afghan grandmother.

The pair had disappeared in a delirium of spring fever and, for some days afterward, I had my first opportunity to witness heartbreak up close. The husband grew pale. He sat alone in the courtyard or in his room drinking dark beers, his head in his hand, probably thinking he could have bought her more things. Some days he sat in his balcony, holding a frothy mug, looking out at the winding gravel driveway. He stopped working.

What were they doing, alone in the open world? Did the student hold her hand as they walked? Did she lose her fingers in his curls? Did they pretend to be Italian and rent a room and share a bed? I imagine he strummed guitar for her on Italian roadsides, spending their meager lire (too few for train tickets) on pizza and Coke to share as he flagged kind motorists, shivered in his thin jacket, and slowly noticed her flaws. Back then, I pretended they were visiting Pisa and Venice as we had done -- I pictured him kissing her on the cheek and I blushed at the idea. At nine, I was curious and opinionated, and I judged her. Her husband was the more handsome one anyway, I decided, and look how he suffered for her sake. I hated her and hoped God would punish her with perpetual wandering, her story never believed.

In time, the runaways returned. They were caught at the border and sent back to the camp with their heads hanging. My memory puts regret on their faces. Only a few months more and they might have been

159

welcomed into a new country, able to leave Hotel Barba with respect and warm good-byes. Now here they were again, back in their old rooms, apart and enduring the silences of the man they had betrayed. Probably their recklessness delayed all three of their visas.

They had no choice but to reconcile with the husband, to eat with him silently every night, to make chitchat about books, to smoke in the courtyard. Everyone watched the spectacle with awe and secret fascination. What gall! Where would she sleep? Of course, she returned to her husband's room, since she was assigned to it. After that, the student spent his days in his single room — as in the outside world, it was his moment to fade away, leaving the couple to suffer alone. Still, at meals, they were the whole of Romania, and they shared a table. Maybe soon a new exile would arrive and relieve them of the burden of three.

As we watched stories unfurl wildly around us, our own unspooled quietly. We had interviews at the American embassy. A soft-spoken woman interviewed Daniel and me. She saw that we had been raised Christians, and she believed Maman's story. We were never accused of lying; we didn't have to shape our story to make it fit their fancies, as others had done.

We were told that things would go faster if we secured a sponsor, a connection to the United States. We didn't know anyone. We had hoped for asylum in England, but Maman's mother, Maman Moti, had, I was told, refused to sponsor us — she had left Iran before the revolution and wanted nothing to do with our postrevolutionary troubles. When I was six and we visited her in London, Maman had attended a church event for an American writer named Jim. She had taken his card. Now she wrote to him asking for help.

Sometime in that turbulent season, when spring was blooming and our restless community was overcome by renewed desire for a country, we discovered why the Afghan grandmother was collecting bricks. One afternoon as the crowd around the mail cubbies dispersed, someone saw her scurry up the stairs with a brick under her arm. The punkish staff member or Zuppa man or somebody followed her and insisted on seeing her room. Soon news spread around Hotel Barba that she had built a shower seat and was spending hours a day sitting happily under the stream, wasting the hotel's water. They dismantled her seat. She threw an epic tantrum. Secretly, all of us cheered

161

her on. The tedium had reached new heights of toxicity. We were drinking it now, mad with it.

A year or two later, we visited that Afghan grandmother and her daughter in California. It turned out they were from an important family, a fact we could easily see when we met them in their own house. "Do you remember that Romanian woman who ran away with the younger man?" the daughter asked my mother as she poured skim milk over my cereal — my first taste of the vile blue water. That detail was all they remembered of a woman who had shared their home for months.

Even now, memories of the old Afghan woman (scurrying behind the hotel with a brick under her skirts, saving our lunches, kissing our cheeks) bring a fleeting smile to my lips. But I wouldn't recognize her in a lineup of grandmothers. Funny, the daily nothings by which an entire person is remembered. Maman wanted me to learn this. The lovesick wife of Hotel Barba might have been smart and talented. But how many strangers knew her only as "that stupid woman"?

Thinking back on this story, I wonder if Maman knew that I was watching, if she saw all that I committed to memory as she erased answers to math problems. I missed Baba, my aunts, and my uncles. I wanted to know why people leave each other. Maybe Maman was thinking about love too, alone as she was after a decade, with no comfort but Jesus. And weren't we all obsessed with love? Despite the daily burdens of refugee life — unfamiliar food, hot buses, lack of school, the possibility of being sent back to face imprisonment and death — I believe that everyone there continued to function on that register. Even when first-order needs were in question, love was all for us, the only thing more basic than home or country.

In May, I had a spasm of devotion and was baptized in Lake Bracciano. Days later I turned ten among my American friends from the homeschool and my fellow refugees. We celebrated with a guitar and homemade cake in the courtyard of Hotel Barba. That summer, in 1989, after sixteen months as refugees, after hours lining up outside embassies and sweating in interview rooms, we opened our letter to the delight of a roaring crowd around the mail cubbies. Maman cried. She received hugs and whispers from mothers and grandmothers. Daniel and I jumped up and down. On our last day in the American church, the congregation sang us a song: "Friends Are Friends Forever."

We said goodbye, packed up our little room. In JFK, we held our breath through immigration. We landed in Oklahoma City in time for the Fourth of July.

III

In summer of 2011 I returned to Hotel Barba with my then husband Philip. We didn't know that this would be the last summer of our marriage, and the twilight of a decade of travels, but one morning we woke up on holiday in Rome and craved to visit the refugee hostel where I had once lived, this place of personal legend — I remember that we both wanted to go. Maybe we sensed a coming exile. Soon I would become a wanderer again, setting off from Barba into a new life for a second time. Maybe that's what drew us back there, the notion that Barba had the power to launch me. Philip had been more father to me than husband, and at Barba I had once before learned that fathers aren't necessary. I had learned to live without one. Now, having forced my husband into my *baba*'s empty seat, maybe I was here to make amends for my silliness, to relearn my lesson, and to give him back.

We made phone calls, but no one in Mentana remembered the hotel. We rented a

164

scooter and drove to the town anyway, on a wet, hot day, through mist and drizzle, Rome receding behind us as we navigated woods and slick highways. I wore a green dress and flats, ready to pick through the rolling fields, to steal an unripe peach, to toe the narrow paths behind the fence. I wished I could buy a Cornetto with lire, so I could remember how it feels to give a *thousand* of something for an ice cream cone and still find it a bargain. When was the last time a sweet felt precious?

Long before we arrived, I spotted the house on a hill from the road toward town. I didn't need confirmation. I knew that hill, that manor on the horizon surrounded by valley. We roared up to the dirt path, our cheeks flushed and windblown. Pulling up that steep, meandering road to Hotel Barba, watching it appear, was a sensation I knew: a jolt of rescue, the feeling that I was plucked by some unseen hand from a fire.

I jumped off the scooter and ran the rest of the way. Philip parked. Were we in the right place? The building was renovated, the courtyard converted to a parking lot and the canteen turned into a restaurant and espresso bar. The fence to the adjoining garden was gone. I imagined it disappeared with the refugees.

If Barba's bones were any more ordinary I would have doubted. But we hadn't followed an address. We had spotted Barba and made straight for it, passing through Mentana (a confirmation) then up the same winding road that, seen from a government car in 1989, had promised new life.

I entered the deserted lobby, my steps echoing dully as a concierge greeted me in Italian. Had I dropped into a parallel universe? "What the fuck happened?" I muttered.

"Welcome to Hotel Belvedere," he said in English. Barba, it seemed, had become a place for businesspeople to rest and eat forgettable meals between breakout sessions. Outside, Philip readied his camera, waiting to capture me in my pretty dress discovering a tree, a bench, as if I were a child in a ballet or having a birthday photo shoot.

I asked to see our old room. I didn't know the number, only the view overlooking the courtyard (now parking lot). The concierge took me from room to room in search of it. It was a slow day. He promised to introduce me to the owner. When we found the room, I stood on the balcony where we had hung bags of sandwiched dinners. I remembered women picking through piles of clothing dumped in the courtyard just below. I said, "A Romanian man used to climb our balcony to get to that one, over there. He was in love with the wife." I had forgotten that detail, the student climbing.

Later, I drank an espresso in my own familiar canteen, now with delicate curtains, tablecloths, while the grandfatherly owner patted my hand and offered me a wafer. I thought: years ago I drank milky coffee in this room, unable to imagine that one day I'd enjoy the taste. I thought of the Romanians. Why do stories repeat themselves in this way? How does love stop being love, and how can I tell if it's happening to me?

"This room is the same," I said. "Those windows . . ."

"It's much nicer," the owner said; the concierge translated. "Big renovation. Do you like it?"

"This room doesn't feel as changed as the rest," I said, looking out at the leafy landscape below the dining room. "Maybe it's the windows."

"Maybe your taste improved at the exact same rate as the renovation," Philip joked. I was so grateful for his presence. He made that first step (of a long journey into my past) bearable, though he seemed so out of place. *We* seemed out of place.

My return to camp was unsettling, no return at all. The cappuccino machine. The tablecloths. The butter cookies. This wasn't Barba. Though we were both done up now to suit Western tastes, I couldn't stomach Barba's familiar frame tarted up for new uses. It felt like fresh homelessness. Barba had been more than a house to us, the exiles it sheltered.

To this day, the name Hotel Barba fills me with dread and nostalgia: that first lick of a Cornetto, the crunch of unripe peaches stolen from the garden, the tinny taste that filled my mouth in embassies. After my second visit, it also conjures images of me as the unhappy wife of a good man, in a green summer dress, trying to find the tree whose peaches I had stolen, the bench where I taught Russian men a few words of English, the sound of a Romanian student climbing over my balcony with his guitar. For years, the characters in Hotel Barba have appeared unbidden in my fiction. Young heroes arrive with milky scars white-washing half their face. Menacing lovers carry guitars and have curly hair — fingers are lost in it. Grandmothers in chadors hide little indulgences under long skirts. Idle women with sleepy eyes make themselves silly with yearning. Back then, the worn-down paths seemed new to me. But I watched people and I began to learn the stories: All love ends. Without a country, a fire is quenched, another flares. Limbo is temptation itself — the itch to make life happen.

People think of the refugee camp as a purgatory, a liminal space without shape or color. And it is that. But we kept our instinct for joy. We made friends and we studied and made a community, as we had every day in Iran. Journalists and aid workers who visit camps often comment on this aspect of the psyche — how can these people carry on with their gossip and petty dramas and daily pleasures? How can they endure the limbo?

Since Hotel Barba, all waiting has been agony for me, and I've been obsessed with the idea of it. Why does it feel like an insult to wait for anything? Why does patience seem like one of those manipulative, sinister virtues invented to debase and subdue, like chastity or poverty? Who waits least in the world? I look for answers in *A Lover's Discourse* by Roland Barthes. Barthes says that waiting robs you of your sense of proportion. It plays out in scenes, in outbursts and calm, like waiting in a café for a lover to arrive. It is the ultimate indignity, to be made to wait; and power is to impose it. "I decide to take it badly," Barthes says. The implication of choice strikes me as a clue: I *could* decide to behave instead. At Barba, we sensed the expectation as we waited: the unspoken chides of our native-born rescuers. The inconvenienced. *Your life is no longer in danger. You could be more patient. You could behave.* The primary sin of the Romanians was their ingratitude, their inability to sit still and revel in their physical safety.

Maman rebelled too, by *not* waiting. She worked and roamed Italy. Perhaps the joys and dramas that arose at Barba were our collective sigh of refusal. To take it well would be gracious. To take it badly, though, would create a sequence of events, heightened sensation: drama and distraction.

In the imagined café, Barthes searches for ways to disrupt or explain away the wait. Then he stops writhing; he watches those who are not waiting and slips into a kind of fog. "The anxiety of waiting is not continually violent; it has its matte moments; I am waiting, and everything around my waiting is stricken with unreality . . . waiting is enchantment: I have received orders not to move."

My defense against unreality in those unmoving Barba days was the movement of other people. Atop that pretty hill, I saw a universe of others, with personalities, secrets, dramas as rich and consequential as mine, battering parallel walls that extended out to the edge of the earth. I learned to care about their stories and the aftermath of those stories. I learned that some stories are a joy to embellish and re-create (as in literature or gossip) and in others, the facts are vital (as in fights with little brothers, or asylum interviews), and that to believe or not believe, the "how" of the story matters in both cases. Sometimes invented stories are true in more important ways — though, despite the allure of fiction and the instinct to create, this wouldn't present itself as foundational for me for decades. What *was* clear then: by watching I could choose who I wanted to be, or *seem* to be, and I could be believed. I could tell my own story convincingly, by convincing myself, by *making* it true. I could put an end to every wait. That's the allure of the Romanians' story — they decided simply to stop waiting; they defied the orders not to move. They remade themselves, deliberately. Is a true thing less true, if you have consciously made it so?

Those were early days in my chameleon life.

Some places travel on with you. They grow

up with you, at the same pace. Though in 2011, I was disappointed with my return to Mentana, and though Barba's assimilation made me recoil (perhaps making my own suddenly palpable), I left with a promise from the owner that I could return one day, maybe with a translator, to dig for details from those two years when the hotel served as a refugee camp. This was a comfort, and I knew that Barba would always tempt me back.

In 2017, the craving returns, not for Barba the brick and glass rooms on a hill, but for Barba the liminal space of my youth. A new obsession forms. I decide to try to find it another way. In retrospect searching out Barba's carcass was foolish, I think. I need the residents, its spirit. I call my mother. She sends photos. She tries to remember names.

I've just moved to London, had a baby girl. I look around for a community. I worry about my daughter, her Iranian face. I watch the new American president, and I try to remember how we thought of America back then, in our refugee days. Reagan was dignified; he made us feel safe. Back then the American government was our savior, an incorruptible Christian nation unlike our own, a nation of free people looking to share their good fortune. I write essays. I contact refugee organizations.

Then, one day, Paul, an aid worker, tells me about LM Village. A UNHCR story from June 2016 says, "A Greek summer resort that closed over five years ago as a result of the financial crisis has been turned into a haven for more than three hundred refugees." The word "haven" strikes me as untrue. Still, I am moved. Here is Barba reincarnated. A refugee camp in the hollowed-out carcass of a holiday retreat, a purgatory inside a playland.

Paul Hutchings is cofounder of Refugee Support, a charity that goes from camp to camp, erecting stores with their own currency to distribute donated food and clothing — to give refugees their familiar neighborhood grocery. He has just left LM Village. He talks to me about dignity, about the humiliation of accepting charity. I listen, realizing that we have both lost sleep over this specific shame. There have been days, months, when I've eaten meals provided by charities, governments, good people. In total, these days have made up a sliver of my life, and yet, after decades of eating well and returning favors, I struggle to accept a cup of coffee. At such times, my behavior is correct (I mean Western) and I accept, but a fingertip to my neck would the ungrateful refugee give me away. There are private things only the pulse can verify: love, pain, illness.

Paul met John Sloan in October 2015 while volunteering in the Calais "Jungle." The two men noticed that the act of offering food and clothing, these undeniably first-order needs, had become so urgent and frantic that "the how" was forgotten. The only people who seemed aware were the refugees; Paul saw it in their eyes, in their gait. Though they had already lost so much, they were losing more with every jacket tossed from a truck-bed and every ill-fitting pair of trousers they would have to barter away. In Calais, provisions were handed out from the backs of vans. One day a van would arrive with, say, large jackets and park in one part of the camp. Another day, a van with men's jeans, or T-shirts, would park in another corner. Refugees lined up as a volunteer tried to keep order, another asked their size. They received one item and were asked to go. Some tried to negotiate, claiming a sick friend, a parent too weak to stand in line. Others fought and yelled and grabbed. Items were trampled. Some went away empty-handed. No one felt good about what had just happened.

"Wouldn't it be nice," says Paul about the early days of his charity, "if we could give people food and clothing without taking away their dignity?"

We're meeting in a London café for a long talk over coffee and cake.

"Why is that so hard?" I ask.

"Because people want every hour and dollar they give to be stretched thin." Paul tells me that his biggest problem was the volunteers, donors, and their lofty expectations. Many donors want to assign criteria to how their food is given out. They want their money feeding as many as possible, to make sure that you spend it only on eggs and bread. They want to police. They don't care about "the how." Paul tells me that there's a spectrum of usefulness for donations. Money without strings, then other money, then high-turnover items like unexpired eggs, oil, flour, diapers, small men's clothes and shoes. But people don't donate these things. They donate worn clothes. Large sizes. Expired things. "Once we got a wedding dress."

"Do they give much strawberry jam?" I ask. He gives me a look.

As for volunteers, even the most good-hearted want to *feel* thanked. They have

175

come for that silent look of admiration that's free to most, but so costly if you're tapped for gratitude by everyone you meet.

Refugee Support began its work in April 2016 at Alexandreia camp near Thessaloniki, Greece. Paul and John set out to open a food store, then a clothing store, a well-designed, peaceful marketplace where a person of note wouldn't be ashamed to shop. At first, residents made appointments and collected prepared baskets of food. Everyone received the same thing, regardless of allergies, habits, or taste. But people didn't have the same needs, and soon there was grumbling, barter, waste. Outside the camp people don't get baskets. Everyone knows how a store works: with money.

They decided to display the goods and give people the respect of choosing. The store's currency would be points distributed weekly to residents like income — 100 points per adult, 50 per child, 150 for pregnant women. Store prices would be pegged to market prices in euros (twenty points per euro). Sanitary items would be free. The camp residents could visit the store Monday to Friday. If they wanted to spend all their points on chocolate spread, they had that right.

Paul has store designs for Katsikas in

Greece, the newest camp, on his phone. He spends time thinking of the aesthetics, whether people will like it — he cares that they *like* it. He has sales data too, and a list of what he needs to stock each week. Yes, the customers (his word) buy some butter cookies, but they don't sacrifice milk for them. They make nutritious choices for themselves and their children. People don't steal. They don't starve.

When Paul finishes speaking I can barely contain myself. He has articulated so much that I know: the quick dread before donated meals. I want to tell him about Barba's glass canteen, how we sat with our tribes, prayed before or after, gave our pork to the Russians, and argued over who had better tea and caviar (Iranians do). The communal meals, complaining about hard bread, cheering for Zuppa man, made us a community.

In Oklahoma, after I fancied myself an American (enough) teenager, I began volunteering at a local food bank. My friend and I were assigned to the storeroom. Poor mothers or single men would arrive in the front, they would sign in at the desk, tell their stories to more experienced volunteers, and we, the teenagers in the back, would receive instruction about which category of

177

grocery bundle to make. Everyone got the same things, with a few extras for babies, some substitutions for allergies. They never saw our faces, the silly adolescents who flirted and sang while we chose their food: tuna or chicken, white or wheat, pulp or no pulp. I gave away all the chunky peanut butter first, thinking I was being kind. I was grateful that I didn't see their faces, that I could avoid the downcast eyes as I loaded their bags into open trunks. My choices inside those paper bags seemed a small tragedy.

Accepting charity is an ugly business for the spirit. It rubs you raw, especially if you were once someone with pride and lofty goals, someone who shook hands and locked eyes. My mother and I used to talk about the irony of so many of the world's refugees coming from the Middle East — we are such prideful people, and a refugee is the most abject creature of all, stateless, homeless, without control over her own food, education, or health. Asylum *seekers* is so mild a phrase — we weren't politely seeking, we were ravenous for it, this creature need for the safety for our bodies. Even as we learned English and swam and erased workbooks, we thought of nothing else. How do we survive the memory of so much wanting?

In my thirties in New York, I volunteered to help a friend, a well-meaning finance type, and his singles' group serve Thanksgiving dinner at a homeless shelter. I showed up in a stained T-shirt and old jeans, my hair in a ratty bun. I stuck ten dollars in my pocket and left my wallet behind. There was no question of what to wear; I knew that tonight I would offer food to a stranger, and that stranger would, for a moment, be humiliated. She would look at my clothes, my posture, for a reason to say, "Who cares what she thinks?" And it was part of my job to give her that reason quickly.

But Manhattan do-gooders don't know the quiet bargains that the poor make in the space of a glance. When I arrived at the shelter, my friend looked me up and down. "Are you depressed?" he joked, eyeing my stains. Behind him bankers and lawyers in Chanel shoes and white silk shirts, leather purses still on their arms, dished out mashed potatoes and uneasy smiles to tired men and women wearing the grime of the city. Later on, when the residents invited the volunteers to join their table (a plea for dignity), the volunteers declined out of concern ("Will there be enough?"). They dashed off to Momofuku instead, ordered pork belly and cocktails and congratulated themselves for leaving ("It would've been overstepping"). They complained about the tourists crowding the door. I confess that I ate a few bites of that turkey dinner that may not have been enough, and I ate the pork belly too, and I let my friend pay. I hated him that night, but I was also grateful to be in his company. I went home and threw it all up.

Now, more years have passed. In 2017, I am starting another new life, trying to make sense of the places that made me. Am I still a refugee after decades spent transforming? I know now that Barba was a "low-hardship camp." Both parts of that term seem dishonest. Yes, it was something other than hell — it wasn't Moria in Lesbos with its raw sewage and midnight wars, its five-hour food lines and shared tents on open soil. And, yes, it was officially a refugee camp. But it wasn't low-hardship. And it wasn't a camp. It wasn't a hotel, either. I call it a hostel. The difference between each pair of words is subtle, a private calculation of shame and place and dignity.

"You know what I love?" says Paul. "When they complain about the selection. Because that means that they've forgotten they're in a camp. They're briefly transported and they're just people in a store, with money in hand, complaining about yogurt."

"I want to go," I say.

"We have rules," he says. "We need to keep absolute equality between people. No hint of special treatment. We don't allow socializing. Volunteers can't even accept a cup of tea or enter the private rooms."

This is to avoid requests for favoritism. It's also to create a microeconomy as similar to the one in the outside world as possible. In the outside world, your store clerk doesn't look at you with eyes that say, *Don't you appreciate what I'm doing?* He expects you to come in, pay, go. He expects you to complain about the lack of whole milk or the staleness of the bread. In the outside world, there is an equality between service provider and customer that doesn't exist when people are doling out charity.

"Are there Iranians there?" I ask. "Or Afghans that speak Farsi?"

"There will be at Katsikas when it opens," he says. "Probably not at LM." He explains that Refugee Support will have left LM altogether by then. Still, I know I'll go there, that I will convince Paul to go with me. This feels like a truer return than my visit to Barba's bones.

"I want to go without that rule," I say, remembering that long-ago turkey dinner

181

that everyone turned down. *If this is about pride, and especially with Iranians, I have to be able to accept a cup of tea.*

The night before I fly to Greece, my grandmother, Maman Moti, calls. She tells us that she has no place to sleep. Her apartment in south London is no longer a refuge. The neighbors are trying to drive her out. I don't have to ask what they're doing. I asked the first time, thinking they are making too much noise, or smoking, bad behaviors that may have nothing to do with my grandmother, but are, nonetheless, believably annoying. "It's the waves again," she says. "I've started sleeping in the attic. It's very cold."

My grandmother and I only reconnected a few months ago, after a seven-year silence. She is an immigrant too, having taken my mother's sister, the youngest of four children, and run away to London before the revolution of 1979, before my birth, when my mother was in her early twenties. The family story is that she left my grandfather, who had never been faithful, to join another man, my mother's teacher. She planned to start a new life with him in London.

In a grimy corner of the city she found a flat and a school for her twelve-year-old daughter. She had brought a little money.

She was young. Married off to my grandfather at thirteen, she had given birth to my
aunt Soheila at fourteen, then to my mother,
Sima, at sixteen. By twenty-seven, she had
my uncle Saeed and aunt Sepideh too. By
thirty, her older daughters stood as tall as
she. She competed with them for clothes,
for admiring looks in the street. In the year
I was born, as she sat by the phone in that
London flat, perhaps looking up English
words she had seen on a billboard or in a
magazine, she was thirty-nine. I was her
second grandchild.

For weeks, Maman Moti waited by the
phone, by the door, suspended between two
lives. Had she left after the revolution, she
might have waited with her countrymen in
a camp. He didn't come. He didn't call. She
waited. Maybe she called her family in Iran.
I'm not privy to the details. I do know this:
After any hope of his arrival was gone, she
continued to wait, and, after that, though
she wasn't a refugee, she succumbed to the
habits of one: she became addicted to waiting, to hope of rescue. She gave her mind
up to it.

Barthes describes waiting as both delirium
and subjection. Illness and torture. My
grandmother has become permanently
delirious, a servant to her waiting. She could

have stepped out of her marital dreams into London, a free city full of all the things she had once loved: poetry, stylish clothes, music. Instead, she found a way to extend the waiting.

She took the name Emma, the first of a thousand small adjustments to make herself palatable to the English. She styled herself the English way, fine-tuned her accent — it isn't Iranian anymore, but something in-between, and very fine — found a church in a well-to-do neighborhood. Perhaps it wasn't so well-to-do then. It didn't have a lot of immigrants. She decided, then and there, that she wanted nothing to do with the past. She didn't want to be defined by a divorce, or by displacement. Certainly, she didn't want to advertise that she had been a child bride — to an almost-child groom, less grotesque, but no less traumatic. On the eve of Maman Moti's wedding, she knew nothing of sex, not even that it existed. They told her that if she got married, she could wear high-heeled shoes, and that's all she knew. When she felt her first baby moving, she thought it was a snake or a worm.

She met Christopher in a singles' group, or maybe it was a parents' group. They prayed. He must have smiled, paid her a compliment. Maybe he took her hand and told her to be strong, not realizing the frailty of her immigrant heart. Somehow in that hour, Maman Moti heard God's voice, a promise. He told her that she would marry this man, that they would build a new life, that all her scattered children would be brought together again in a great house in London where she would serve the best Iranian dishes on antique Wedgwood, where well-heeled daughters, thin in elegant dresses, would serve tea, where grand-daughters, still married to their first hus-bands, having not wasted their hard-won Ivy League degrees on middling writing careers, would sit at her feet waiting for wisdom, bring her melon and mint in a glass with a long spoon. In my fantasies, Maman Moti is always asking for a long spoon. Probably it's just some broken fragment of a memory. I work it back in this way or that.

All she had to do was trust. Trust and wait.

Nowadays, like Barthes's waiting lover, she sees Christopher in the street, in the faces of passersby. Later she cries, knowing that the man who glanced up from a news-paper in the park, or the man who held the door to the supermarket, was her betrothed waiting for her to acknowledge him. But she has forgotten his face and so she has failed; he is disappointed, heartbroken. Each morning, she sits in a park, stricken with unreality. She writes poems, letters, family histories. She signs them "Emma" and mails them to him. He never replies, but the letters aren't returned either. Someone is collecting them, these precious family stories, my inheritance. I wish I knew Christopher's last name, so I could search for them. He is married now; maybe he has moved, or died.

She has waited for him for roughly three decades. How many times has she fantasized about the house, the dinners, the return of the prodigal children? She experiences the waiting no less urgently than those in camp, though hers is invented. She lives in it, still. She is no less crippled by it. Every day life's smallest choices (traveling, moving churches) are made unthinkable by the remote possibility that today an answer will come.

Meanwhile, she craves drama, to heighten the sensations around waiting. Years ago, Maman Moti confided in the family that certain members of her church are offended by her certainty of her future. The church has divided into factions. There are political machinations afoot, much like the early days of the church. She prays. She asks us to pray.

Arriving in London, she had a small bundle of money. She bought her flat. Prices rose. A few decades ago, her feet began to itch again, another symptom of the exile disease. But she didn't recognize it as that. "They've hired the downstairs neighbor to drive me out," she told her daughter, my aunt Sepi, now grown into the very offspring she craved: a Londoner with a pale blond husband and three tall, handsome sons who dreamed in English.

Now and then, friends from church came around, but all Maman Moti saw was that no one believed her.

Each time Maman Moti sold a flat, she lost around fifteen thousand pounds, moving to a slightly less desirable location. Each time, after a few years, the neighbors began to conspire again, sending smoke into her home, vacuuming at night, sending children to scream and fight in the yard.

She moved again and again, always writing Christopher with her new address. In each new flat, her hope returned for a time, and the itch in her brain calmed. Maybe this would be the living room where Christopher would sit, where she would bring him a cup of tea, where he would take her hand and say, "I'm sorry you waited so long."

In 2011 when news reached the family that I had moved from my home in Amsterdam to some workshop in Iowa without Philip, and later when we decided to divorce, Maman Moti stopped speaking to me.

For her, Philip was proof that, even though her daughters had fallen into exile, her granddaughter hadn't. Philip was white and handsome. He made money (never mind that my earning power was equal to his, that we had met at Princeton, that I had better grades). His feet were rooted. What more could a silly immigrant girl want? And besides, Jesus did not allow divorce, and she was a Christian now, so.

In 2015, I became pregnant and moved to London. It took two years of living in her city before she contacted me. Maybe it was Elena, her great-granddaughter. Or kernels of news planted by my mother or aunt, telling her that my new partner, Sam, came from a good family, that he was an artsy version of Philip, much better suited to me. That he had graduated with highest honors from Oxford, so let him have his man-bun. God bless him for having those curls after forty. His mother was a faithful Christian, did you know? She was French, like Philip's mother, but an artist too.

When Maman Moti phoned, I was angry. I didn't want to welcome her back. How dare she reject me for the very thing she did at my age? How dare she abandon us in Iran for an English life, then judge us? And how dare she refuse even to sponsor us out of Barba? We were in limbo — without an inkling of our future. We could have ended up in rural Australia, or deported back to Iran. No one speaks of this part, but Maman Moti could have brought us to England. Why didn't she?

Then there's her casual sexism: to my grandmother, an unmarried woman is wasted, and so she is in a perpetual in-between space, a time between marriages. Being man-less is the same as being stateless. If you have no husband, even if it takes forty years, you are only waiting for one.

By February, the night I'm preparing for Greece, my first true return to "Barba" (whatever that means now) after that false start in 2011, Maman Moti and I have had a handful of visits. We dream aloud about bringing our family together: Maybe a reunion! What can we do to convince everyone? We scheme together. She is kind, but she lives entirely in her own invented world. Sometimes she glimpses out at us from inside, but mostly she's decorating the corridors and rooms inside her mind.

I understand her more than anyone else

in my family. She is me in old age. I can see her struggling with the itch in her brain. I can see it just as clearly as I see it in the mirror, or in my daughter when there's an extra fold in her tights, or when one arm of a sweater is tighter than the other. When I'm my grandmother's age, will the itch open up to reveal a fantastical universe full of church espionage and radiation guns? And when Elena is her age? Will she too invent a home for herself? Are there homes that I have rejected because the itch wants me to be ever on the move?

At 9:30 p.m. we're still waiting for Maman Moti to arrive. I am furious. This trip is full of small ironies. Our sofa will arrive while I'm gone, completing our home. It seems ugly to reach this final step now, after decades of wandering, just as I'm visiting the freshly uprooted. Elena is asleep. I expect that Maman Moti will call from the train station, but she doesn't. Instead she gives my address to some strange man who walks her to my flat. She is at our doorstep at 10 p.m. I hear her chirping gratefully at him. I never see his face. We were robbed two months ago. I grow nervous, then livid. "God sent me an angel," she trills as she takes off her boots.

"Don't give my address to strangers,

please," I say, instead of "Welcome." Then quickly, I add, "Welcome."

We make tea for her. "What happened?" I ask.

"They're sending the waves again," she says with a long sigh, as if she's telling me the dishwasher is busted. "I can't sleep. I can feel it poisoning me. They turn on the machine, and I get headaches, nausea."

The downstairs neighbors are sending waves up through the floor of her flat. They are radioactive, or electromagnetic, who knows. But she feels them in her body, inside her head. It makes her heart flutter. She gets palpitations and shortness of breath. In the evenings, a low-grade buzzing starts up and keeps her awake until morning, or until she gives up and moves to a sleeping bag in the attic. If anyone visits, the neighbors know to turn off the machine so that they can make her look crazy.

I ask if she's seen the machine. She dismisses the question. It's large, aimed straight at the ceiling through to her floor. "What if it's not radiation but an allergy?" I ask, "Or something else in your body?"

"I'm not sick or crazy," she says, sipping tea. She's said this so often.

I ask her if I can come and see her flat. She says that they never send the radiation

191

if someone else is in the flat. "What if someone else stays there with you for a while," I say. She perks up. Then I have the answer; how could I have missed it? "I can call a friend at Amnesty," I say. "Refugees are always looking for a place to stay. I can find someone young and strong. And you'll have someone to watch over you. It's a win-win!"

Her face falls. "No, I don't get involved with refugees," she says. "I don't want to have anything to do with any of that anymore. No."

I remind myself that she was forced into marriage at thirteen. That she is old now, losing her grip on reality, and has reason to distrust.

We make her a bed in the living room. She thanks us and goes to sleep. In the morning, the flat is chaos. We make breakfast. We feed Elena and dress her for day care. I pack my suitcase. I'm so nervous. Here I am about to visit people who have lost their homes and families, young mothers and lone travelers and elderly couples who live in metal boxes, people so displaced they can't even imagine the landscape of their future. A majority will be depressed, some suicidal or drowning in fantasy, and I can't even handle my grandmother and her inhospitable flat. And what a waste — she *has* a passport, a place to live. The doors were flung open for her and yet she made herself into a refugee.

I'm late for my train to the airport. I decide to run ahead. I kiss them goodbye. We reach for our coats, our shoes. Elena says, "Bye-bye, Mummy! See you next week!" My chest tightens. She's parroting "see you next week," but she means "see you tonight." Maman Moti chuckles at Elena's English accent. "She's darling," she says.

As I'm leaving, I see Maman Moti struggling with her boot. She leans against a wall, taps her purse, checking for something. She says, "Dina *joon,* bring me a long spoon." I freeze. Then I run and fetch her a dinner spoon. She plunges it into her boot like a shoehorn.

IV

"The complicated thing is that dignity changes as different needs are met," says Paul Hutchings as we drive on a pitch-black road, slick with rain, away from Athens. "When you arrive from Lesbos, dirty, tired, starving, dignity is that prepacked package of shampoo, deodorant, eggs, coffee, bread. So we offer that on arrival. Then, when you've showered and slept and cleaned up, that package becomes humiliating. You want your tea, not coffee. You remember you hate eggs. That's when you want choice. After you've lived in a camp for a few months, the store with fake money and strict friendship rules becomes humiliating too. Why *can't* you befriend the clerk? There's a shelf life to this. We don't want to contribute to camp becoming permanent for them. They need to be a part of communities."

I'm terrified of what I'll see and remember. The rain is ominous, and I want a thick piece of chocolate and Elena's hot sugary breath on my neck.

I have a sofa now. How enormous this seems. It's a good sofa, handcrafted in a workshop. I also have a bed that I bought, and this too seems like a wonder, because, like my grandmother, I like to set fire to my habitat. I don't buy furniture. I'm addicted to resetting, to the in-between.

We are driving toward Kilini, to LM Village, the former holiday resort. I imagine a modern-day Barba. For Paul to accompany me is pure kindness. Refugee Support has left the camp, and my *Guardian* photographer, Eirini, is scheduled to meet us at Katsikas — our assignment is there, and the two camps are hours apart by highway. But

I'm drawn to LM, to the shell it inhabits. I tell everyone I want to see the aftermath of the stores.

Our hotel is rough. I wake up itching, convinced that it has bedbugs. Sam has texted that Maman Moti called. His message makes me itch more — that's how I know there are no bedbugs. I have this survival trick: Some nights when I'm afraid, I don't brush my teeth. When I was two, my father operated on them. In an early memory, my uncle chases me around Baba's dental office, forces me into the chair as Baba comes at me with a needle the size of my forearm. Now, when I don't brush my teeth, they throb in the night. Fear makes them throb. When I wake up with no pain in my mouth, I know that it existed only in my mind. And if *that* wasn't real, then I know that all the other nightmarish things that I saw weren't real either. The toothache is a coalmine canary; when it goes, other pains follow. Without it, I wake up disoriented, unable to sift through my fears or to soothe myself.

I've also missed a call from Minoo, a refugee woman from Isfahan whom I have befriended in London. She is around my age and has two excellent children and a chronically ill husband. Minoo's call will be about housing; she's been brushed aside by the housing authority for a year.

I dress for the camp in an old shirt and a loose black skirt that hangs down over my muddy boots. I am ridiculous, even to myself.

The gate into the camp opens onto an office, then old, fenced tennis courts. They're littered with dead branches and debris. A dog growls at us from inside the court. Clusters of tree stumps skirt the fences. The court isn't surrounded by pavement or stone or grass, just raw ground. Beyond the courts the ramshackle village looms in muted yellows and burnt sienna, colors that may have once been cheerful. They blend down into the dirt. We walk through LM Village in the rain. It's deserted, ominous gray clouds hanging over the complex. Scattered hedges line the walkways. People peek out of numbered buildings. They drift in and out, glistening with idleness. I want to knock on doors, but, first, Paul takes me to the site of his old store. Though it's not meant to be a residential space, it serves as a bedroom now. One wall is window, looking onto the man's bed, his toiletries, and his books.

We visit the clothing store. It hasn't been shut but put in the hands of local workers, to sort and distribute donations.

A Greek woman sits in a chair near the door, her eyes locked on her phone. Piles of clothing lay discarded on the floor, boxes overturned onto them. Children play in the piles. Bare hangers are strewn everywhere, and rows of mixed winter clothing are jammed together on the racks. A boy and girl rummage through the piles, trampling the clothes. A toddler runs in. The worker doesn't look up. I stare, transported to Barba, the donated clothing strewn in the courtyard. Paul walks from the racks to the piles, picks up a jacket. He shakes his head, shoulders dropping.

We visit a recreation room, a big empty space with a television hanging in a corner, a toaster in another, and a few scattered remnants of a game room. On a wall beside an empty shelf, a label says *coffee, tea, sugar.* Beside another empty shelf, *glasses.* A fire extinguisher leans against a painted sign: *To be different.* A teenager smokes hookah and watches soccer as a younger boy fiddles with the pipe, waiting for him to find some energy. The floor and the benches are soiled from months of dirt.

Near an abandoned play area, a pool full of twigs, the commander of the camp joins us. He follows us around, nervous. He speaks a lot, tells jokes, mostly for Paul's benefit. I disappear into the background. The play area is a creepy mangled version of itself. No children play in it. It reminds me of something out of *Stranger Things* — this is a holiday village from the Upside Down. Paul tells me that the residents call it "a holiday from hell."

There are 219 people in this camp, most from Syria, and yet there's nothing to see but dogs and children and naked gloom. Everyone has a foot in bed, and I remember how very little there is to do in a refugee camp. You're not allowed to work. You're not welcome in local schools; native parents are forever nursing fears of foreign disease. We find our way to the day care. The teacher tells us about the toddlers in her class, their fragile shaken minds. One girl, she tells us, refuses to remove her backpack.

This girl, I know, is toeing a road without end. I've refused to take off my backpack for thirty years. Her teacher tells us that she won't put the bag aside to sing or dance or play. The adults have tried every tactic, suggesting that she keep the backpack but empty it in her room, so it'll be lighter. I chuckle. The backpack is about one thing: holding your diminished identity, the pieces of your life. The glossy pink receptacle is meaningless.

Now the skin inside my throat loosens, my body's crude warning sign from my schoolyard days, at first grating, like an unreachable flap of skin, then maddening. I don't want to be here. I have a home now; why did I return to this wretched limbo? Why am I not living my life, grateful for every minute I'm allowed to come and go in the free world? What if I'm stuck at the airport? What if my passport gets stolen? What if I'm detained? Where is my Elena? I breathe in as deep as my breath will go, until my lungs are full and I force the thing in my throat back down into place.

But I *do* know why I'm here — I've come because the world is turning its back on refugees, because America is no longer America and Europe is going the same way: these once-Christian nations have abandoned duty in favor of entitlement and tribal instinct. I'm here because I have a skill, born out of my own idle refugee days. I've watched people when they're ordered to do nothing, and I know just how life reasserts itself, like that first bubble in still water before the whole pot comes to a boil. I'm here to make a few stories leap out from the tepid simmer of information, and to carry those stories to the West, a mother who once

199

adopted us, the exiles and outcasts, and now needs us to intervene as calluses harden fast around her heart.

And there is another reason too. Now that I have a daughter, it's time I made sense of my own story and identity so she can be certain of hers.

I've been told that refugee work is harder for former asylum seekers. It's easier to volunteer at a homeless shelter or hospital ward; going back is anathema to instinct. My grandmother isn't the first Iranian to want nothing to do with her countrymen. And plenty of immigrants would shut the door once their own family is through, out of survival instinct. (What villain will follow them out?) The ground is never as solid beneath the feet of the displaced. You are told that the good and the honest will get out somehow, that looking back will turn you into a pillar of salt, that now you must put your energy toward building, belonging, repaying. No one needs you to return to camp and stir up futile hopes with your presence.

I long to find Barba. Not its bones, but its residents, the locals, the staff. What miracle to find them all prospering — if I can just locate a few names, a few heartening stories, proof that we were worth the trouble.

Greeting passersby, we find an aid worker who speaks Arabic and English. He has an open wound below his lip and claims not to have permission to translate except to and from Greek. Still, he agrees to help. He suggests a family whose space, he promises, will surprise me.

Amina from Aleppo opens the door. She is built like my mother, round and petite, with bottle-red hair and a neat blouse. Her intimate movements are like Iranian aunts; their welcome warms the limbs. She takes my shoulder and pulls me in, puts on tea without looking away. "Come in, come in. Sit. Have tea," she says in Arabic. When her daughter runs in with her pleated skirt over tights, a fuzzy star on her shirt, it's as if I'm sitting across from my former self, my young mother.

We kick off our shoes on the mat. Inside, all sign of camp is gone. What am I seeing? The translator explains that this couple takes great pride in their space. The husband is a furniture maker. The first thing he did was ask for a paint roller. He repainted the rooms, fixed all the peeling parts, nailed down the broken boards. She scrubbed for days and decorated with whatever she could find. "And now look. Beautiful."

Above the midnight blue laminate of the

kitchenette hangs a yellow floral curtain, calling out the yellow of the turmeric in a jar. Big yellow serving spoons hang on the wall beside a ladle shaped like a sunflower. The dishes are washed. It seems heroic to me, every scavenged and scrubbed item, the toil to keep her family's dignity in this wasteland. What stores of willpower it takes for this couple to commit to making these rooms a home. The very air in a camp is heavy, making you listless, pushing you into your bed. Their refusal to sit and wait is a daily resistance, a gift to their daughters. These childhood days at LM will not be marred by poverty and anticipation for them. LM Village will be just another chapter of their lives. They might have their next birthday here. They might learn to read here.

Then my eyes are drawn to the most peculiar feature of the house: Teddy bears of all sizes are mounted to the walls, in the kitchen, above the bedroom doorframes, on the banister to the lofted space above our heads. Teddy bears are nailed to every wall. An enormous one hovers above me. The bears are funny and sinister. Over the coming days I will see many rooms with mounted teddy bears, both in the brick and mortar of LM and the metal Isoboxes of

Katsikas. They overflow from donation bins. Americans and British well-wishers apparently are always sending bears.

What can I accomplish here when there is such distance between good people? When a heartfelt gift can twist into a gruesome reminder of all that you still need? When you're forced to make use of it anyway? Why weren't the bear donors told to send calculators or tablets or English workbooks, dictionaries, and box sets of Roald Dahl and Beatrix Potter and Julia Donaldson? No one wants a bear. In Iran, bears (like sheep) get decapitated in airports. Here, they get hung on walls.

As Amina prepares tea and a plate of boxed cookies, I crane my neck to see into the bedrooms. Everywhere there are touches of yellow and blue.

Unlike us, today's refugees have smartphones. This woman knows that blue and yellow are fashionable now. What tantalizing self-harm to google "house décor" and be confronted with London showrooms, to see that the decadent world outside gorges while complaining that you exist, that you might come too near. Outside, they scream for borders. You might take what is theirs. You might forget your place, grow entitled and bold, accustomed to rich yellows and blues. And what about death breathing on your cheek? That is a guilty puzzle.

Mustafa arrives wearing a neat button-up shirt and a houndstooth newsboy cap. Their younger daughter flings herself at him. I like them, how they refuse to relinquish their spirit after nearly drowning in a smuggler's boat, dressing their clever daughters like British schoolchildren.

Mustafa is losing his sight. The keratin in his eyes is destroyed, and he needs injections that cost over a thousand euros. "I tell them, just make me glasses. They say, we can't make you glasses." Syrians come into these camps, all claiming health problems. They want care for their teeth, ears, backs. They are not believed. "I just want to fix my eyes," mutters Mustafa, who has papers from his doctors in Syria. I wonder why they think a person would lie about their keratin. Do they want a needle in their eye for sport?

Later, I follow Shiva, a speech therapist, to her cabin. Her family is tightly packed, three, maybe four twenty-somethings and an elderly mother. No one cares about making a home here or creating a semblance of a life. No one wants to take pride in this temporary space. No one has tiny memories to protect or childhoods to shape. The space hasn't been cleaned for a while. Now I see the state of the cabins before Mustafa got his paint roller and hammer. A pot boils atop an old hot plate splattered with sauce. Other pots caked with yesterday's meals wait beside the sink. The counter is chipped and cracked, broken in places. Mold peeks out from every corner of the walls. The cupboards and walls too are chipped; a chunk of wall is gouged out, as if with an ice cream scoop. The mold enters my sinuses.

Shiva's mother sits on a bench between the kitchen and the stairs, at a small table where the family eats. She is a sprawling woman wrapped in a chador, cleaning runner beans. She could be Maman Masi. She stares, then breaks into a smile and welcomes me. They don't get many visitors here.

I learn that she was once mother to eleven. One died, maybe recently, and her ten living children, ranging from forty-four to twenty-one, are strewn across Europe and the Middle East. Her youngest has brought a handsome fiancé who refuses to acknowledge me. I hear him in the loft, bubbles popping in his water pipe, the throaty murmur of Syrian music.

We sit looking at each other. Without a translator, we communicate in gestures.

They bring tea. Syrians, I'm learning, like their tea migraine sweet. They think I'm refusing sugar to be polite and stir a full tablespoon into my tea. It's hot syrup. I sip and look around, trying to place myself. If Amina was fiery and determined like my mother, this lady is like my bricklaying friend, the Afghan grandmother. I watch her hands work quickly as she glances up at the ceiling, gesturing that she is praying for her children to be reunited with her in a single country.

The commander breaks our silence. He knocks, enters, sits without invitation. Our few interactions have shown me that this man's ego is intertwined with LM. He reminds us again and again that he has been here every day for two years. Still, he doesn't have the experience to run the camp, and there have been problems. He shows favoritism, enters homes, fights with refugees. People are afraid of telling the truth when he's around.

He takes a cup of tea. We chat with single words. He tries to translate.

During a silent beat, Shiva's mother looks up, says an *Alhamdulillah* for her absent children — it is a tic. The commander bursts out in English. (Is it for my sake?) "What do you want me to do? Should I go to Syria and get them?" It's a bizarre display. Shiva rubs yogurt on it, as Iranians say.

I text Paul the cabin number and he appears in minutes.

But when I get up to go, Shiva's mother begins shaking her head, as if something unfathomable is about to happen. She looks around, sees my backpack, then grabs it and hugs it tight to her breast.

And here's another memory from camp: you become dramatic. You mean to scold, you shout. You mean to tap, you punch. Waiting amplifies your responses. Maybe this explains the commander's outburst too; he's lived here all this time, catching the symptoms. Now I remember that at Iowa, a famous writer told us that we must taste life more than we write about it, that we shouldn't publish while in this preparatory bubble. When you're waiting for life to begin, you're prone to spectacle, to theater, and, as any asylum seeker who has looked into the cold eyes of an immigration officer knows, no one believes melodrama. In life and in fiction, hysteria is the ultimate lie, and the waiting are most prone to it.

I want my backpack. It's not that I think she'll open it. But it's my bag; it goes with me everywhere. I can't eat an entire meal while it hides under her chador (where she's stashing it now). Shiva whispers to her mother and they agree to put it on the bench beside the old woman, within my sight, and to lock the door instead. They've gone mad with boredom.

Now I find something else to worry about. With the commander happy to stay, they have taken on three extra mouths. I can't bear to eat up their food, bought with precious euros now that Paul's store is gone. I try to refuse again, but now I'm insulting them. Shiva frowns. I'm bordering on "this isn't good enough for me" territory. And yet, this isn't like that New York Thanksgiving, the well-to-do fretting over the shelter's rations. Shiva's family needs this food. After we're gone, the fiancé will come down from the loft and expect a plate. But pride wins, and we stay.

Shiva's sister, the twenty-one-year-old, perhaps preparing for marriage, has made the entire meal on the hot plate. Lentil soup. Chicken with mushrooms. Watery rice. A small dish of yogurt. They serve us first, and too much. I'm embarrassed for us, and for them. I know the competing instincts. They want us here; they long for guests. But they will be hungry before bed. No adult can be satisfied on a few tendrils of a chicken thigh.

Shiva's mother has put an entire drumstick on my plate. No one else has a whole drumstick. To distract from the serving, I ask for the recipe.

Shiva's sister beams. She starts listing ingredients, and when she's lost for the English word, she gestures. She shows me an empty can of mushroom, points to the chicken with a laugh (chicken, of course!), shows me the peppers. She searches for a word, then opens the fridge and shows me an open tin can of tomato paste. The sight of an open can in the fridge rouses my every itch. Words I learned in pregnancy return now, and they're all I can think about: listeria, metal poisoning, what else? No. Stop. This isn't about the can. I'm not one of those local mothers who think refugees are carriers of disease and vermin. I'm looking for an excuse to leave because the camp is bearing down on my heart. I feel trapped in the waiting place. I want to grab my backpack, unlock that door, and go breathe in a field.

I eat a big spoonful and tell little sister it's very good. For twenty-one, she is a skilled cook, though she needs to be more patient with her rice. If she were my sister, I would teach her to lower the heat, to measure the water up to the first segment of her finger, to wrap the lid with a towel. I'm fascinated by this quiet, dutiful little sister, the haughty young man she keeps upstairs. There is a physical mismatch between them, and I'm interested in that too. She smiles shyly and tucks in.

I'm sitting beside the mother. Now and then she touches my left hand, which is resting at the edge of the table. Her fingers are warm, filmy, and wet, like almonds soaking in hot water. When she touches me, I feel her skin sliding off bone. I like her attention. She reminds me of Morvarid and Ardestoon. Then, as I'm talking to Paul, the length of my left pinky touches something cold and slimy. I glance over, recoil. Shiva's mother has built a mountain of tiny chicken bones outside her plate, a centimeter from mine. My pinky is mingling with the debris, touching a discarded chicken skin. She sees me looking. I grin madly, squeeze her hand, and look away. She smiles at me with childlike curiosity, even affection, then licks the rice off her spoon, plunges it into the chicken bowl, and serves me another piece.

There is absolutely no fixing this. My every reaction is American, urban, obsessive-compulsive. This is who I am. Her manners aren't so much Syrian as they are those of a village grandmother of a huge family — my own Maman Masi would behave exactly the same way. She would kiss my cheek with her mouth full, leaving a ring of oil. She would use her dress to wipe my mouth and cheek. She would serve me yogurt from her plate, use her own spoon as a serving utensil. She would get into a bath with me. Maybe on her way out, if her boot stuck, she would ask for this same spoon.

It's in my head. It's in my head. It's in my head. I remind myself that Sam's aunt, a French film director, once served us hummus using a spoon she had just licked. The woman has won a César, but she's a villager too. Her habits are the same, but her village is in Europe. Why should this help? And yet it does, because I have internalized all the biases that were once used against me. European heritage neutralizes dirt and germs. So do wealth and education. I remember believing as a teenager that if I got into Harvard, I would erase the traces of the refugee life from my body.

I recall something else: days ago, I got into a bath with Elena. There is no chance she didn't pee in it. My queasiness wanes, like toothache in a dream. The itch lives inside my mind; I banish it and eat my chicken. If you are a mother or ever had one, you have shared in another body's grime.

211

■ ■ ■ ■

I drive as Paul searches for music. The road to Katsikas is new and pristine and empty. The cellular networks are patchy, so instead of music, we talk about our shared obsession with shame — no, not shame, which is entirely contained within. We're obsessed with the public manifestation of it for some knowing or unwitting beneficiary: humiliation.

"I'm afraid to hear their stories," I say. "The way Iranians tell stories is so vivid, so slow and detailed, you get dropped into the nightmare."

When the music blinks on again, we talk about our phones, how everyone in the camp has one. The number one request when they arrive to any camp? Wi-Fi. The number one complaint: bad connection. You can get a phone for almost no money, and yet, hostile natives often use the presence of phones as a sign that refugees are pampered, wanting and taking too much. Back at Barba, we kept an eye on our mail cubbies; we watched each day for the postman. We didn't think of our mail as a luxury.

I tell him that I read that the Trump administration is proposing a plan to replace a large portion of food stamp benefits for the poor (SNAP) with a prepackaged box. The box is the same for everyone, a humiliation. It will reduce choice, efficiency, dignity. It reminds me of other measures in recent years limiting what the poor can buy with food stamps (no shellfish, for example). To some, help must always come with a slap on the wrist.

"They don't care what happens to these people's spirit," sighs Paul.

V / MAJID AND FARZANEH

"It was just casual talk. People talk," said Farzaneh, frantic, when the Sepâh came for her. It was 2017. The girls, three and nine, watched their parents pace and fret.

"What were they wearing?" asked Majid.

"Street clothes," said Farzaneh. "It's Sepâh. No one else does this. Mohammad must have sent for me." She was shaking. Farzaneh's brother was high up in the revolutionary guard — he had a "thick neck," they say in Farsi — and he had decided she was an apostate and a brazen, unreligious woman who must be broken. She didn't pray. She was mouthy and lax with *hijab.* Now and then she asked questions: Should faith be a prison? Why must I hunger for thirty days? Why can't I choose

213

my own clothes? Her brother called her godless, a Christian, a Jew.

"If they come in street clothes," said Majid, "it's serious. If you go, you're not coming back. Then they'll take me and the girls will be orphans." Farzaneh started biting her thumbnail. "We have to run."

Their street was at the dead end of an alley. The window in the back looked out over a parking lot that opened to the next street. The family snuck out onto the terrace. On her way out, Farzaneh grabbed her purse and a flask of cold water. They took nothing else. No clothes; no toiletries or treasures. The girls left their backpacks, their toys. Sarah, the older one, watched stunned as her mother put three-year-old Shirin on her lap and slid down the fire ramp into the parking lot. Majid put Sarah on the slide, sat behind her, and pushed off. When their feet hit asphalt, they ran.

They drove to Urmia, a city bordering Turkey. They rented a room, tried to sleep. Farzaneh bought toothbrushes and a new neck brace; she had suffered from neck sprains for years. As the girls were preparing for bed, washing socks and underwear in the sink and hanging them up to dry overnight, Majid stepped outside to make a call.

"Your brother went to see my parents," he said, when the room was dark and humming with girlish sleep. "He said he'll find us and kill us. He said, even if the government lets you go, he'll never let you go. Farzaneh *joon,* he's a two-fire revolutionary. We have no future together in Iran. Let's not doubt. Let's get out together."

They weren't running from the Islamic Republic whose interest is cold and finite, but from a brother whose rage could cross borders. In the morning, they changed their SIM card. Majid found a smuggler and prayed he wouldn't leave bread crumbs for his brother-in-law.

They drove to the border at midnight. They waited in the dark, whispering to the girls to quiet their breathing while a guide crept ahead to await the shift change of the guards. The smuggler disappeared with his fee; he would go no further. When the guide signaled, they shuffled to him, keeping their heads low. The guide lifted the girls onto a horse, then grabbed the reins and gestured for Farzaneh and Majid to follow, and they began climbing the Zagros Mountains into Turkey, to a safe border village. They walked for five hours in pitch-black silence, though that route takes a fit man half the time. They made stops, the horse treading quietly, as if it knew. With two children, they couldn't risk being shot at in the night. The guide left them partway through; he wouldn't cross into Turkey. A Turkish guide met them a few paces into the country to take them the rest of the way. The girls didn't speak. The gravelly mountain wore through Farzaneh and Majid's unsuitable shoes in a few hours. Only the guides, with their accustomed eyes, could see through the gluey black night. Majid and Farzaneh glanced back toward Iran; they had survived thirty-six years of a brutal regime to watch their home melt away behind a peak, into darkness.

They reached the village just as the sun was rising. In a small room, they waited for the smuggler's group to complete. The girls slept.

In Istanbul, Majid arranged for another smuggler.

Getting out of Iran was dangerous, but nothing compared to crossing the Aegean by boat, entering Europe illegally. What they had to offer the final smuggler would drain the family. Majid decided to settle for a less vetted one, in order to have money for another try. That night, they sat in an inflatable boat made for fifteen with forty-five others, held their daughters tight, and watched as the smuggler turned on the motor. "You, over there," he said, pointing to a young man near the top of the boat. "You're the captain of this boat. You hold this here. It works like the motor of a car. Those are the lights of Greece. Go toward it. Don't turn. Don't stop until you reach the lights."

Then the smuggler stepped off and they were in open water, forty-five unlucky runaways, with no sea training but no other choice, no country that would take them back. They were caught within the hour. The boat began to sputter and die out, then came to a complete stop in Turkish waters. A coast guard ship caught sight of them and shone a light on the boat, blinding the children and ending the journey for that night. For a moment, they dared hope the ship was Greek or English, but they hadn't traveled far enough. And soon, the men yelling in Turkish ended all such hopes. The men loaded them onto the ship and took them by car to Izmir, in Turkey.

In the car, Majid, who spoke Kurdish, befriended a young Arab Kurd. He told his story and was believed. "Sir, if you tell them you're from Iran, you'll spend three months in Turkish prison," said the man. "The prisons here are spilling with Afghans and Iranians. Syrians are released, god knows why. You must say you're Kurdish Syrian. Don't worry, I'll register for you." He gave Majid Arab names to use. Then he said aloud, to those sitting near them, "No one will say this family is Iranian. They are Arab like us. Everyone here is Syrian. Understood?" Some nodded. Majid paused and shook the man's hand. The man leaned in. He whispered, "You're lucky; no other Farsi speakers here. If the girls keep quiet, you'll be believed."

In Izmir, they were fingerprinted. The man registered them as Syrian Kurds. They kept their gaze to the floor until he was finished. They were taken to a tiny windowless room in a caravansary hotel. They counted the money for the next smuggler. Days later, they were back on an air dinghy, looking at the lights of Mytilene on Lesbos as the smuggler assigned a ship captain and explained that the controls are much like the ones in a car.

The girls held hands as, once more, the shoreline receded. Soon they were on open water, headed for Greek lights. But the night was windy and waves rose up high around them, rocking the dinghy hard. It swayed from all sides, terrifying the girls, making Shirin cling to her mother. The boat took on water. Soon they were soaked through, their shoes waterlogged. Some wanted to turn back, screaming that their lives were worth another try, but others insisted it was rain, not seawater, filling the boat. Men used their clothes to drain the boat. Shirin wept. Someone vomited in the sea, and Farzaneh wondered if it might all end here, in Turkish waters.

Just as another wave crested, a searchlight tore through the dark, lighting up their faces again. Shirin's grip on Farzaneh was so tight now that she barely had to hold her. The Turkish coast guard began yelling into the boat. This time, it seemed, someone had left their cell phone on.

An officer boarded the dinghy and ordered the refugees to mount the ship by rope ladder, one by one. "The children have to go separately," he said. Shirin clung tighter, gripping Farzaneh's hair, her legs wrapped around her mother's hips like a baby koala. Every muscle in her arms and legs had contracted, and she wept on Farzaneh's shoulder.

"I'll take her myself," said Farzaneh, rubbing Shirin's back.

"That's not possible," said the guard. He grabbed Shirin by the waist and tried to pull her off. Shirin screamed. Majid stepped in, whispering to his daughter to let go, to go up with the guard and Maman would join her. She wailed. Farzaneh tried to imagine those five minutes in her daughter's life, when she waited on a different vessel than her mother, watching, imagining the two boats parting. Those five minutes would scar her for life.

"I'll take her," said Farzaneh. She put Shirin on her back and began to climb. "Hold on tight, *azizam,*" she said. *This is how monkeys transport their children,* she told herself. *Shirin's animal instinct will make her hold on.* Still, every step higher against the side of that ship, every inch between her daughter's body and the sea, meant a more disastrous injury if she fell.

Farzaneh tried to climb with one hand, holding Shirin's bottom with the other. The officer kept yelling, "You can't do that! The child can't go with you! Trust us to take her up!" But Shirin was glued to Farzaneh's back, her breath hot with fear, and Farzaneh had to release the other hand and climb the ladder, trusting Shirin's arms and legs to hold her. Her grip wouldn't loosen all at once, right? Farzaneh would feel it weakening.

On the ship, Shirin continued to cry in Farzaneh's arms — big breathless hiccups, fits of screaming, ribbons of tears. An officer approached and hovered over them. "Calm her!" he said. "Do it now."

"I can't," said Farzaneh. "She's scared out of her mind."

"What kind of mother are you?" he said. "Calm her!"

It was enough. Weeks of wandering in unwashed clothes, daughters wasting away, two failed sea journeys, with death waiting at her doorstep, and this man was yelling at a crying child. Farzaneh began to scream. "You animal!" she said. "You're no human. She's three. What does she know?"

Now the captain rushed toward them. Majid tried to step in, but the captain pushed past him. He pulled the officer away and slapped him across the cheek. "They've lost everything," he said. "What's wrong with you?"

Shirin spoke one word before falling asleep. "Maman," she mumbled. "Maman, Maman, Maman." Then she nodded off on Farzaneh's shoulder. She wouldn't speak again for ninety days.

In Izmir, they were fingerprinted and freed again.

On the third trip, Majid stood up and told everyone to turn off their cell phones. "No silence or airplane mode," he said. "GPS sends signals. Switch off. Off!" It was nine o'clock, and the Greek lights were visible again.

Today's captain pressed ahead, straight toward the lights. No one spoke. Shirin hadn't spoken for days, not since the rope ladder. Now she spoke in secret syllables when hungry or when she needed the toilet. After some time, they began to wonder if they had left Turkish waters. But land was still far off. They pressed on. The land drew closer. The refugees held their breaths and began to whisper about the journey on foot. Where were they to go to report themselves? Half a kilometer from Mytilene, the familiar harsh light appeared and Farzaneh released all hope. *I can't do this again.* She looked up, despairing, whispering soothing words to Shirin. "Oh god, let it be," said Majid. The ship looming nearby wasn't Turkish. Was it from an EU country? "I think tonight is the English watch," Majid whispered. "I think we're in European waters." On board, Farzaneh listened to their words and tried to learn something from their uniforms, their hair and skin. Their talk was melodic, with clipped consonants giving way to long vowels, elegant, like the men and women in English movies.

The officers held them on the water for hours, as the refugees were transported onto rescue boats three or four at a time, their flimsy life jackets exchanged for coast guard vests, and taken to the ship.

They waited in a bus till morning, without food, water, or blankets. The girls shivered all night in their wet clothes. Their lips turned blue. A driver arrived, and the bus set off. At eight o'clock, they were unloaded in Mytilene's refugee camp, known to its residents as "The Hell of Moria." "You won't be here longer than a week," someone said as they were pushed into quarantine. In the distance, grimy travelers from Africa and the Middle East waited in lines for food. Toilets ran over, and people bathed in buckets near them. Arab and Farsi men fought with broken glass bottles. The line for toilets was two hours; three hours for an undercooked meal.

"I don't know," muttered Majid. "I'm like Rostam. Everything seems to take me three tries." Only his wife chuckled at the dramatic reference to the poet Ferdowsi's legendary Persian hero. They were given a mattress in a tented salon packed with bodies. No blankets; they'd have to bargain or fight for those. *Like animals,* thought Majid. He looked up; they were right below the Wi-Fi box. From then on, their sleep would be interrupted by men hovering over them,

223

looking for a signal that would connect them to home.

Moria would be their home for ninety days.

VI

In Katsikas, I am walking by a row of Iso-boxes, when I hear delighted shrieks in the language of my youth — children playing soccer outside. I say hello. "Are you police?" a young girl asks.

"No," I say, "I'm an Iranian lady looking for other Iranians."

"I'm Sarah." She points to her Isobox. "We live in that." I knock, and Farzaneh invites me in. I struggle to strip off my boots. As I jump around, knocking into the table, Majid hears my accented Farsi and rolls out of bed. He seems happy to cut up the day with some talk. "Come in, come in, sit with us," he says. Farzaneh dashes to the kettle. "We'll tell you stories that will make you grow horns." I laugh. My mother uses that expression.

Majid is wearing pajamas — the day has no shape or rhythm here, no reason to change clothes. Sometimes you shower after soccer. Sometimes in the morning. Far-zaneh pours us Iranian tea in small glasses and they tell me about escaping from Iran;

the boat disaster, the mute child, Moria.

"The first thing we did when we got this Conex was to strip off everything and go straight for the shower," says Majid. His accent is deeply familiar. He's around forty, a well-educated contractor. A long scar cuts across his eyebrows and makes him look angry even when he's smiling. He picked it up in Moria camp in Lesbos, a place he compares to a Guatemalan prison. "That first shower was so nice. We just wanted to wash Moria off."

His wife nods, a tired smile blooming. "Then we made eggs and slept."

"Then, OK, yes, we asked about the Wi-Fi," Majid laughs.

It takes no talent to coax out the stories. Everyone wants to share theirs, maybe to cut the boredom or in case someone knows someone who might help, or most likely as practice for that day when they will perform it for a jaded and skeptical audience — it is widely understood here that, in becoming an asylum officer, you relinquish all imagination and wonder.

Just before Christmas 2017, 450 refugees from ten countries including Syria, Afghanistan, Lebanon, Iran, and Iraq arrived in the empty camp at Katsikas, near Ioannina. Awaiting them were residential Isoboxes, converted steel shipping containers in a gated field, each outfitted with kitchenette and bathroom, beds on metal frames. The Iranians call them Conexes. Almost everyone was arriving from Moria, the hell in Lesbos, and from similar inhospitable camps on the islands.

Preparing for their arrival, Refugee Support store workers didn't worry about chaos. They knew that when you treat people with dignity, they are dignified. Refugees — former doctors, teachers, craftsmen — browse the store. They choose olive oil or sunflower oil, the one they prefer. They don't have to hurry off with a basket and barter half the items away.

I work in the store and observe. The space is clean and whimsically decorated, cheese graters as light fixtures, small plants here and there, vegetables piled in neat rows. It looks like a section of a food cooperative in Brixton. An iPad is the sole point of sale. Volunteers fetch diapers and extra bags from the open storeroom behind the produce. No one worries about theft. Outside, a long hallway features art by the camp residents, including a haunting sketch of a laden boat at nighttime, refugees on open water. Tables and chairs are set up where families wait their turn. Here are some differences between this store and any other: only one family can shop at a time. And no one, no matter how compelling their story, gets an exception.

One afternoon, a pregnant couple returns after their shop. The husband has counted the items, and he came up fifty points short. Nothing can be done. "It's not a question of truth," says Paul. There can be no whiff of case-by-case judgments, the possibility of favoritism, in the camp.

For most of my time at the store, I bag groceries, just as I did in Oklahoma. This time, I have no say in what goes into the bags. But after the second family passes through, I notice other peculiarities of this store: in a way, we do tell them what they can have, because we control the points. The envelope full of paper money is largely symbolic, since almost everyone spends all that they have on the first market day after the points are issued. They hand over the entire envelope and the volunteer keeps track of their shopping. At some point the volunteer says, "only ten left," or "you're ten over," and the family begins to make tradeoffs. Private discussions are had. Children jump in, biting their nails. Olive oil is traded for sunflower. Children beg for bananas. Juice boxes are sacrificed.

The first time this happens, I realize I have bagged too soon. I have been overzealous. I have to stop, wait to see what will be put back. I have bagged the children's bananas, and now I remember how rare bananas were in Iran, how frantic I was for them and how that desperation lasted all through my teenage years, after bananas became ordinary. I want to ask Paul if we can just let them have it. I stand by, feeling useless and ham-fisted as the parents explain that the bananas will have to go back.

A man pokes a soft tomato. Another claims the last medium onion is defective; are there better ones? I glance at the corner of the store, where a smile is creasing Paul's temples — he loves it when people complain. "Please get real rice," says the tenth Iranian that day. "Basmati."

Later, as a young Syrian mother and I are trying to arrange her six sacks in a chubbily occupied buggy — the baby leans forward, accustomed to sharing his space — I hear the familiar, easy sounds of Farsi. An older Iranian couple enter, handing over their envelope (two hundred points, so no children). I listen as they speak in the language of everyday shopping. "How much" is this or that? "Is the olive oil worth the price?" Once, I hear them say "five tomans," tally-

228

ing their purchases in Iranian currency. It is beautiful to enter this brief fantasy they share. For ten minutes, they are a couple in their own city, doing their weekend shopping.

They go ten points over; the wife bites her lip. "The cookies then?"

The husband scans the items. "Yes, that's the best thing." Then he adds, "But we'd be five under." I imagine them back in their Isobox with their cups of tea, the cardamom they have smuggled from Iran. Butter cookies are just the thing with tea — but they put back the cookies, take a tomato paste, and wait at the register.

Then I do something stupid. I say hello in Farsi, wish them a good day. They stare at me, stunned, say polite hellos. I realize I have punctured the brief fantasy of a normal life that Paul envisioned; maybe this is the reason for the no-chat rule. My intrusion into their private negotiations makes plain that they are part of a charade, that this is a charity shop. I have heard and understood the cookie debate, the talk of "tomans." I know about their ten-point shortfall and can see the play money in their hands. I beg the universe to rewind, so I am not the same as those Thanksgiving volunteers in New York, the ones whose help came at such high costs.

I start bagging their things, grateful again for my shabby clothes.

When the store closes, I walk through the rows of Isoboxes, knocking on doors. I think about that pregnant couple. Did they lie? Were they believed? Refugees are always battling to be believed. As a white-skinned woman with an American passport and education, I am believed by default, and when I was pregnant, no one questioned me even when I was delirious. In a village in Italy, people crossed themselves as I passed. But to be pregnant in a refugee camp — what a curse. When you're pregnant, you agonize over details. My obsessions and tics were at a peak during pregnancy, and I would have gone back for a miscounted fifty pence. If the couple returned for their points, I believe them, though I also believe that they might have miscounted, because pregnancy also makes you imprecise.

Knocking on doors is intimidating and thrilling. Who will answer? Will they speak Farsi? Will they invite me in? I have a list of the Farsi households, and soon I memorize their door numbers. Word spreads about the American-Iranian woman walking the

Conexes like a ghost. They stick their heads out and say, "Come over!" "Come to ours." An Afghan boy says, "Come to my house, lady," and I go. For hours, I am a wanderer in a strange land, a lapsed countryman, and everyone wants me in their home. One afternoon, as I walk the field of Isoboxes, a Syrian boy approaches. It's raining. He takes my hand, but by now I'm used to these strange overtures; I am learning that displaced children change in different ways than adults. They fixate on anything concrete, and their responses are almost entirely physical. We walk. The boy stops and reaches for the hem of my Refugee Support fleece, zips me up with great care. He says something, maybe a mother's advice about zipping up. Then he takes my umbrella. I let it go, thinking he must be getting wet. He gets on tiptoes, struggling to hold it over my head. I duck a little. We walk. He says more things in Arabic. His tone is polite and careful, as if I'm his elderly aunt visiting from afar.

Every day I walk and I accept invitations, sick with shame for my adopted countries, my neighbors, safe in their homes, born in prosperous countries, crying out for walls. Soon I don't even have to knock anymore, or remember who lives where. The residents know me. People offer meals, familiar smells wafting from their windows. They offer tea. It's the other side of the looking glass, a village dropped whole into the bleakest desert.

VII / VALID AND TARAA

Valid married Taraa so young that they could have raised a family twice. Maybe they made this joke too often. Maybe that's why fate forced them into it. After they married, Valid got a clerical job in the Afghan government. They had two sons in 1992 and 1993. Then, in 2002, a third son, Pooya, completed their family while they were still young and energetic. Taraa was plump and beautiful, with light hair and a fair complexion; Valid's mother saw her in a bathhouse and promised him as much, and after they married, she delighted him in a thousand ways. She was fun, wittier than his friends and brothers. She could cook, sing, and dance. And when she laughed she threw her head far back and clapped her hands. She worked hard to make him laugh, too, and this moved him. She said she couldn't bear that the edges of his eyes turned down, grieving even when his heart was at peace.

They lived in a big square house that Taraa painted blood orange and mint green, in a mountain village in snowy Parwan

Province, north of Kabul. In the Salang Mountains, the air was always crisp, and one might forget the history of the place, the thousand and one ways Afghanistan had conjured to kill you. They found small joys; Valid kept his own turmeric blend. He fried eggplant and tomatoes. He stewed lamb.

September 2001 brought a new war to their doorstep.

But Valid never thought of leaving. He had a duty to his country and his family. He had his snowy mountaintop, and his tiny sons, to protect.

In 2004, Afghanistan prepared for its first presidential election since the ousting of the Taliban after 9/11. Taliban fighters, however, had vowed to disrupt these "sham elections" and to target anyone who supported them. This included workers, security personnel, poll takers, even voters. The Taliban vowed to dispatch their *mujahedeen* to foil the Western invaders at any cost. Valid, a government worker, soon became a target of a local Taliban operative. When men showed up threatening death and dismemberment, he knew he didn't have much time. The Taliban don't quibble or dither. Still, he didn't expect them to act so soon. And he expected a confrontation: men with guns.

The next day, Valid and Taraa, along with

233

their three sons and Valid's father and sister, loaded their car and started toward Bamyan Province, where they often traveled on Fridays. Two-year-old Pooya sat on his aunt's lap. The mountain roads were covered in bright powdery snow. Though the family had often traveled this path, everyone hushed near Shibar Pass, a winding road feared for its deathly drop-offs, steep curves, and rocky terrain. Famous as one of the world's most dangerous roads, it had killed many, and yet it was often clogged, though no barriers separated the narrow road from the deadly cliffs. At three thousand meters above sea level, the road was an icy, rocky thoroughfare braved only by experienced drivers.

Taraa had crossed it many times. That day, she drove as the family quieted down to allow her to concentrate. Partway through the mountain, a ball formed in the pit of her stomach. The car felt unstable, like the reinforcements on the tires had been adjusted.

She whispered to Valid. Only a few words, but enough so that he knew. They had tampered with the car, and now they were navigating the death pass with their children on wheels fit only for city streets.

Maybe she would have made it if her

confidence hadn't been shaken. Maybe knowing made her more agile and determined, enabling her to get past the cliff sides. At a sharp turn inside the mountain, the tires gave, the car veered, then flipped, turning again and again down a hillside. The screams of the children rang out in Valid's ears as he lost consciousness. Somehow, he was sure, his family was alive. He would wake and find them. If that patch of road had been any steeper, everyone would have died.

A while later, Valid woke. He pulled himself to his feet. He found his sister's and father's bodies first. When he found his older sons, dead at eleven and twelve, Valid fell to his knees and wept, pressing their faces to his. How far from the car they had fallen — in their final moments, they had almost flown, birdlike. He could hardly bear to search for his wife and youngest son. He wept and bled and stumbled along the rocky terrain, slipping on patches of ice in torn shoes. Why didn't they just shoot him or cut off his head? Why remove the reinforcements from his tires? They wanted him to suffer. Perhaps they wanted help from someone in the government. What fools to think he would crave anything but death now.

Just as Valid was considering stepping off the edge of the nearest steep cliff, he saw her. Her skin was shredded, but she was moaning. She kept pointing to something a few paces away, behind a pile of stones. Valid rushed for the rocky patch. Pooya lay there in a pool of blood, unable even to scream. He moaned, his tiny lips trying to call for his mother. Valid lifted him into his arms. The meat of his leg had been shredded clean off. His face was bloody. So many jagged pebbles had dug into his face and legs that Valid didn't dare try to pick them out. He dragged his two living family members to the road, where someone picked them up.

Taraa was in the hospital for weeks. Metal rods and clamps were inserted into her spine and on both sides of her pelvis. A line of stitches, thick like a suitcase zipper, bisected her back. For days, Valid collected X-rays in a file. Her foot was mangled at the ankle; she would spend her days hovering near her wheelchair; trying to walk a few paces farther from it.

Years passed. Pooya healed and grew. Scars lost their terrible sheen, and Valid and Taraa became accustomed to Taraa's new body. One leg was completely without feeling, limp from the pelvis down. Her ankle folded in on itself as if someone had hammered the anklebone and stapled it shut. Scars crisscrossed her legs. She grew plumper around the enormous stitches up her spine, but this new fat tissue didn't obscure the scar or push it away from her bones; the zipper sat taut against her spine, dividing her back into two distinct pockets of flesh.

Valid and Taraa had their second family. When Pooya was seven, a son, Naser, was born. A year later, their first daughter, Nushin. The new children clung to each other like twins. They were big-eyed and stony-faced and watchful, like children in Persian films.

For years Valid battled with Taliban leaders, staying their hand in whatever way he could. They lived in a war zone, each night preparing for death and the death of their children. One afternoon, Taraa was sitting in her chair, lost in thought as she unraveled an old sweater, when a hard knock startled her. The knocks grew louder and more urgent. Then, she heard commotion on the roof. Someone was stomping around above her head, trying to get in through the roof. She struggled to get up, to tell them that Valid wasn't at home. Outside, she heard them yelling. "Valid! Come out now!"

She heard a window shatter, and as she moved toward the noise, she saw the barrel of a gun entering her house through the window.

Before she could run, they shot her through the shoulder, just inches from her heart. Then, seeing she was alone, they left.

Valid moved his family to Iran, where they lived in hiding for years. Though they had torn her body apart, Taraa was serene, if no longer joyful. Valid could fit a finger in the bullet wound in her shoulder. Then a letter warned that he had been found. In 2017, Valid and Taraa took their children to Turkey. They were eight, nine, and sixteen, able to walk a long way, to help their parents. Though they had already lost two sons, they put their replacement family on an inflatable dinghy to Moria. The Aegean seemed on that day as murderous as those winding mountain terrains, whose open maw was, at least, the devil they knew. When they reached Lesbos, Valid kissed the ground. "I've been running for fifteen years. Finally, we're done with escaping." Over the coming months people would ask, "How long has it been?" and he'd begin the story with post-9/11 Taliban plots to stifle democracy. Often, he'd find that they meant *how long has it been starting from this day,* the day his foot touched European soil.

In Moria, Pooya fell in with thugs from home. Valid worried. Once he tried to intervene. But he was too weak to quarrel with young men. He only wanted to endure this phase and find a roof in some forgotten corner where he could fry eggplant in turmeric and care for his broken wife.

One morning a cheery, stout-legged widow appeared behind Taraa's chair and started chatting. Hajira looked decades older than her thirty-five years. Back home she had taught literature. "I raised my children with the power of my pen, under the eye of the Taliban!" she said, and Taraa smiled and said, "You are a brave woman, my friend."

VIII

"We are abandoned," says Majid. "But they're telling everyone this is paradise. It's maddening." He tells me that a senior official from Amnesty or UNHCR visited the camp. A school was hastily set up and passed off as part of an improvements program. It was in session for a day and never returned. A doctor visited too, that day. This seemed less a lie. A pop-up clinic can achieve a lot in a day, but a school cannot. Still, the residents played along. They sent their children. No one dared complain. They didn't know who was responsible, or whom they would anger if they made a fuss.

Besides (everyone always says), this isn't Moria. Thank God this isn't Moria. That hell is over. Now we don't sleep in mud, or bathe our children while wading in sewage. We have linoleum planks below our feet. We sleep in beds. We might waste away without work, study, or any purpose at all, stuck in this shapeless, colorless half sleep, but we don't wither in the rain waiting for our food; no one hurls rocks at our children in the night.

Before I leave, Majid shows me videos of Moria, toilets overrun by sewage where people also bathed, tents on raw ground, children begging to leave. He tells me how he got his scar, a stone to the head during a routine nighttime brawl between Arabs and Iranians. He huddled over his daughters in a tent erected atop the mud, and when he stuck his head out to beg for quiet, the rock struck him, cutting a gash over his eyebrows.

"The fights are terrible," says Majid. "It's because they give everything to the Arab-speaking refugees." He means Syrians. "The media is watching them. If you're from Iran, you have nothing, no one."

"Can I come back tomorrow?" I ask.

"Yes," says Majid. "Actually, you'll come back thrice. Things happen to us in threes. Three boats to Moria. Three tries to get here. Always three."

"Is there anything you can do to speed things?" Majid asks. He means the asylum claim. I don't know what to say — his cell phone videos are scenes from a nightmare, and I feel cruel and silly for having revealed my own asylum story, my impossible passport. Paul keeps his face neutral. "I'm sorry, we can't help. We don't know asylum law. But we'll look into basmati rice," he says. Later he tells me that it's a mistake even to provide reassurance, because when you're staring at years of waiting, you grasp at every hope to circumvent it. You want to act, to cut through the void. I tell them to be patient. They won't be here forever. Recalling my hand-erased workbooks, I say, "Don't let the girls miss school. Teach them to read in English."

From here on, the videos and pleas will greet me in every Isobox.

Outside, I find a few moments of solitude. It's chilly and wet and most of the adults are in their Isoboxes, cooking or reading or playing on their phones. Many are visiting neighbors — since arriving in groups from island camps, cliques have formed by country and gender and age. A few children play in the distance. Laundry lines connect metal boxes. Bags of garbage await the next trip to the dumpsters. Heavy sacks hang from flimsy doors, to keep them from slamming open and breaking windows.

A young man approaches me. "What are you doing?" he asks. I tell him I'm collecting stories. He offers his. "I'm Darius," he says. I follow him to a room full of single men from Afghanistan and Iran. Each Isobox holds four adults, but several of them, like this one, have become social hubs. On seeing me, the men jump up, offer me tea. They are young and polite and deferential, and they receive few female visitors. Still, I am something of a novelty, and they allow themselves to ask questions they would never ask another woman: *What is your passport? How old are you? What's your accent?* When I tell them I'm from Isfahan, the Iranians start joking in Isfahani accents. I haven't heard it in so long, I burst into laughter.

I'm dying to hang out with these guys, but Paul has rules. I text him. He joins us in half a minute and works on a laptop as we chat in Farsi.

Their window is broken. Darius tells me that, a few nights ago, there was a fight between a group of Afghan men and Iranians. He shows me a knife scar on his arm. Pulling up his sleeve, he reveals much older scars. In camp, midnight battles are routine. Idle youth grow restless; factions form. Earlier Majid told me about disturbances by "the layabout boys without families." He heard the Afghan raid at Darius's Isobox — the shouting, the windows shattering. "These boys are the source of every problem. They drink, smoke, fight. They disturb the single women." And most damningly, they are economic migrants. They had no trouble at home, so why did they leave? If you're a man, you can tell the Islamic Republic or the Taliban whatever they need to hear, right? "Don't tell me about ethical or religious stirrings," he says, "those are luxuries. These boys are bored and underused and they think they'll have a better time in Europe." What he means is that if you were born a Muslim man in these countries, you are already privileged. You're not a rebel woman. You're not Christian or Baha'i. If you're gay or an apostate, you can hide that — you shouldn't go looking for problems. If you're here in the camps, either you left a good life for a better one, or you stirred up trouble on purpose. "They are lying!" Majid says, "They make it hard to believe those who had real trouble in Iran."

He is choosing to forget mandatory service, a deadly requirement that traps primarily poor young men, the ones who can't pay their way out. Military service aside, though, shouldn't wanting a better life be enough on its own? Isn't being "underused" in your twenties the greatest tragedy for the mind and the spirit? I would have considered it so, when I was studying at university and falling in love for the first time. Why should these men have to spend their lives idle and mediocre with no hope of accessing their potential? Isn't a wasted life also a life that is in danger?

The men tell jokes and prepare a bowl of fruit for me as the water boils. Their eyes sparkle with intelligence. These are no layabouts. I wonder what they might have done, if they had the privileges of the average American, even the poor ones. Would they be engineers or writers or dancers or chefs? Darius was a tailor in Isfahan. Would he own a New York atelier? As I wait for my tea, I imagine what they might have become if they had, say, the same opportunities as the Trump children. My mind conjures Pulitzers, heart surgeries, books of poetry and philosophy and history. There is no logical or just reason for a mediocre few, shielded from competition, propped up by inherited riches and passports, to feast on the world's resources under the guise of meritocracy. Meanwhile, these clever young men are offered no country, no home, no right to work or study, no basic right to health care, no future. They are shunned from every society, their talents wasted — *why?* If they are offered charity, they are told exactly what they will eat, that it cannot be the luxuries of the more deserving.

Asghar has been a refugee for a decade, since he was a teenager. He keeps smuggling himself out of Afghanistan, making his way through Iran and Turkey, sleeping in roads and under bridges, finding menial work until he reaches Italy or France. There he finds friends, earns enough for a flat, buys a couch, gets a girlfriend. Within months, he is deported again. It's these tendrils of root — the address, the girlfriend — that give him away. Suddenly he's seen, investigated, tossed onto a plane. He visits his mother. He escapes again. The last time Asghar was deported, he left behind a baby. Now, he must get back to her. Now, he has a specific destination, not just a better life, but *that* French town, *that* building, *that* small room with pink curtains. This has been the work of his twenties, staying fastened to France.

Hamid has spent nearly a year in Moria, the longest of anyone they know. In one year, he has aged a decade. He is scarred up and down the arms, neat rows of cuts and cigarette burns. "It's the only way to remember that there are worse pains than living like an animal," he says, "You need to feel something. To try to change things." It's common among the men, to try to release energy they should be using for work, for falling in love, and caring for families. I know that privately Hamid hopes that the burns will make someone take notice, but that's not how Westerners think. I want to shake him, to tell him what I know. *They don't like the damaged,* I want to say, *especially if they think the disease is in your mind. Trust me, the Americans and the English, they like triumphant stories. They want to be a part of the stories. They want to find excellent people, luminaries, pluck them out of hell, knead them flawless. They want to congratulate themselves for something re-markable. Keep yourself undamaged.*

I remember the day when I was eleven, when I willed the tic in my neck away. Even if the itch threatens to make me faint, I will not move. I swore in my bedroom: *I will never let an American see into my mind again.*

I say, "Don't hurt yourself." And he looks at me with wide, watery eyes. All over the camp, people look at me the same way, like I am a pinprick portal to America. What an unnatural thing waiting is.

Meanwhile their tea is brewed to a glassy amber. They quote Rumi. They talk philosophy. They talk about love.

I ask Darius why he fled. He tells me the story of the woman he didn't love, but could have loved: trying to date a worthwhile girl. He tells me about the outings, the beating by the moral police and his three-month coma. Their stories often go like this: caught in this or that small joy, they run. He shows me the marks on his body. Now, in camp, he's found himself more woman trouble. He befriended an Afghan girl, angering the Afghan men. "It's always about ladies with you," I say. He shrugs, eyes laughing. He's not harmful to women. He doesn't deserve his three-month coma or his banishment from home, his worried mother, or this forced inertia, his wasted hands. Despite the ban on work, he sews clothes for his friends at the camp. He's just young, with charm and a skill, and he wants to live.

But Afghan-Iranian animosities run deep, not only at Katsikas. I imagine those boys have their own convincing tale: she was a misplaced thing, blown far from home, and what could this young cad give her but a broken heart? At this age, every man wants to lay waste to a heart. What injustice for these underused boys to see it happen to a woman who is already suffering the waiting place — Barthes's waiting atop the one doled out by a cowardly world; it can kill someone. I think of the Romanian wife; how did she survive? To fall in love as a refugee would be a nightmare.

"It's as if you're playing with their sister," says one of Darius's Afghan friends. "She needs protection. She's foolish to go into a man's Conex."

So, the Afghan boys broke in through the window. They cut Darius's arm, broke his things. His Iranian friends came to his aid. To the neighbors it was a gang fight. There was drinking, maybe hashish. There was blood and glass, and for a night, they were all quenched.

The next day I knock on a Conex door and stumble onto a morning gathering from decades ago. I peer into the window. Eight or nine Iranian and Afghan women sit around a worn rug, sipping hot tea from water glasses, gossiping, rolling dough on round wooden slabs, like chopping boards on legs. They've turned the Isobox into a rural kitchen from home. Now I'm looking into Maman Masi's window in Ardestoon. Now I hear my aunt's laughter, my grandmother's reedy voice that sounds very much like it could be mine in old age. What rivers of memory flow quietly in the veins, waiting for a note, an image, a smell, so they can gush up to the surface.

A hush falls when I knock. The door opens and every eye is watching me. When I greet them in childish Farsi, they wave me in, everyone at once. Two jump up to make a space on a cushion on the floor. "Bring cake!" someone says. There's cake? Peeking in, I spot a plate of white lemon cake, cut into squares, entirely possible from the ingredients in Paul's store.

"Are you making bread?" I ask, glancing at the wooden kneading board that one of the husbands has made. The board isn't for making bread. They're turning everyone's flour into thin noodles for Iranian noodle soup, a staple. I look up and see the oldest of the women putting the dough through a rickety pasta maker. "Where did you get *that*?" I can't hide my shock, and they laugh. This grandmother doesn't live in the camp. She has a flat in Ioannina. She and her family have Greek papers, and her son, Davood, teaches the camp's makeshift school without permission or pay. This mother and son come to the camp every day, because here are countrymen who need neighbors. And because they too need friends from home. "I found it in a market," she says about the pasta maker.

I start to ask where the noodles are drying. It's raining outside; they can't hang them on the clotheslines. She points to a small room. A mattress leans against the wall, and thin ropes of dough are drying on the metal bars of the naked bed frame, enough for many families. "This is genius!" I yell into the room. "Come, take a tea," someone shouts back.

I can't wait to tell Paul about the noodles. Here in this Isobox is everything he has been working for, people cooking their native food, providing for their community with their own knowledge and ingenuity.

Amid the movement, I lose track of how the cup of tea got into my hand. "We heard about you," says Hajira, a great-auntie type, a sprawling woman with a rural skirt, a flat, sun-worn face, "the young lady writer."

"Not so young," I joke. "I'm thirty-eight." I have to say my age so they'll take me seriously. The approval of Iranian mothers is my weakness.

"I'm thirty-five," says Hajira. This time I

hide my shock.

"Do you have children?" I ask. She does. They are grown. Her husband died when she was young and she raised them alone, because who wants to marry all those hungry mouths? She became a teacher of humanities. One of the other women says that she knows everything worth reading in Farsi. Hajira tells me that, a week ago, she married another man.

"Married? Here in Katsikas?" Why am I surprised? Everywhere people fall in love, they marry. Hajira tells me that he is a family friend she met on the phone, that he lives in France and came to the camp to marry her. Now she is applying to live in France, close to her children in Germany.

She shows me a wedding video on her phone. Men circling the empty recreation room that Davood uses for school. I recognize two of the Afghan men who served me tea. Hamid, the one with the cuts and burns, is dancing as others clap. The bridegroom sits in a chair, wearing a suit, accepting well-wishes and congratulations. The women are celebrating elsewhere.

"What did you wear?" I ask.

"A dress. You can't get a wedding dress here," she says, and I recall Paul's complaint about the donations. *Once we got a wedding dress*. The irony almost knocks me onto my cushion. Later, when I tell him about Hajira's dress search, he slaps his forehead. "I wish she would have told us! Even if we didn't have that dress, we could have found one. We could have found things for the reception." Refugees have secret lives; often that robs them of the vast stores of kindness people like Paul have to offer them. But camps have so many rules, and asking for things could have consequences.

Hajira tells me about her husband, Abdul. He is much older, and kind. He is making a home for her. I ask again about the way they met. She repeats, "On the phone." And I say, maybe too girlishly, "No, I mean, what did he say to court you? How did you fall in love? What's the story?" She laughs and takes my chin. "Listen to you, you little devil."

I get comfortable on a pillow beside a shy woman at a kneading table. She has lost the use of her legs, something to do with the Taliban.

Davood, the teacher, pops in just before school hour. I follow him.

The children sit dinner-style at a table in the center, boys and girls together, surrounded by their own hanging art and by a handful of parents at the periphery of the schoolroom. Davood writes Greek, English, and Farsi pronouns on a worn dry-erase board. One of the mothers asks if she can add an Arabic row. He offers her the marker. Her son speaks no Farsi. He sits quietly beside another boy, squinting hard, trying to force himself to understand. Later I learn that her row contains basic mistakes, but Davood has no way of checking this. He drills each student in front of the class.

Afterward, I greet a nine-year-old Persian boy idling by the table. He asks, "What's your card?" He waits, smiling at me. "I have a friend who left," he says. "He got a German card." He tells me about soccer and winter in Greece and Davood, his new teacher. "Davood has his Greek card now. He comes and teaches us. What's your card?"

It's difficult not to react. To this child traveler, the world is made up of cards of different value, each representing the worth of its owner.

Another boy joins us. He tells me his name, Naser, his younger sister's name, Nushin. They are eight and nine, both exceptionally beautiful. They have an older brother, sixteen, who wants nothing to do with school.

Later, as I walk the Isoboxes again, Naser

sticks his head out of the window. "Come to our house now, lady," he says. He disappears from the window and the door swings open to Nushin's giggles. I glance back.

There's something serene and civilized about the rows of metal homes against the backdrop of the misty mountains beyond Ioannina. The savagery of Moria still haunts the place. During the day, Katsikas is still, children playing outside. At night, the adults share meals, a dozen women around a *sofreh* that covers the entire floor, eating, praying, reciting. The men drink and smoke, too. Both groups gossip, they dance. I imagine one unlucky teenager in an Isobox down the row, watching twenty children.

Inside, a wheelchair is propped by the door. Hajira and Taraa are making tea. A man with a kind face sits cross-legged on the floor. He jumps up to greet me. Naser and Nushin settle on cushions to study. They ask their mother if they can make popcorn for everyone, and she says yes. "These are your children?" I ask Taraa, and she proudly confirms.

I chat with her husband, Valid, about the camp, the store, their journey here. How has it been, this in-between life? "It's not new," he tells me. "We've been running from the Taliban, it seems, for fifteen years."

They launch into the story without fanfare. They don't spare details, and it feels wrong to hear it with the children just there, sitting with their books at their father's side, hearing that they are divine replacement for their two dead siblings. Sometimes Hajira jumps in, reminding Taraa of details she has forgotten. "Did you know each other in Afghanistan?" I ask. They didn't. They met on the way, maybe in Moria, like everyone.

They speak openly about Pooya, the sixteen-year-old smoking outside the community room, the toddler who was flayed, his small body tumbling down the mountain. "He's a layabout," says Valid, eyes on his bare toes. "He has no education. His future is done. We've wandered too long."

I start to argue, but I stop. His eyes are drained of hope. "The most important thing is that the children are learning English," I say. "Use your time here. You don't know when it'll end, and when it is over, you won't want to have wasted it. The worst thing is to sit and wait."

Nushin draws closer to me. She shows me a book of English words she's reading. It's a book for infants. A single photo and word on each page — apple, car, tree. "Yes, exactly," I say and give her a squeeze.

Then Hajira asks the question I've been

dreading. "Can you help this family? If you wanted to help anyone here, it should be them."

I say nothing. Do they think I'm going from home to home, *choosing*? The idea sickens me. I'm making their lives worse. I want Eirini, the photographer, to interrupt us. She knows how to handle this. She's photographed every camp in Greece, even Moria. Hajira insists that I look at the scars on Taraa's body. Taraa lifts up her shirt, shows me the long scars up and down her back, the place where her back seems to have been pieced together, badly, from spare parts. Her flesh grows around the cuts so that she looks like meat bound tight with string.

I turn and look at her husband, his kind eyes. The children watch me.

"Have you seen a doctor here?" I ask. No one will give them an appointment. Every phone call takes hours, and they need a translator.

Taraa pulls her shirt back down. She shows me her mangled feet. We sit silently for a beat. Then Hajira says, "You should take Naser."

"I'm sorry?" I say. Naser looks up. He seems unmoved.

"Take the boy with you to England. He's

nine. He still has a chance to make a life, to bring his family later." I see now that she's been considering this plan since the moment she saw me.

"You want me to take her son?" I've lost my filter. "Are you crazy?"

"What other solution is there?" Hajira says. "They've been running for fifteen years and they're stuck here. Do you think you'll find someone who's suffered more?" I look around the room. Valid's head hangs so low, I want to sit beside him and prop it up. Taraa is worrying the fabric of her shirt. Hajira grows more resolute. "If you don't want him, drop him off in a camp in England. He will figure out what to do. He will learn English." His mother nods at the ceiling. His father pulls a foot close to his haunches and rests his chin on his knee. He stares at his toes. Naser watches me, his playfulness gone, as if he's trying to decide whether I'll make a good mother.

"That's not what will happen," I say. "The camps are the same everywhere. It's worse there, if you end up in detention."

"They will take unaccompanied minors," says Hajira. "The state will raise him. He will have an English education and human rights."

My voice is feeble. "It's a good plan, my

friend. But I can't smuggle a boy without papers into the country. He needs his own mother." Briefly I entertain the idea. Do I adopt him? Do we take trains through Europe? Do I flash my own passport and claim that his is with his father? Do we pretend he's unaccompanied, and I watch over him from afar as he sneaks his small body through the pores of the English border?

None of us speaks. A minute later, Eirini knocks, curls falling over the threshold as she reaches for her shoes, her breezy voice calling into the room, "Hello there!" I am overcome with gratitude. I ask her if she knows Greek doctors, perhaps former classmates, people who will visit this family. She offers some ideas, and the room breathes out. The women make more tea. I glance in the corner, where Naser and Nushin are sitting on tiny haunches, their backs rigid, huddled diligently over their closed books.

I spend dusk wandering through the camp, trying to figure out what I've done wrong. Is it cruel for a person who's come unstuck to return to another's purgatory? Did they truly offer me their son, or is this Barthes's loss of proportion — the desire to cut the waiting into pieces, to manage it. *I decide to take it badly.* How much worse could you take it than this?

Someone told me (perhaps they read it somewhere) that refugees are forced into cement shoes and told, "Now you have roots." But being held down isn't roots. They are told not to move, to build a life for a year, two years, to learn a culture they may soon leave behind. But the knowledge that you haven't been accepted hardens the soil. This in-between country hopes you will leave, and so do you. In the meantime, they keep you in holding pens. You aren't meant to mingle with locals, to get by too skillfully in this land. You aren't meant to take root through your cement shoes. Once accepted, you don't wake up with feet unbound — you are still a foreigner who speaks feeble Greek, who lives in a bad neighborhood, has darker skin, can't find work. Perhaps that's what draws Davood and his mother, who have a flat in Ioannina, to return again and again to Katsikas.

Ioannina is a tourist town. A short walk from the barren lot of the camp (which Google Maps calls a "hospitality center") is a boardwalk with chic restaurants, cocktails, good espresso. But who wants to witness the spectacle of vacation when there is no work to give days shape or meaning? For the stateless, what is rest? Acting out a fiction. The vacationers too are acting in a play, a controlled wait with a known end. But tell them that their vacation is indefinite and watch them abandon all manufactured calm.

Unknown waits combine dangerously with finite resources. Boardwalks don't soothe the frenzy. Who wants to walk into town and risk the children pining for pastas and gelatos that cost a week's budget? This too is a nightmare that won't end with asylum. Each morning, for a long time, you will wake up a little taller, your sheets never covering your feet.

Better to stay in your quarantine. The camp or the holding pen.

"I forbid myself to leave the room," says Barthes. If he leaves the room, the lover might call. The hardest part of leaving Hotel Barba was drifting from the mail cubbies — what if our letter was lost or stolen? Today's refugees wait by their phones, hitting refresh. Barthes writes, "*To make someone wait:* the constant prerogative of all power, 'age-old pastime of humanity.' "

I think of my grandmother, frozen in London, the way she recoils from refugees and their tales. I think of her decades of anticipating this one ordinary man, all the many times she has told her stories of sabotage and church politics, the theater that enables her to survive the waiting. She has no more proportion, just the faint hope that one day, finally, she will be believed. Maybe it won't come to that. Barthes, reflecting on a lover's vigil, writes, "A mandarin fell in love with a courtesan. 'I shall be yours,' she told him, 'when you have spent a hundred nights waiting for me, sitting on a stool, in my garden, beneath my window.' But on the ninety-ninth night, the mandarin stood up, put his stool under his arm, and went away." The Romanian lovers of Hotel Barba defied the order to wait; they, too, got up and left. Will my grandmother's vigil end? Will it drive her to madness?

Is it a taunt for me to return here, as Davood does? Does every exile want to run backward after a time? I've moved every two or three years since I turned eighteen. That isn't displacement anymore. It's a compulsion.

As evening settles over the camp, washing the walkways between containers in pretty shades of orange, I hear music. Eirini has joined me and we stop outside a door and try to look into a window, but the curtains are drawn. The room is lit, though, and bustling. We knock. The door opens and a bolt of voices unfurls at our feet. I know almost all the women inside. "It's a birthday party!" says Farzaneh. "Come in, come in! Here you are again!" says Hajira. She is back to her teasing tone from that morning's pasta party. Taraa, too, looks relaxed. She is sitting on a cushion against the wall with her tea glass, and she summons me in with her hands. She adjusts her skirt over her useless legs.

They bring out homemade presents. Familiar music from someone's phone strains to fill the packed room. Teenage girls gossip quietly as children run underfoot. Mothers serve the lemon cake again. Two grandmothers, both having chosen to live at Katsikas, look serenely at their displaced offspring — they remind me of my own mother, how she follows me everywhere even when I don't want her there. A girl from the noodle morning gets up to dance. Her body swings about brazenly, expertly, and when she asks me to join her I'm embarrassed. I can't dance like that. I don't have access to . . . *that.* Others feign shock. There are clucks and titters. I was raised in America, after all. My life should be all disposable income and sexy clothes and inexplicable connections to asylum officers.

And, look, I'm acting like some silly village girl. "Didn't your mother teach you to dance?" Farzaneh asks me. She jumps up now to dance with her elder daughter. She takes her hand and they move in exactly the same way, the girl's narrow hips keeping time with her mother's. I want them to think differently of me — that I haven't squandered my freedom on a joyless life. But maybe it's time they learned some things about the powers of refuge: it can't transform you, at least not in the exact way you'd like. There's no such thing as a single redeeming story. And money can't buy moves like that.

My bones ache from the work of this year, of this decade. Someone cranks up the tempo. Everyone cheers. Taraa, the grandmothers, and I lean on cushions and watch the others dance. Am I this wilted? I want to sleep. Taraa tucks her twisted feet under her skirt, pats my hand, and signals for my tea to be refilled. Three women in kaftans who, just that morning, I had mistaken for sixty, dance like restless thirty-year-olds, fresh from divorces.

On my last day in Greece, as the store is closing and I am saying my goodbyes, a bewildered Iranian man in his midforties wanders into the waiting area. I greet him in Farsi and he looks relieved. He tells me that he has just arrived at the camp. He has no clothes, no food. The volunteers register him and agree to keep the store open so he can shop. They tell him to return at 3 p.m. and they will open the men's store so he can have his ten items. He is larger than average. I hope he will find something.

Since he knows nothing of the points, I help him choose his food. He gets eggs, rice, a kilo of bananas, oil. He puts back the oil — he is starting to understand how shopping will go here. He gets cookies, pistachios, milk. He puts back the milk. He doesn't buy much else. Since his last twenty points won't buy oil, he settles for four juice boxes. He leaves happy, nodding thanks.

What did he expect, this new arrival? The chaos of Calais? The horrors of the isles? Is he ready for his heart and mind to erode, bit by bit, as he waits? Does he have children in Iran? Will he send for them, or will they be born in a foreign place? Will they learn German, Italian, or English? Will he work in his old profession again? Will 2030 find him lecturing in a university, or driving an Uber, washing dishes, cleaning homes whose shelves hold a fraction of the books he once owned? These questions torture the mind, and yet the world will say, "He made it out! He is safe!" He has a metal container to live in, food to eat. But charity and welcome are different things. Why do we ask the desperate to strip off their dignity as the price of help? You never forget the moment you were part of a shivering horde, when another human threw you your food, when you slept in mud alongside your confused children, when you shoved and grunted beside other faceless people, some of them former architects, doctors, teachers. It can break your spirit as fast as hunger. And yet, it seems too much to ask, in these hard-hearted days, to suffer the minutia.

From November 2017 until February 2018, Refugee Support was at Tombru camp in Bangladesh, a no-man's land where people live in bamboo and tarpaulin structures, where they suffer severe malnutrition, poor sanitation, and lack of medical care. Many are rape victims, and there abound conflict injuries, cholera, diphtheria, overcrowding, sexual violence, to say nothing of the local opposition. It is a living hell. We must do better. These camps are filled with humans, just as intelligent and interesting as our best citizens. In some of their cultures, the *how* of things is as vital as a roof.

More and more, as I write these pages, I am confident that, though refuge is undeniably today's battle, dignity is tomorrow's.

The night after tea and popcorn at Taraa's, I heard my name called from a nearby window. "Dina *khanom.* Come here." It was Valid, Taraa's husband. As I approached, I smelled Iranian eggplant, my favorite, with turmeric and olive oil. I calculated it in points: olive oil, forty. Turmeric, perhaps ten or twenty, from the "one week only" shelf. "Come and eat with us," he said. The sky was darkening. I was exhausted from walking the Isoboxes and heavy-hearted and I missed my daughter. I was afraid of looking little Naser in the eyes again. I declined, and though he repeated the offer thrice, as is customary, I thanked him and said I needed to sleep. He nodded, his eyes sad, and I knew I should have stayed. He was trying to make up for the uncomfortable tea, the hysteria, with a dish from home. Back in my bed, after a stale fish dinner, I wondered what could compel me to reject Iranian eggplant. Once again, I had behaved just like those Thanksgiving volunteers at the shelter in New York. I had come to this camp expressly to accept cups of tea from their hands, to sit with them and eat a bite as friends. And yet, I couldn't face that room again, not because I was afraid of their need — I didn't want to see the shame pulling at Valid's eyebrows.

On the way to my rental car, I think of how nervous I have been to revisit this strange waiting place, this limbo that shaped me, that is now shaping thousands of others from my home. We will be forever linked and defined by it. Maybe one day soon, I'll find one of my Barba neighbors, the scarred soldier who kicked the soccer ball with me, the Romanian wife, or the bricklaying grandmother. More and more often now, I conjure Barba in my memories. The refugees I knew in 1988 are thirty years past their trials. I wonder what they've done with their days. Was anyone tossed back? What about the American homeschoolers who gave us workbooks? Or the Italian pastor and his family who visited us bearing small luxuries and comforting prayers? I wish I could bring Barba back to life for a day, or an hour.

As I clean the coffee cups and candy wrappers from the backseat, I remember a final errand. I jog back into the camp, find a door, knock. I have knocked on this door twice already. Yesterday, Majid said, "No need for goodbye. Remember? Everything happens in threes." Now I stand at that family's doorstep a third time, waiting to be invited in. No one answers. A neighbor pokes a head out and says, "They're out. Maybe playing soccer."

"OK," I say, "I guess I have to come back then." I don't like this unfinished feeling. I shuffle around, trying to decide what to do next. I scratch my neck, check inside my backpack, and my pockets, for nothing. I think maybe they'll return in a minute, or five minutes.

"Next time in England," says the voice, releasing me from my wait. She recedes behind a makeshift curtain, a light blue fabric that might have been medical scrubs, and I recall that we used to say that too.

■ ■ ■ ■

Part Three:
Asylum

■ ■ ■ ■

(on stories and the alchemy of truth)

I

We landed in Will Rogers World Airport on a stifling July day in 1989. Jim, the American writer Maman had met in Maman Moti's church in London years before, came for us at the airport. We loaded into the car, jet-lagged and confused, unable to take in the details of our new life. The Oklahoma landscape seemed like miles and miles of nothing, like we had landed on Mars. It was the barest, flattest land I had seen. Jim took us to his house. We met his wife, Mary-Jean. They gave us their loft, a wood-paneled space decorated in russets and browns, and left us to rest in a big bed.

The day we arrived in the United States, Baba sent Maman a letter demanding the return of his children. It was as if he hadn't believed we were gone until some asylum office took us in. Maybe he hadn't mourned us yet.

271

We rose early the next morning and lined up to see a parade — it was the Fourth of July, but it seemed that all those families on beach chairs waving American flags and eating watermelon were celebrating our arrival. The parade weaved down residential streets, house after house of *actual* white picket fences. Some had porch swings, American flags. We were in a film.

Jim and Jean were right-wing evangelical Christians — I marvel now that they agreed to sponsor a family of strangers from a place they knew from a hostage crisis and a war. They spoke to Maman about her plans, making clear that she wouldn't take advantage of any of the resources available to refugees. ("We're hardworking Republicans," Jim chuckled; he wasn't joking.) He would instruct her how to hunt for a job, a car, a driver's license, an apartment. In the meantime, we would live in their attic.

Jean wore tube tops far above her shorts, sprayed her hair with Aqua Net, and made bologna-mayonnaise sandwiches on plastic plates with stacks of Pringles on the side. She took Daniel and me to Toys "R" Us and to an ice cream shop with an unfathomable array. There is nothing, nothing, like ice cream on an Oklahoma summer night, cicadas and twangy music tickling your ear, beside a mouthy grandmother with a bare midriff and no moral police to witness it. No *hijabi* teachers shouting. No bullhorns thrust in your face. We drove to the Edmond Public Library, where she got us library cards, and we checked out thirty books each — stories about rebellious sisters, and bodies in puberty, and Indian ghosts, and shameful history like slavery and the Trail of Tears — that would have been banned at home. I spent the next year consuming stories. I was voracious, and the huge gaps in my English closed like a shallow wound. I learned to put myself in another's skin: a kid with freckles, a girl called Blubber. I thought of Khadijeh who had given up and sprung many leaks, and I wished I had sat beside her and said that we were all afraid, even me and Pooneh.

When I wasn't reading, I was watching television. After every Friday-night lineup (TGIF!), I had a dozen new words in my mouth. In those early days in Oklahoma, the show that captured my imagination was *Perfect Strangers,* an American sit-com about distant cousins, one American, one seemingly Greek, who became unlikely roommates. For me, the show wasn't about their friendship. It was about Balki Bartoko-mous, a funny, hopeful, lonely immigrant.

Every day I would sit on the floor of Jim and Jean's Oklahoma living room and watch him fumble through American life without losing his joy, and for half an hour, I was comforted. For Balki, any country would be easy because he knew how to love, to be kind. Balki didn't have an itch in his brain. He didn't need to count. Balki was my hero.

One day Jean announced, "Today I'm getting you the best treat you've ever had in your life — the best sweet in America, hands down."

We squealed. *The best sweet in America?* It would have to be better than saffron ice cream, rose water cream puffs, and pomegranate fruit leather, better than honey baklava and sugared window-bread and crunchy fried tendrils of dough drenched in honey and covered with cinnamon. It would have to be better than pistachio cookies and chocolate walnut cake and crème caramel and the queen of all desserts, the unbeatable *sholezard:* chilled saffron almond rice pudding. "Really?" we said. "Thank you!"

So, when, after a hot, nauseating thirty-minute car ride, we took our first sip of a blue slushy, we were a little annoyed. We didn't complain, because she was being kind; she just had no clue that we came from a pastry-making people. "Thank you,

Jean!" we said, as we had practiced, and we drank enough of the blue ice water to please her. We would experience this moment again and again in our American lives. Always we kept silent and nodded our thanks, acknowledging that this was better than what we had known, that we were lucky to be here. We did this when we first tasted hard-shell tacos. We did it with iced tea, bland winter fruits, sugary yogurts. We did it with children's stories and songs and jokes and riddles. And some things did delight us: Tex Mex. BBQ. Corn Chip Pie. Bulgogi (I'll get to that). Soon, whether our immigrant amazement was real or pretend, we came to believe that Iran had never had much to offer, that America was simply better — with one exception. The spell broke when it came to math. After almost two years without formal schooling, I expected to suffer to catch up. But it took my American classmates another two years to reach the math lesson I had abandoned in Iran, that day when we heard the sirens, dropped our pencils, and fled.

Jim had a dog called Cuji — aptly named after Stephen King's terrifying Cujo. Unless it was TV time, I stayed in the attic to read and avoid the dog. Now and then, I meandered into Jim's office and we played a drawing game on his computer. One day, he asked if I missed any snacks from home. "Jean can get anything at the grocery," he said. "Just name it." I did badly crave one after-school snack. I tried to explain it: you fry spinach in olive oil and put it in cold yogurt with a bunch of salt. I wanted it very much. "Good lord, grody!" he said, holding his nose, "Didn't you have Twizzlers or jelly beans?" I said those things were grody, and he laughed.

School began while we were still at Jim and Jean's. I counted down the days, itching to study and learn and prove my worth. "Do they have *dictée* here?" I asked Jean. She shrugged. I tried to explain that there existed two kinds of tests in the world: the easy kind and terrifying shouty-speedy *dictée.* Soon I would learn that everything in America was the easy kind, and yet Americans constantly spoke of their superiority. I began to think that I might excel here, once I learned to *sound* American. Wasn't this, after all, the reason my brilliant mother was working in a factory? Sounding American, in all the various ways, would be the great project of my youth.

At school, children *ching-chonged* at me. I was confused — where did they think I came from? They whispered things about cat-eating and foot-binding. They said in Iran we didn't have showers. I was terrified, recalling on the one hand how London boys had pummeled my stomach and sliced my finger, and, on the other hand, the brutal consequences of confiding in teachers in Iran. I flinched a lot and remained silent. In my fantasies, I had answers: about Ardestoon picnics under leafy canopies, fussy old women with turmeric fingers, cream puffs, Maman's seventeenth, our *hammam* in Isfahan with its many showerheads that could swivel and point to one spot, so that you could pretend to stand in a waterfall. Once I told a group of girls my favorite riddle about two guards ("one always lies, one always tells the truth . . ."). They stared at me like I was foaming at the mouth. I took these stories home to Maman, and we laughed about them over chickpea cookies.

We learned that you cannot talk about Iran this way. "Tell them about the Three Miracles," said Maman. "I bet some are believers."

"They're all Christian," I said, burying my head in her lap.

"No, they're not," she said. "In Iran, it was dangerous to call yourself a Christian. Only real believers found their way to our church. Here, everyone is just born with that label. It doesn't mean anything. It's not faith. It's habit. Here, the Christians are like the Muslims in Iran . . . praying out of habit."

In our school, poor children stood in a separate line to get their free lunch cards. Every two weeks, the kids with money bought theirs with bank checks for fourteen dollars. To spare us the humiliation, Maman convinced a kind secretary to take her checks from us, which the secretary then tore up. She gave us normal blue lunch cards, accounting for our aid separately in her ledgers. I didn't discover this ruse for three decades.

Within weeks the children told their parents about the Iranian kids in school. Then the insults became a touch Middle Eastern: turbans and camels and such. They made fun of me for wearing certain clothes too frequently, for not owning enough pairs of jeans. After years in a uniform, I didn't know how to choose clothes. Maman didn't either: once she sent me to school in a yellow knit bonnet. I missed Isfahan, my gray *manteau,* even my headscarf. The itch ravaged me at night, and I developed a tic in my neck. I grew too fat, then too wiry. Once I stole a toy from the church general store, to see what would happen. A few months after our arrival, a cheap barber chopped off all of my hair. And when my Iranian nose began to sprout, the children grew merciless. My pretty face was gone. I missed my friends and Baba, and I became obsessed with grooming my teeth.

Meanwhile, I battled with my teacher, Miss White, over a papier-mâché topographical map of the United States, a frustrating task that was strangely central to her concerns about my education. When I tried to explain that only a few months before I had lived in Italy, at a hotel for refugees, and the whole subject of social studies confused me, she looked at me sleepily and said, "Awww, sweetie, you must be so grateful to be here."

"Yes," I said, though I was struck by a dislike in her tone. Iranian culture relies on hidden meanings and subtext. Important things go loudly unsaid, and children are taught to hear them. My American teacher, though, was accustomed to being taken literally by children, even when the gaps in her words brimmed with meaning. She was prone to sarcastic asides she thought we wouldn't understand. Once when I asked for "a rubber," she smirked at me, then said, "Lord, you're serious. Say *eraser*, honey."

"OK," I said. "What's 'rubber' mean?"

Miss White squinted. "It's a material used

in making *erasers.*"

Her eyes told me that "rubber" is the American word for something wicked. Chasing up that mystery on the playground is how I first learned about sex, a fact that my mother, the doctor, refused to confirm for years. I also cemented my status as a blacktop pariah.

"She's a perv *and* a cat-eater!" said a curly blonde named Dawn.

My reactions only made things worse. "But where did you get the cat thing?" I pleaded with the popular girls.

"So, you admit to being a perv?" said Dawn.

"No," I said, "but I know where that came from."

Again, I had no place to look at recess. I sat near the jungle gym facing the building, reading, trying to avoid the gaze of children and teachers. And I learned something else from the rubber episode: that teachers are the same around the world; that the kind ones aren't clustered in America, as I had expected. Every school the world over is full of *khanoms* or *misses.*

One day, when a clump of papier-mâché fell off my map, Miss White said, "Don't be lazy. We work hard here, do you under-stand?" I nodded.

In that first year, I expected Maman to move mountains. She had set a high standard in Iran ("seventeenth person, not percentile"), and I expected her to quickly start a medical practice, to buy a big house, where we could live, just the three of us, free from the whims of men. Maman had learned English in medical school, finishing at the top of her class, but with her thick accent and Iranian medical license, no one took her seriously.

She accepted a job in a pharmaceuticals factory, working alongside other immigrants, former doctors and PhDs, sorting pills into bottles late into the night. Every day her bosses questioned her intelligence, though they had a quarter of hcr education. They pretended not to understand her accent. If she took too long to articulate a thought, they stopped listening and wrote her off as stupid. They sped up their speech and, when she asked them to slow down, they sighed and rolled their eyes.

On weekends, Maman struggled with the daily nothings of life: where the mail was delivered, how to buy groceries, where to wash our clothes. Our first visit to a supermarket lasted hours. Maman stood bewildered in every aisle, trying to decipher the dozens of options for bread, cheese, milk. It dwarfed Dubai markets. *Who needed all this choice?* In Iran, we had butchers and corner shops. We had messengers on bicycles who delivered one kind of milk, one kind of white cheese, one kind of fresh-baked lavash bread, and a variety of fresh vegetables from local farms.

Maman took solace in the church, where she continued giving her testimony to some group or other every week, shilling the skeleton of our story for a few moments of acceptance. People loved hearing about the Three Miracles, about the moral police and Maman's arrests, about the underground church and the brutal *hijabi* schoolteachers. They got bored or confused when we spoke of Hotel Koorosh schnitzels and sour cherries and hikes. Still, friendships didn't come. Once, as she was walking alone in a park, Maman found a friendship bracelet on the ground. She wore it home. When I asked what it was, she said it was a sign of friendship from God.

Around that time, Maman met an Iranian man named Rahim. He was a convert and had friends in an Iranian church in Tulsa — exactly the sort of man Maman had wished for. Though he didn't come from an educated family like hers, he was young and handsome. They had nothing in common beyond country, apostasy, and age. He worked as a programmer, tinkered with his car until morning, and was obsessed with Korean culture and cuisine, a strange fixation that accompanied his black belt in Tae Kwon Do. To this day, the detail that baffles me is how much kimchi I ate in my first Oklahoma days, the glass bowls of bulgogi, the many intense reds, marinating in our fridge, how we perfected it by serving it on Persian rice.

Jim and Jean forbade a friendship between Maman and Rahim.

But Maman was done listening. She was tired of being told what to do by Americans who didn't know her, who probably never would. (Would she ever be her old self again? Was that person lost?) She tried to explain to Jim and Jean that she valued their friendship, but she would make her own decisions, as she had always done. They advised her to be humbler, to show gratitude to her new country instead of isolating herself inside the Iranian community — why did she need him? She had *them,* Jim and Jean. She had the church. Besides, didn't Iranian men treat women horribly?

I sided with Jim and Jean — I didn't need a new father; that wasn't part of the dream.

This man could never understand me, or my potential. He wouldn't storm into a schoolyard for me, make a teacher cry, and ask her where she went to college. I needed stubborn Maman to listen to the Americans with the big house, to learn the rules and how they managed to succeed here. Jim had published books! But, having settled into her job, Maman said goodbye to Jim and Jean, thanking them for their months of hospitality. Though we had grown to love the couple, we moved into a cheap apartment in a part of town we hoped drew other immigrants, the kind with busy hands, like in Hotel Barba. But it was a corner for the disenfranchised, drug addicts, welfare mothers, the ill-fated. On the school bus, children sneered at me for living there. When the church youth group paid a random visit, as they did with all newcomers, I burned with shame.

Sometimes Maman complained of slights and insults from Americans, people at work telling her that she didn't pay attention. "Maybe you didn't listen hard enough," I said. "You have to learn English, listen hard."

She stopped confiding in me, or reminding me of her university days in Tehran, how she had breezed to the top of her classes.

She enrolled in night classes at the University of Oklahoma and earned two master's degrees in public health and health policy. She worked in factories and clinics and a hospital. Once or twice, I heard about technicians who harassed her, or blamed her for their mistakes, and I chastised her.

"You probably made a mistake," I said.

It took willful blindness on my part, since the children of these same people teased me constantly in school. They called me cat-eater, terrorist, sand-nigger, camel-fucker. But I refused to believe that the world operated this way. The adult world was my sole hope for the future — it had to function as a pure meritocracy.

"There are things you don't see now," she said. "There are ways people communicate. Things they tell you, without words."

Maman married Rahim. Baba married the woman who had stretched Maman's clothes. He stopped sending money. We moved into a smaller apartment, though we were now four. Sometimes Rahim's daughter stayed in the room I shared with Daniel. I couldn't breathe. On the day we moved in, I sat reading in the empty closet. Something glinted in a corner of a shelf. A first-place medal. I put it in my backpack. Maybe if I showed it to the girls at school, they would find me interesting. Maybe they'd want to be friends.

The next day, Dawn grabbed the medal from me as I took it out of my backpack. "What is *that*?" she said. "Oh my god, do you wrestle?"

I didn't know the meaning of the word, so I nodded.

"Oh my god!" she squealed again. What was happening? Was she impressed? All day, children asked me about the medal. After recess at the water fountain, Dawn's best friend bounced toward me. She said, her voice kind, "Do you wrestle boys or girls?"

Which was the correct answer? "Girls?" I said. Yes, it must be girls.

"Oh my god, that's even grosser!" She ran off to tell her friends.

I looked closely at the medal, at the etching of the two figures intertwined. I knew now what wrestling was, and it didn't seem so gross or shameful to me — weren't Americans into strength sports? Maybe the girls here didn't do sports. Or maybe just certain ones?

Fifth grade passed slowly. My accent changed. I failed geography. I daydreamed through math, waiting for a new lesson. I wrote a story about Cuji and won "most creative story," only to learn later that I had imagined the same terrifying dog as Stephen King, because, let's face it, Cuji *was* Cujo.

Money was a constant worry. Rahim switched us to a discount grocery where sickly onions rolled underfoot. He regulated the air-conditioning. I was always sweaty and tired of having the toilet paper monitored. In Iran, it seemed that money didn't exist. People just did things for each other — the butcher sent meat, Baba fixed teeth, I studied. That was my job. Here, though, I decided, I needed to find a way to make money.

One day, in Sunday school, we learned how to embroider a coaster onto plastic canvas. The front read "MUG RUG," and it had fringe, like a mini *ghilim* carpet. Soon after, during an Iranian church outing to Tulsa, a man saw me embroidering. He owned a Persian rug business. "That is clever," he said. " 'Mug Rug.' I should give them as gifts to my customers."

"I can make you some," I said.

"Oh yes?" he chuckled. "How much do you want for them?" I considered it. Should I ask for ten dollars? Forty? "How about $2.50 each?" he said. "I'll take as many as you can make."

"Great!" I started calculating: I could

make five dollars a day. More on weekends. "I'll make a hundred." He laughed and wandered away.

The next day in math class, I took out my sewing — this would be a way to keep busy while the others caught up with mixed fractions. My teacher gave me a strange look. The next day, I did it again. This time she said, "Dina, put your sewing away. In this country, girls have to learn math just like boys. You can do your sewing at home." I burned at that comment for days, wishing I could articulate all that she had wrong.

I made about eighty Mug Rugs in two months, borrowing money for materials from Rahim. I took them to the next Iranian church meeting. The rug merchant was dumbstruck. He muttered about what a resourceful girl I was. I thought he was disappointed that I hadn't reached the promised hundred. He took out his wallet and paid for the rugs, but said that his needs had been met. My first business was finished.

I began looking forward again. Oklahoma wasn't a promised land. It was hot and mediocre and lazy. And I could never satisfy these people.

We went to work, to school, to church. Maman baked American cakes and replaced the rosewater in her pastries with vanilla. Some say, that's the natural cycle of things. We learned what they wanted, the spoken and unspoken language that made them comfortable. We told our story the way they wanted to hear it, the *China Cry* way, full of melodrama and miracles and villains, but without the small beauties of Isfahan and Ardestoon. Without Baba's jokes, the photos under his glass desktop. We started to understand that in America, you can choose your story and make it true.

One day in late spring, I was in the Edmond Public Library stacks, looking for new fiction. Someone had left a book splayed open on a seat. It was a university entrance book, complete with profiles and rankings, average scores, acceptance rates, and tips on writing a successful application. I flipped to the front, where the top fifty were ranked. I had heard the name that topped the list on television and in movies. *Harvard.* If I wanted to go there, the book told me, I'd have to win my own medals, earn perfect scores in every subject, be exceptional according to American standards. It said to choose sports wisely, maybe ones that aren't so oversubscribed. I touched the cold, hard medal in my pocket. The odds were low, the Harvard page warned, and I'd have to begin at fourteen. Lucky for me, I came from the land of screaming *dictées,* from a school where there was no place to look but the blood mural or the class rankings, a mother who loved riddles, a father who thought every girl needs a worthy rival — I was itchy and angry, and I was only eleven.

II / KAWEH

Before the police arrived, Kaweh stood in the town square, filthy and hungry and unshaven, and he watched the passersby. A young girl yelled to her brother, "Jack, hurry up." The boy sped up. *Hurry up,* Kaweh repeated to himself, its meaning apparent from the boy's response. He stored it away as the first phrase in a long education.

The police station was vast and clean. When two blond officers greeted them, Kaweh whispered, "My God, we're at Buckingham Palace."

They were searched and questioned in separate rooms. The others chose Kurdish interpreters, but Kaweh asked for a Persian one. He spoke both languages, and fearing that the Home Office would claim he was an Iraqi Kurd, he opted for the translator who could verify his accent, his true country. Though he knew little of the asylum process, Kaweh had listened along the way.

In Turkey, he had claimed asylum from UN-HCR and had met more than a hundred refugees. All day in Kurdistan and Turkey, he read books and newspapers. He understood his party's history, world politics, the aims and singular logic of European asylum. Like his Kurdish heroes, Ghassemlou and Sharafkandi, who read widely and spoke calmly and knowledgeably, Kaweh tried to know his adversary, and the field of battle.

After almost losing his precious documents in the water, Kaweh had entrusted them to a friend in Turkey. He had boarded the first truck carrying nothing, reasoning that documents are useless for illegal border crossings. His friend would keep them safe and scan or mail them later.

"You have entered the United Kingdom illegally," an officer told the group. "You may be prosecuted. Do you have any family in the United Kingdom? Do you have friends here?" Kaweh didn't know the addresses of anyone in the party, though some did live in the United Kingdom. He had a single phone number, which he kept to himself for now.

Asked if he needed a lawyer, he said, "I only want to claim asylum."

That night he slept in a cell with another refugee. The next day, he met with a female officer and a Kurdish interpreter who would translate by phone. "Are you OK to speak Kurdish this time?" the officer said into the phone and passed it to Kaweh, who listened and nodded.

"What is your name?" said the man on the phone.

"Kaweh Beheshtizadeh," said Kaweh.

"No," said the interpreter, not bothering to interpret. "No, that's not your real name. We need your real name." The man was an Iraqi Kurd, and Iraqi Kurdistan has different naming conventions.

"I assure you," said Kaweh, "This is my name."

"What's your father's name?" said the man.

"Mohammad Khaled," said Kaweh.

"And your grandfather?" said the man.

"Mahmoud," said Kaweh.

"Then your name is Kaweh Mohammad Khaled Mahmoud."

"If you call me by that name," said Kaweh, "I won't recognize myself. I understand that in Iraqi Kurdistan this is the convention, but as you know, I'm an Iranian Kurd, and in Iran our system is: first name, family name."

The man was unmoved. It seemed that on some level, he was eager to out Kaweh as an Iraqi Kurd. Casting doubt on his Iranian name wouldn't help him, given his current lack of papers. What was his aim here?

"Well, before all else, we must agree on your name," said the man.

"What do you suggest?" said Kaweh, struggling to remain calm.

"We agree that your first name is Kaweh, yes?"

What madness — on the first day of this new life, having given up his country, his language, he had to negotiate to keep his own name.

The man thought for a moment. "How about . . . we cut the name in half. Your middle name can be Beheshti and your last name Zadeh?"

Kaweh wanted to ask, What does this have to do with following Iraqi rules? Wasn't Kurdish authenticity your purpose a moment ago? Now you're just cutting up my name to fit the Western standard. And I'm neither Iraqi, nor Western. "But that's still not my name," he said.

"Yes, but let's write that for now and we can sort it out later."

Kaweh thought it unwise to object. For years after, his identity card would show his name cleaved in two, the beautiful Persian construction "heaven-born" cut up so that his last name read simply as "born." *Hello, Mr. Zadeh,* people would say. But *Zadeh* is only a suffix. Alone, it is unrooted, having been shorn of a birthplace, a poetic reminder of home.

The officer asked, "What is the basis of your asylum claim?"

Instinct said, *Clean hands won't help you. Don't hide anything. These things happened. Surely asylum decisions don't involve moral judgments.* He began telling his story. "I left Iran illegally. I was a member of the Kurdish Democratic Party of Iran for over three years. I was approached by Iranian authorities to be a spy, and I refused. They gave me money that I accepted and used for my personal needs. I never repaid them. They found me in Turkey. My life is in danger in Iran, and also in Iraqi Kurdistan and in Turkey, too." Now the officer chuckled. She didn't believe — maybe it was the drama of his words, or the detour from the narrative to explain things that (fiction writers know) should be *shown.* Kaweh carried on. Sometimes in life, impossible things happen, and they are nonetheless true.

Kaweh and his fellow travelers were boarded onto a van. When they saw that they were headed to Dover, they dropped into collective despair. "I swear," said a

Kurdish man. "If they deport me, I'll kill myself."

Hours later, the van stopped in front of an old building in Dover. Two interpreters emerged. The Kurdish one said, "You will be accommodated here, in temporary lodging, for, at most, twenty-eight days while the Home Office sorts out longer-term housing and considers your asylum claim."

The relief was palpable. "We were dying of anxiety," someone said.

The interpreter laughed. "No one will be deported to France today."

Kaweh shared a four-bunk room with a father and son. They had a bathroom, towels, sheets. They took showers and headed for the dining hall full of refugees — Russians, Turks, Iranians, Iraqis. In this camp Kaweh decided to lie, for fear of Iranian intelligence still pursuing him. "I'm an Iraqi Kurd," he said, noting that he must disclose this tactic in his interview.

An Iranian newspaper journalist said, "You speak very good Persian."

"I lived on the border," said Kaweh. "I watched Iranian cartoons."

"What's your claim?" asked the journalist.

Kaweh became uncomfortable. He thought, better not to be taken seriously by this reporter, better to be thought an opportunist. "My claim," he said, "is that I've come here to drink alcohol and sleep with women."

"What a stupid person you are," said the journalist, his mouth curling with disdain. "There are people with lives in real danger."

In the hostel, Kaweh took English classes twice a week. He spent his days in the Dover public library, looking at words in English children's books. He called his parents from a friend's phone and told them he was safe in Switzerland. He borrowed a second pair of underwear from his roommate. Each night, he washed his clothes in the sink and hung them up to dry, since he couldn't go to the laundromat naked.

Kaweh hired a young solicitor, a trainee in immigration law, who told him he would be removed to Turkey, since he first claimed asylum there.

"No," he said, "you have it wrong. I didn't claim asylum in Turkey. I did it through UNHCR. That makes a material difference." When had he learned this? He hardly knew; one of the many long nights of reading and obsessing. When a senior solicitor insisted on the same error, an instinct said to move on. "It's fine," he said. "It's better if you don't take my case."

When Kaweh returned to his room, he

learned that his roommate's brother had arranged a London solicitor for him. Kaweh asked for the solicitor's phone number; maybe he would take Kaweh's case, too.

He borrowed money and took a bus to London, where the solicitor's interpreter met him at the bus station in Victoria and took him to his own home for the night. That night a more senior interpreter, another Iraqi Kurd, heard Kaweh's story. "Your case is complex and this solicitor is busy," he said. "Let me prepare it for you tonight. We'll take it to him to complete."

The next day, the solicitor read the statement and asked a few clarifying questions. In two hours, it was signed and sent to the Home Office.

Christmas in Dover was just as he had imagined it from childhood cartoons: twinkling lights on wintry trees, shoppers in bright colors, the smell of pastries. He read for hours and walked the streets.

He called his friend in Turkey for his documents, and for a letter confirming his party membership. For fifty days, he lived in the temporary hostel, awaiting word from the Home Office. On January 10, 2005, Kaweh gave his asylum interview. It took six hours, with two breaks. The asylum officer was a Muslim in *hijab,* the interpreter an uncovered Persian woman.

He presented his papers, his photos at KDPI headquarters, articles he had written, his acceptance by UNHCR. They asked a thousand rapid-fire questions: *What is your name, date of birth, who are your parents, siblings, where did you grow up, how much schooling do you have, why did you leave Iran, what did you do for the party, why did you leave the party, what did you do in Turkey, why did your asylum claim fail there?*

"Why didn't you move to another part of Iraq?" the officer asked.

Tired and frustrated, Kaweh said, "By another part of Iraq, do you mean the territory controlled by Saddam Hussein?" She nodded. "If Saddam Hussein is such a nice person," Kaweh snapped, "why did you attack him?"

The interpreter paused. "Are you sure you want me to say this?"

"Yes," said Kaweh. "Please translate."

But the interpreter made a slight change. "If Saddam Hussein is such a nice person," she said, "why did the *United States* attack him?"

Kaweh broke in, speaking English now, "*And* the UK."

Years later he would think back on this day and regret his arrogant Iranian style:

answering a question with another to high-light its absurdity. A wiser, older man would have reminded the officer that Saddam was a brutal dictator, that Kaweh wasn't an Iraqi national and might have been branded a spy, that many Iranians died under Saddam's torture.

Later, the interpreter tried to call out an inconsistency. "You said before that the Iranian authorities promised to send you to Sweden if you spied for them," she said, "and now you said Canada. Are you lying to us?"

In fact, the Iranian intelligence officers had contacted him many times, each time with new promises. Instead of clarifying this, Kaweh said, "You're only an interpreter. Please just interpret what I'm saying."

Maybe it helped that Kaweh made no effort to ingratiate himself to the two women. He knew that this was a game of logic, not emotion. He told a story in great detail, clearly, in his own way. He didn't perform hysteria.

He was moved to Cardiff, into a house with three other men. He was given ninety pounds for necessities and a card (bearing his broken name) that he could use to collect a weekly allowance of thirty pounds from the post office. With their first small sums in hand, the four men stopped at Lidl to buy food. "We should eat together," said Ali, an Iranian. "It'll buy more." They agreed, each giving him five pounds. He bought chicken, salt, tea, a few vegetables. Kaweh wondered if they could have ice cream. Ali made the purchases and produced a receipt — a very un-Iranian gesture, but comforting among poor strangers. It seemed this arrangement would work.

For a total of about thirty pounds at Peacocks discount store in Cardiff, Kaweh bought a jacket, two shirts, socks, underwear, a pair of jeans, and a pair of shoes so ugly that he repeatedly refused to describe them. Later, he discovered Primark, an even cheaper store, to much regret. For years, Peacocks, Primark, and Lidl were the only stores he entered.

Every week the four young men walked twenty-five minutes to Lidl, carrying their purchases on foot. Penniless and forbidden to work, they busied themselves with household chores. His roommates were younger, and Kaweh did all the cleaning. He spent his days in the public library in the Cardiff city center. They went to parks, fairs, markets — free places. In the third week, Kaweh bought a soccer ball — this is how the men befriended their neighbors, kicking their ball into yards and bashfully knocking on doors. Kaweh enrolled in English courses. One day at the Sunday market, he bought a television for fifteen pounds, which he carried for an hour and a half. "I need a television," he said. "I have to learn English."

He read Penguin English readers for eight hours a day, working his way through the levels. He wore through his dictionary, memorizing twenty words a day. Each time he finished a book, however simple, he felt the possibility of making a life here, of becoming someone new, maybe even the person he would have been, had he lived in a free Iran.

Within three months, Kaweh was reading letters for his housemates and handling all that required English: shopping, correspondence, house maintenance. The housemates no longer allowed him to do the cleaning. After a while, they chipped in for a DVD player and danced to happy Kurdish songs, remembering Kurdistan together.

When he was fluent enough to attend college four days a week, he bought a Walkman radio to listen to the BBC, because the fifty-five-minute walk was a waste of time and the Walkman was a smarter purchase than daily bus fares. He was eager to understand news and politics. He listened to everything — news, commentary, music, debates. He caught words. Then, he discovered *Friends*. Here was a show about everyday things, full of familiar words and the opportunity to learn new ones. Every few minutes, an invisible audience laughed (how completely bizarre, this intrusion into the fantasy). He didn't understand the jokes, and he felt an affection for Chandler, who was, even in his own country, so misunderstood. One day, watching with dictionary in hand, something magical happened:

An ecstatic Rachel hung up the phone with her mother. "Emma just said her first word!" she said (or something like that). The friends gasped, eager to hear the word. "She said 'gleba'!" Everyone went back to what they were doing. " 'Gleba' isn't a word," said Ross. "Of course it is," said Rachel. And when Ross asked for the definition, she said, "I don't know *all* the words!" When Ross asked her to use it in a sentence, Rachel said, "Emma just said 'gleba'!" Then she stomped off to look it up in a dictionary, and Ross shouted after her, "While you're at it, why not look up 'pptthhhhhhh.' "

It had been a while since Kaweh couldn't

stop laughing. Was it that he understood an entire American scene? That he got his first Western joke? Or was it the pleasure of watching someone else, a native New Yorker, struggle with a dictionary, try to divine the meaning of a word, admit that she doesn't know *all the words*? Whatever the reason, it delighted him.

The next day he asked his English teacher, "Bella, do you know what 'gleba' means? It is the fleshy spore-bearing inner mass of certain fungi."

And so, *Friends* became a crucial part of Kaweh's language studies.

Sometimes the housemates called home and listened as their families worried. One family didn't believe their son wasn't allowed to work and kept begging for money. He would hide in his room, dreading their calls, desperate to work but afraid to jeopardize his asylum application — people had been rejected for doing charity work out of boredom. "You worked," the Home Office would say. "You broke the rules."

One day Kaweh used a discount phone card to call home. His brother picked up and started to panic. "Why are you calling from Tehran? It says you're calling from an 021 number." Kaweh spent half the call convincing his brother that he hadn't been caught and thrown into prison, that this wasn't a forced call, that the caller ID had his location wrong.

Kaweh lived for twenty-one months in that house. Within six months, all three of his housemates were gone. Rejected by the Home Office, they returned home or lived illegally on the streets, or in homes of friends. The next three were gone in five months. Twenty housemates passed through the house during Kaweh's stay. All were rejected and left. Kaweh never saw most of them again. Now and then he heard of a death or a return home.

In September 2006, one year and nine months after his arrival by truck, Kaweh was granted asylum and recognized as a refugee. His acceptance meant that in twenty-eight days, he would lose his home and his allowance. In four weeks (minus the time the Home Office takes to provide new identification), he had to secure a bank account (which requires proof of address), a new address (which often requires a bank account), and income. Thanks to this impossible window, refugees often spend their first weeks after being welcomed into English society sleeping on the street. Kaweh was lucky. In January 2006, having passed the IELTS English exams, he had applied (speculatively) to university. He had been accepted in April for a foundation course. If his asylum hadn't come through a week before the start of classes, he would have lost his place.

The moment he had his papers, Kaweh applied for student loans. He was rejected. He borrowed from a friend, a butcher, and begged the university for an installment plan. When they agreed, he secured a room and a night job at a Peacocks factory, cleaning and loading clothes, five nights a week, from 11 p.m. until 7 a.m. Mondays were grueling as classes met right after his shift and carried on all day. But the numbers worked, and that was enough — his weekly pay from Peacocks paid for his rent, tuition installments, food, bus fares, and basic necessities.

Years later, after he had changed the name on his ID cards back to Beheshtizadeh, after he had an office, a home, a wife, he would stumble on a tabulation of the allowances the British gave him during his twenty-one months as an asylum seeker. It was an official document with his name still broken at the top, a figure in the two thousands at the bottom. Now he paid many multiples of that in taxes each year. Not everyone survives — you can tell yourself, *I'm never eat-*

ing out, never buying a bag of chips or a bus ticket, but you can't deny your pleading child. You think you've made it to England. Your pain is over . . . until the first time your kid begs for Nando's.

Kaweh thought of the twenty men who had passed through the Cardiff house, all turned away, sent back into danger or destitution. Many such men and women had died, lost inside brutal regimes or to despair. One man, he read, had set himself on fire. How close Kaweh had come to that fate, how unlikely to sit here, in this office, *believed,* waved into a free civilization, able to throw back his tie and join in the great public work of sustaining a neighborhood, a city, a nation. It felt right to toil alongside the British, whose language came easily now. And it felt right to use his talents to help the next hungry, unwashed traveler picking through the mountains.

It was satisfying, too, the day the British called him one of their best . . .

III / KAMBIZ

If Kambiz had an Iranian passport, he tore it up and flushed it before going to Ter Apel for his first application. A man named Hadi had a home in Almere, near a camp, and sometimes Iranians gathered there for dinners or tea. Kambiz arrived there in 1999 for a dinner. A dozen or so legal and illegal Iranians from nearby ate chickpea cookies and broken pieces of sesame candy; they dipped sugar cubes into their tea and sat against cushions and talked of home. Hadi slapped the newcomer on the back and asked what he could do. "I can do electrical work," said Kambiz. "I speak Turkish and Arabic, a little English, too." Hadi said that he could easily find building work for him if he was any good as an electrician.

The women had brought dishes from home: Iranian chicken salad, meat cutlets, herb frittata. Kambiz offered to make something next time.

"Where are you living?" asked Hadi.

"At the camp," he said. "I'll have papers soon, then I'll buy a house."

"God willing," said Hadi, and he sipped his tea. "First you need money."

Kambiz let a chickpea cookie crumble on his tongue — the taste of every Persian childhood. He missed his older sister, whom he had promised to call even if he didn't call their mother. His sister was a lawyer, the child who had fulfilled their mother's hopes. Maybe now Kambiz would too. Maybe he'd bring his younger sister to study. She was a child. She could still learn perfect Dutch and English and be a Western lawyer — imagine that.

"What case are you giving?" someone asked. It was a man named Parvis, an aspiring restaurateur whose own case would soon be settled.

Kambiz considered the question, as he had done for days — there was the woman he had befriended, her angry husband, the menace always at his door. "I'm part of a circle of journalists," he said. "We've had arrests."

"Are you a journalist?" someone else asked.

"Not me," he said. "I'm just part of the circle. It's been unsafe for us."

"That won't be enough," said another voice from the *sofreh*. "You should say you're Christian."

Kambiz shook his head. "I'm Muslim," he said.

"Yes, but you should say —"

"I'm Muslim," he repeated into his cup. "I won't lie about religion."

"Well, maybe you'll meet a Dutch woman, then," Parvis joked.

Kambiz sipped his tea. "It would be nice to have a family. A kind Iranian woman." Uncomfortable laughter followed. They thought he didn't have a chance at asylum.

Regardless, he wouldn't claim to be Christian, or gay — he feared the regime; claiming apostasy might endanger his mother and sisters. Surely having a Sepâh come to your door and threaten your life is enough for the Netherlands' immigration authority (the IND). Surely, the Dutch don't turn away the able-bodied and the eager who want to light their homes and cook their food.

Over months and years Holland stamped his hopes into a manageable size. He learned Dutch. He didn't fall in love — sometimes he talked in bars with tourists or Eastern European women he suspected were sex workers, but a respectable Iranian marriage eluded him. He told his asylum interviewers about his journalist friends, his woman friend, the moral police who came to his door. The IND dismissed his story once, then again, and his status fell from asylum seeker to "illegal." Without a passport, the Dutch couldn't send him back. They demanded that he request one from the Iranian embassy. He refused, as many do. The IND informed him that, with his case now closed, he was no longer welcome at the camp. Hadi offered him a room and steady electrical work. He made a decent living on the black market and easily paid his own way. Still, he couldn't purchase a phone plan, rent his own home, or carry proper ID.

After a while, Kambiz had a stream of steady cash clients, and he went in and out of their homes, the homes of their friends and family. He excelled at his job, priced fairly, spoke softly. Sometimes he over-charged the rude ones, the entitled ones, and undercharged the poor, the honest, the sorrowful. Dutch culture drained him — what a lonely country he had landed in. "You know this about the Dutch," Parvis said, when they were both fluent (Kambiz's fifth language) and Parvis had his papers and a plan for a restaurant. "You can't expect friendship from them. A Dutchman's mother calls, you know what he does? He checks his appointment book and says, 'Tuesday at 4 p.m.' He doesn't go to her, because 'she lives all the way in Utrecht.' What do *you,* random Iranian asshole, expect from that man?"

Kambiz laughed. Such behavior was un-heard of in Iran — there, you visited your mother daily, even if she lived three hours away. There, if a lost friend called in the middle of the night, you threw on a jacket and got into your car. You'd never think to say, "Call a taxi," as every last Dutchman would. Kambiz had never been invited for a dinner or a tea in the home of a Dutch person. He was thankful for the Persian community. He would say sometimes during dinner at Hadi's, "I can't wait for the day Parvis's sons are doctors and I have my own. I can't wait to be *proud* of the children."

The waiting began to take its toll. "It's a terrifying place," he said to Parvis. "Pressure from the past, pressure from the future. They say too much of either is a mental illness." Parvis nodded. This was a common complaint among refugees: the future brings anxiety because you don't belong, and can't move forward. The past brings depression, because you can't go home, your memories fade, and everything you know is gone. "I'm standing on a thin border between the past and future, waiting for madness to come." Kambiz missed his big family, all noisy and living on top of each other in a small house. He missed his sisters running around, making a mess of things. He even missed his mother's daily moaning about his aunt.

Some days, Kambiz worked twelve hours. He sent money to Iran, and soon his family believed that he had made something of himself — he told them he was studying. This satisfied them. One day, about a decade into his stay, he decided he had had

311

enough. "I'm tired," he told Hadi. "I can't stand this waiting. I want a family. I have to get my answer and start my life." He planned to present himself again at Ter Apel or to the police, this time with more details about his affairs in Iran.

"It's a watery story," said Hadi. "They don't kill people for unwitnessed affairs or friendships with journalists. You know Dutch logic. They pretend the Islamic Republic is clean and by the book, like the court in The Hague. Do you really want to do this?"

"What do you want me to do?" said Kambiz. "I won't say I'm Christian." In a few months Kambiz's cheerful demeanor had vanished. He had taken to self-pity and long bouts of complaining. He knew his friends were tiring of him. "You have a wife, kids, a car," he said. "I'm not allowed to have anything of my own. I want to restart this damn process and become a legitimate human. Is that too much to want? Am I asking for so much?"

"Of course not," said Hadi, "You deserve those things. But you *must* say something new for the case to be reopened. At least go and see Pouri."

Ahmed Pouri was an activist, a translator of cultures. He helped Iranians understand

Dutch logic, to present themselves the European way. One day Kambiz accompanied a friend to Mr. Pouri's office. He listened for a long time as his friend took Pouri through his case. Then he left.

Soon after, he presented himself to the police, explaining that his case was closed but he wished to tell his story again. He was thrown into a cell.

Kambiz spent nearly a year in detention. After a decade in the Netherlands, after all the waiting, the toil, the aimlessness, the anxiety, he was idle now, with nothing to do but sit and suffer. He was confined to a box, except for a daily hour or two outside. He heard from no one. He became depressed and began to dream of death. Why should he go quietly and unseen back to a country where he would wither and die anyway? What a waste of a life that would be. Night after dark night, he considered the ways. Each time, he put it out of his mind, chastising himself for indulging in drama and fantasy.

In late 2010, some months into his imprisonment, word reached Refugee Aid about Kambiz, that he was alone, without family or proper legal aid and that he had been held in the Schiphol Detention Centre for a long time. Fearing he might be lost inside the system, they asked Frank van Haren, an asylum lawyer, to visit him.

The detention center is a huge, boxy building near Schiphol Airport. On approach, it gives the sensation of a white boot ready to stamp down. Van Haren endured the usual entry theater, though he was a regular visitor. After security, a guard brought him to a room with a phone. He dialed a prebooked interpreter and waited for Kambiz to be escorted in. He introduced himself, asked if Kambiz would like to discuss his options.

"I want to reopen my case," said Kambiz.

"I'm happy to do that," said Van Haren, "But you need something new to present to the immigration officers. You need evidence, documents you didn't have before. If you can prove your case, we can possibly win."

"Do you really believe that?" said Kambiz.

"Yes, of course," said Van Haren. He noted Kambiz's quiet misery.

Kambiz had heard this before. Van Haren wasn't his first asylum lawyer. But two months later, he asked to see him again. He looked worn, as if he had spent his nights agonizing over their talk. He had nothing new to offer, only the hope that he had missed some vital detail, and if he heard

Van Haren's advice again, he would find the solution hidden in the words.

What else was there to do? Any ordinary person, if instructed to wait five hours, will find something else to do. But for ten minutes, most people sit and wait. If that ten minutes becomes twenty, they might still find it pointless to try to accomplish anything substantial. In this way, a rational person can be made to squander those five hours, minute by minute. This is the life of a refugee. Madness in increments, by an ever-shifting endpoint.

A few months later, on a Friday around five o'clock, Kambiz showed up at Van Haren's office with a hopeful stride and papers in hand. He had been released from detention (having refused to obtain an Iranian passport) and had dug around, calling old friends and acquaintances, until he had found new facts and documents linking him to various journalistic circles in Iran. He asked Van Haren's assistant if he could see him without an appointment. "It's urgent," he said. "I have the new documents he wanted. They're good enough to start a new proceeding."

Van Haren stepped out from his office. "I'm very sorry, Mr. Roustayi," he said. "I have a client and I have work till seven o'clock. I can't see you now. But you can come back. Shall we make an appointment for Monday?"

On Monday, moments before his appointment, Kambiz called the office in tears. "What's the matter, Mr. Roustayi?" asked Van Haren.

Kambiz wept, his sorrow and confusion carrying through the phone line. "I swear, I'm cursed. I put the papers in the carrier of my bike, and I forgot them there. I went back outside in the morning and they were gone."

"I'm very sorry," said Van Haren. He believed Kambiz, remembering that Kambiz had carried those papers in with every intention of having them examined right away. Whatever he had held in his hand wasn't a prop. "I understand your panic. But we're back where we started. If you lost your new proof, we have nothing. I can't take your case."

Kambiz decided to appeal to Ter Apel one more time, to start proceedings on his own behalf. The legal aid lawyer on duty sat with him. She explained that his case had no chance. Still, he remained there for several days, crossing paths with other refugees. "If I get another negative," he said to whoever would listen, "I think I'd like to die."

In the long, gray days following detention, he stayed up with Parvis late into the nights, letting his tea go cold. "Maybe it's better to die."

"Go back to Iran," said Parvis. "It's not worse than *this.* Your spirit is destroyed. It won't get better here."

"I can't," said Kambiz, dropping his face into his hands.

"Come now, let's go talk to a new lawyer. Say you've lost faith with Islam. Apostasy is enough," said Parvis. "You don't need a Christian case."

"I can't say that," he said. "I'm Muslim."

"Kambiz *jan,* you have to do something about your mind."

"What can I do?" he said, "They put me in a cage like an animal."

"But you're out now! Do something. Go to Germany or England. Go start over with a new story. Kambiz *jan,* are you hearing me?"

"It was a year of hell," said Kambiz. He was speaking to himself now. "You sit and think and the answers don't come. Everything gets dark." Parvis sat back and listened as his friend tried to piece together his thoughts. "Do you want to know something? They try to get a passport for you from the Iranian embassy, but the embassy says no, because you have to request yourself. The only exception is if you're wanted by the regime. Then the Iranian embassy helps the Dutch deport you. So, it's a trick. If the Dutch request a passport for you and the Iranians say yes, that's proof you're in danger. Otherwise, to hell with you. Go die on the streets."

"God forbid," sighed Parvis. "What a world."

"I think I'm going mad," said Kambiz.

A few days later, on April 6, 2011, Kambiz left Hadi's house in a fury. He slammed the door behind him, ignoring Hadi's call. He jumped on a train to Amsterdam, stopping at a shop to buy a box of lighter fuel. He stood in the center of Dam Square, the fast-beating heart of the city, surrounded by cafés, watching tourists and local workers pass by. A family of pigeons pecked at the ground near his feet, and he thought, even the birds have a corner of this city to make a family. He lifted the container over his head, dousing his hair and clothes. He didn't wait long enough for anyone to notice or question him. He said a prayer, and when he was clear of bystanders, he said goodbye to his mother and sisters and lit a match.

Parvis was at soccer practice with his

younger son, listening to the radio, when an announcer said that a madman had set himself on fire in Dam Square. The manner of the death made him uneasy. He phoned Hadi. "Where's Kambiz?" he said.

"He got angry and left," said Hadi. "Why? What's he done?"

"Turn on the radio," said Parvis. "He said a dozen times that he'd kill himself. What if he did it?" Parvis took his children home and went straight to the police, who were in the process of identifying the victim. "If it's him," said Parvis, "he wasn't mental. He was a refugee."

"There are a lot of people in this city," said an officer. "It's probably someone else. But we will call you." The police took Parvis's name and address. *It's him,* thought Parvis. *It's a death only a refugee would want.*

That night he got a call — the police wanted him to come to the hospital to identify the body. As he entered, Parvis tried to think of other places Kambiz might be. *No,* he thought, *it's him. It's him.* The man in the bed was wrapped in bandages, his face so swollen its features were an indistinguishable mass. And yet, it was Kambiz. Parvis nodded. An officer held Kambiz's papers in one hand. He went to call Ter Apel for fingerprints. "You must call the embassy so they can notify his family," said the officer when he returned. "We need to know what to do with him."

Parvis looked at his friend. He was attached to a catheter, but the liquid pooling in the urine bag wasn't yellow, or even red. It was black. It was ash. His face had ballooned, and oxygen was pumped into his body through artificial lungs that inflated and deflated beside many other machines. He was burned from so far inside, nothing worked anymore. People had tried to stamp out the blaze with their jackets. Did Kambiz know that he was buying a liquid that couldn't be extinguished? Or did he hope someone would save him? Now the doctors said that, even if he survived, he would never be human. He couldn't live without the machines doing his body's work. His last natural functions were gone.

The next day, the police called again. Kambiz would be taken off life-support. "The team has said he has no chance for a life."

Kambiz Roustayi died at thirty-six, having wasted twelve of his strongest, hungriest years, the years when people crave to build and to give of themselves to each other, to their communities — years for work and family. Why did he choose to die this way? Maybe he wanted to remain in the country's psyche, to be a part of their news, to appear in art installations and writings, to be remembered each April for a time. He had been so forgotten. In his darkest nights, Kambiz had grappled with those who had cast him off. Is it so hard to imagine that he wanted to burn his image into their memories?

After Kambiz was buried, his family called Parvis and asked for his belongings. Parvis packed a small bag of clothing and Kambiz's cell phone and shipped it to Iran. When the bag arrived, Kambiz's brother-in-law phoned. "Is this all?" he said. "This is all he has after twelve years in Holland?"

"What do you expect?" said Parvis. "He was illegal, living in a rented room." It was painful to say to this family that their son's life had amounted to nothing. Iranians believe that Europe is all villas and wine. To think that after a decade, a man would own a sack of work clothes, full of dirt, an old phone, and some underwear — *that* is the tragedy for them. Kambiz's life in Europe was small. He visited two homes. He confided in two friends; he socialized with five or six. After prison, back at Hadi's, he had no one.

The day after Kambiz's death, Parvis spoke to the radio station. "Don't call him crazy," he said. "That is the wrong word. He was a refugee." And despite the media's many mistakes in reporting Kambiz's story (calling Van Haren his lawyer, claiming he met Parvis in an asylum center, that he was homeless on the streets), from then on, at least, they called him a refugee. The IND never did even that: "Immigration and Asylum Minister Gerd Leers called Mr. Roustayi's death 'very tragic,' but says all the procedures were followed correctly and that the man was given proper legal assistance." Soon, talk died down and the story was forgotten.

But some people couldn't shake Kambiz's memory. An Amsterdam artist named Sara, my cousin by marriage, began drawing his face. She made a notebook for him, saving every news clipping. Amsterdam Iranians gathered in Dam Square to sing songs and to remember him. Many Dutch people also came to pay respects. "It wasn't right," they said. "He was part of this society now. After ten years, he should have been believed." No one stays in limbo for so long if going home is a safe option. People asked about his life in Iran — no one knew much. He kept his stories private. My research turned up only a grainy image of that time.

That spring, Ahmed Pouri organized

protests. He asked the mayor, "Do you question your system at all?" The mayor replied, "What could be done? He used his democratic rights." He had moved on from Kambiz.

Ahmed Pouri raged. "Living without perspective, like a worm. Waiting for Godot. Who can live like this? Humans need meaning. Kambiz broke because he needed purpose and family and progress."

Some mornings, Frank van Haren looked out his window at the spot in Dam Square where Kambiz had set himself alight. "He passed by my asylum practice, without leaving a clear trace, only a very sad feeling. He died three hundred meters from my office. I was in the office when it happened. I will never forget."

IV

The day Kambiz set himself on fire two kilometers from my apartment, I was planning my second escape. It was April 6, 2011, only about a month after I had heard from the Iowa Writers' Workshop that I could take refuge in a small cornfield town, far away from Amsterdam.

Back in February, my husband and I had been spending a rainy Sunday afternoon in our favorite café, Two For Joy. He read

Monocle. I read Ishiguro. We wore matching Lacoste shirts without irony. We held hands. The instant before the phone rang, I was staring at our fingers and thinking of the many intersecting uses of the word "sterile," how it is good or bad but always frightening. Old age. Hospitals. Fire. Our fingers were a little older and thinner now than those early college days of chewed-up pink nail polish and review session times penned onto palms. We had grown up.

Then my phone lit up. An Iowa number (I had been waiting for that area code for weeks; 319 still registers as rescue, literary outings, cheap wine on a Tuesday night, real friends, freedom), I ran out into the rain and listened to Samantha Chang offer me a place. She spoke about the long arc of a writing life and about the peace of living for a time in a small creative town, but I only heard half her words, the ones I recognized from my asylum-seeking days. Freedom! (to imagine and create), refuge! (from the grind), support! (the writing kind — *simmer down, Dina*).

For six months, I had suffered a desperation so profound and all-consuming that I was always winded. I battled the metal bar, my Sisyphean boulder, and I kept struggling to push it down. The physical symptoms of the OCD returned. I stopped writing. I lost fifteen pounds — one day I woke and they were gone from my bones, like a misplaced earring.

As in Iran, a necessary part of me was stifled. I felt it shrinking. What if I let it disappear, this thing I couldn't even name or articulate?

I was mired in ennui and narcissism and boredom, itching to get out of my marriage and Amsterdam, but too cowardly to pack a bag and go. I was married to a decent, kind man, but the prospect of escape plunged me into psychotic fantasies. I imagined him caging me in the basement, or calling embassies and having my citizenships revoked. My heartbeat quickened at these thoughts, as if my body believed them — I would spend my mornings looking through our documents, taking my passports from our filing cabinets and hiding them in my underwear drawer.

In early April, I was searching for an apartment in Iowa City when I heard the news. An Iranian man, an asylum seeker who had been knocking on doors for a decade, had set himself on fire in Dam Square. His name was Kambiz Roustayi. It seemed that in an instant, my obsessions and fears had a place to go: who was this man? I read everything. I asked around. I dragged Philip to a vigil for him in Dam Square. I watched the video of Kambiz's death almost every day, until I knew its morbid choreography. I imagined myself in the square, part of the spectacle. What if I was there with a blanket or with one of the rain-soaked towels Philip kept in the scooter to wipe the seat? What if I had known Kambiz and could have talked him out of it somehow? I wondered if he had someone to cook for him — Iranian men had no clue how to cook. I kept returning to the core of the mystery: why did nobody believe him?

I asked Philip. He said, "Stop worrying. You're adopted by us French."

I asked my aunt. She said, "It's so often the translator. Did you know they pay more respect to translators with English and American accents?"

I asked my mom. She said, "Only God knows."

I asked someone in the Iranian community. She said, "The Dutch are racist! Haven't you heard Wilders warn about Nether-Arabia and fire up all their vilest nativist instincts? They treat this man like a real candidate; they give him legitimacy when he should be slithering around on the fringes."

"The trouble is," said a Dutch finance man at one of Philip's company parties, "that opportunistic migrants give the same stories as the true refugees. Real ones are rare. How is the IND to tell them apart?"

I thought of how I would soon board a plane to Iowa City — my own opportunistic escape, the one in which I finally have agency and power and ambitions. In a few months, I would become a wanderer again, but definitely not the same kind as I had been when we escaped. I was so tired. "I don't think 'opportunism' is the right word," I said. "Escape from a shitty life is still escape. They're not coming here to run pyramid schemes."

"Of course," said the man. He took my empty glass and put it on a tray. He was very kind. "I mean those leaving for economic reasons. The ones whose lives aren't immediately in danger. Do you see?"

"Yes," I said. I was too tired.

"Dina's family were refugees," said Philip. I didn't add that I was a refugee too — it didn't happen a generation ago. It wasn't forgotten. But that didn't feel right. These were kind men. And I was wearing too lovely a dress; that night, it was my passport to joy, all that burnt coral silk.

Shortly before I left, I had another shock.

A friend in the Persian community told me that she didn't believe our escape story. She spoke tenderly, as if she were telling me that she had seen my mother shoplifting at the Albert Heijn market. She said that someone cast doubts on it: a talking head of sorts, a man, in the Armenian exile community. My mother wasn't a publicly known minister, he argued, like the one who had been shot in the streets. She was a wife of a savvy Muslim who had purchased plane tickets under the nose of the Islamic Republic. She was being melodramatic. Maybe she was lying to get out of Iran — for a better life. An economic migrant, that's what she was. Where were her arrest papers? The records showed that we boarded a commercial plane out of Iran, that we had a visa, a sponsor. How could this be if she was about to be executed? Why wasn't she sent to Evin, the larger, more terrifying prison in Tehran? How could she have boarded that first cargo plane? Surely an educated lady in Iran wouldn't be reckless enough to distribute tracts in city streets. Surely no dentist inspires such loyalty that a patient would risk his job and freedom to smuggle his fugitive family.

It was a boot to the gut. I felt like I was dropped in front of a tribunal of asylum officers, unhappy white men openly hating me for coming in and taking too much, wanting too much, their birthrights. Now they would tear up my passport and send me back. I raged at the gall of this man — an Armenian from Iran should know better. Casting doubt as if there is no universe of unseen and unrecorded favors and threats. As if, in Iran, only the guilty are hanged. As if every credible threat of death is recorded in triplicate at the ministry of intelligence. Memory is a tricky thing, I thought, but I have albums, I have vivid scenes in my mind, I have trinkets I carried in a backpack across the ocean. My life *happened* — how dare they question that. What's more, the Three Miracles had *made* me; they shaped my identity. I thought of all the hours spent retelling that story for the approval of Americans and Europeans and even fellow Iranians, for parents of friends and admissions committees, anyone who cared to listen. I thought of Kambiz and how he had an Iranian community that had likely heard his story dozens of times, but was powerless to help him. Had they tried?

Thank god that Home Office interviewers aren't former asylum seekers. What great temptation to roll up the ladder behind you and move on, to question every story according to the narrowest standards, trying to match its peculiar details to your own. Every true story has strangeness, things that can only happen to *those* people at that time — the unbiased listen for it, trying to imagine an unknown world. But the biased look only for *familiar* oddities, the ones that match and validate their own story.

And there is another complication. To offer a "true" story is a guilty business. I understood this only after becoming a writer. Every memory falters, skips, adorns; the story takes on mythic or hagiographic qualities because the mind is thirsty for meaning. How tricky our memories, how inconvenient their gaps and contradictions, how vulnerable to desire. Knowing this, how can a lucky petitioner believe those who come after?

And even if the former refugee had no trouble with his own story, his memory flawless, his papers in place, there's the sense of entitlement and heroism that follows escape, the desire to keep his story pure, to enforce that purity in others. And this desire is complicated by all that he knows of Iranian culture. "Iranians exaggerate; that is the main problem in preparing them for questioning," says a stellar Iranian asylum lawyer I met in London. "I won't tolerate a lie."

For years I obsessed over this man's doubts. When my relationship with my mother was strained, I doubted my own memories. Some of the man's questions were easy to dismiss, like motive: my mother has been a faithful, hard-practicing Christian for thirty years since immigrating. She is brutal in her judgment of new arrivals who claim faith but don't practice, who don't know the language and the secret codes of the underground church. "Yes, they deserve rescue, but they should tell the truth!" She is also not an economic migrant, or else a terrible one, since she moved from the respect and comfort of a doctor's life to poverty and factory work. She pulled herself up from that new starting point, working as a medical researcher, organic farmer, pastry chef, Peace Corps volunteer in Thailand. But never again did she enjoy the material comfort she had in Iran. No more Diana haircuts and leather bags and black-market Nivea Creme — Maman rubs lemons on her face and plants basil and reads her Bible.

And yet, if one were to swim deep into the dark waters of the psyche, would one find in my mother a pure and guileless love of Jesus or a desperation to please her own mother, to escape a bad marriage, and to find some agency after a lifetime of obedience? After twisting into knots to reject every radical desire of her heart — to be seen, to be held equal to men — she couldn't become a feminist, but she could rebel against most extreme injustice while making her mother happy; she could claim liberation while remaining a good girl who serves male ambition. Can such desires make the love of Jesus true? Well, who knows. Devotion is always murky. Anyone claiming pure love is lying.

Hence the absurdity of at least one kind of asylum interview: the religious devotion test (and its cousin, the sexual orientation test). The very notion of it requires falseness. What is faith when it's so mired in fear? What is devotion? Or desire? Terror can conjure or stifle any emotion. Fear can render it true in the moment, convincing in some, false in others.

It is often a question of whether the storyteller herself believes. So maybe a practiced ear *can* know, if he's listening well, if he understands the language of truth. I take the question to that stellar asylum lawyer in London. He is Kaweh Beheshtizadeh, former runaway, teacher and archivist for the Kurdish Democratic Party of Iran, who arrived outside of Birmingham in the back of a truck and is now one of the most accomplished young asylum lawyers in London, winning Legal Aid Lawyer of the Year in 2017. When we meet in his Croydon offices in 2017, Kaweh has only heard of Kambiz in passing, but when I keep pressing the subject, he humors me. "It may have been a weak story, or maybe he had no evidence. Or there was a contradiction somewhere." Since 2011 Kaweh has worked on over seven hundred refugee cases from at least thirty countries. He has lost fewer than ten cases in the last two years. He still has the political ambitions of his youth, and I won't be surprised if one day he's a member of parliament (MP).

"Those who lie do so for three reasons." When he can, Kaweh numbers his answers — *There are three issues here* or *let's establish four points of context* — I can't imagine a time he wasn't a lawyer. And I can't imagine speaking to him in Farsi. Our interviews are all in English, and neither of us gives it a second thought, until a Persian dish or a Farsi expression is mentioned. "First, bad advice from friends. Second, success stories taken out of context. Third, experience in other countries, which they assume will apply to the UK. I don't let my clients tell lies. Before anything I want to sleep at night. This is people's lives. It's *my* life."

I ask Kaweh to take me through a mock interview. "I want to see if I can pass it. Interview me as if I'm a Christian asylum seeker."

"Haven't you already done this once?" he asks, chuckling. I have — the fact that Daniel and I spoke like Christian children, the fact that we were obviously raised in the faith was a deciding factor for our family.

"I want to experience it as if it's 2017," I say.

He shrugs. "What is your religion?" he says. The questions come quick and easy, like memory verses. He has heard them a thousand times.

"I'm a Christian," I say — it was true once.

"When did you become a Christian?" he asks.

"When I was six." I think of my first night in London, decades ago.

"When did you become a Christian?" His expression doesn't change, except for a small squint in his eye, and I almost don't register that he's repeating his question. He doesn't believe me.

"When I was six," I repeat, more emphatically.

"OK, then please tell me about it."

"We were visiting London in May 1985. My grandmother told me about Jesus. My mom converted on that trip too. Then we returned to Iran."

"Did you go to church in Iran?"

"Yes, it was an underground church."

"Which church?"

"It was a home church. It rotated. It didn't have a name. I don't think."

"How often did you attend and for how long?"

"Three years. Sundays and Wednesdays. Christmas. And sometimes when my mother needed to talk . . . I probably shouldn't go into this . . ."

"Does anyone there know you?"

"Yes, of course. I mean, I don't know how to reach them now."

"What's the name of the pastor?"

"Brother Yusuf . . . what was his last name? My mother would know."

"Did you get baptized there?"

"Yes . . . No, actually, because my father wouldn't agree and they had these sexist rules . . . I got baptized in Lake Bracciano, Italy, on May 7, 1989."

"Do you have a certificate?"

"Somewhere . . . OK, I understand. When do they stop?"

"When they're satisfied. Hours. Days. Often after they find enough contradictions." Kaweh doesn't say it, but they're not looking to rescue. They're looking to reject.

"You'd need documents for as much of this as possible," he says.

"I don't know if my mother had all that. She probably did."

"It was a different time." He sits back in his chair.

The questions are straightforward. They can be believably answered in many true and untrue ways. How can you separate a studious liar from a person who has stepped into that church, shaken hands with that pastor? I can't tell. If you ask me, the biggest stretch of the imagination is that underpaid bureaucrats have such profound insight into the human heart.

Since I met Kaweh, Kambiz has become more insistent in haunting my writing hours; I've so conflated his fate with Kaweh's that the two men move side by side in my imagination — everything Kaweh accomplishes, every ounce of talent and pound that he spends on helping refugees and the English, is a triumph Kambiz will never have. Every fruitful minute in Kaweh's life is a minute Kambiz spent aimless and waiting. Would he have become a the ungrateful refugee successful contractor? A chef? An electrical engineer? Why was one believed, and the other sent away? How did each tell his story?

V

Twice in my life I have been instructed to tell a story that, if believed, would open the door to a new life, a chance to remake myself. Children know instinctively how to tell good stories, especially true ones, and so my asylum interview wasn't the burden it is for adults. I didn't agonize over it. It didn't tickle the itchy spots in my neck and palms. The interview didn't make them worse. I hardly remember it now. I know we were interviewed in spring 1989 in the American Embassy in Rome, traveling there by bus from our refugee hostel in Mentana. I know I had not yet turned ten.

My second petition for a new life was at the Iowa Writers' Workshop, after I left Amsterdam and started over as a writer. Again, I had landed in Middle America with its white porch swings and hot summer nights. My disorientation was so similar to those first Oklahoma days. I dragged my body. "I have exile sickness," I said to no one, and I tried to hold in the tics.

On the crisp autumn afternoon when my

novel was first workshopped, I was consumed with fear that I had told lies. Of course, I had lied. I had written a novel. A running joke in workshops is this: a novice submits a story and it falls flat. It isn't believable. In defense of his story, he shouts, "But it happened!" *Too bad,* our teachers say; that's why the novelist has a tougher job than God. God can have coincidences and melodrama and silly, pointless scenes that don't move the story forward. That it happened doesn't make it true enough for fiction, and, like the asylum seeker who isn't believed, novels that are seen to lie are doomed to death.

"What makes a story *true*?" we would ask in seminars and workshops. There were many answers: vulnerability; a singular, unashamed voice; surprising inevitability; originality. Orphan details, Charles Baxter told us once, bring a story to life. These details are specific and strange and they seem not to belong. A naked woman wandering in the rain, a child gnawing a chicken bone on a bench — our protagonists pass by them, sometimes reflecting on them, sometimes not. They are part of the world. In *How Fiction Works,* James Wood asks, "How would we know when a detail seems really true? What guides us? The medieval theologian Duns Scotus gave the name 'thisness' (*haecceitas*) to individuating form . . . Because thisness is palpability, it will tend toward substance — cow shit, red silk, the wax of a ballroom floor, a calendar for 1808. But it can be a mere name or an anecdote; palpability can be represented in the form of an anecdote or a piquant fact." I scribbled in my notebook: *Korean ribs on basmati rice.*

"What makes a story *important*?" we'd ask. This seemed more urgent.

In a seminar called "Undoings," Charles Baxter told us that the stories worth telling are the ones in which someone's world tilts on its axis, and they are forever changed — there is no undoing what's done. He told us to aim for stories that, though they cover a day or a week of a life, allow the reader to imagine *everything that came before and everything after.* Most lifetimes only have a handful of stories like that — you must slice out a "wedge" from the arc of a life. The wedge is that life's most vital story. The consequence of choosing the wrong wedge is that your story strikes false.

I spent those two years confused. Here I was trying to dial back my life's biggest lie (that I had turned myself into someone's European wife), and I had chosen a school for making up people and inventing stories. Still, in 2012, I started writing the kind of stories Baxter told us would strike true — moments of undoing, however subtle. And I populated them with the orphan details I knew, the ones from my home, my family.

I started writing "autofiction," staying close to stories I had lived, but used the tools of fiction, combining characters, collapsing time, inserting invented images. It was, I believe, the purest, most powerful way to tell honest stories. Autofiction removes any impediment to vulnerability, so that the writer can focus on creating a fresh, compelling voice and a moving narrative. At the same time, it stays close to the raw story that only a single person can know and contains all the power of that lived reality. It is a chance to rewrite the facts in service of a larger truth.

My mother, on the other hand, believes in facts as they happened — one universal, irrefutable reality. She is brutal in questioning new refugees; sometimes she embarrasses me. She thinks that, if something is true, we should all remember it the same way. If we don't, someone is mistaken or lying. So, when I choose from her traits for my fiction, she believes that I'm writing about her, the real her, and that I owe my invented story the perfect truth of who she is. "Is this what you learned in writing school?" she said after reading one of my stories. "You lied about me!"

"It wasn't real! It's fiction." I said.

"Yes . . . but it was *still* full of lies," she said.

My mother and I have been having this same argument for years. She keeps saying that the facts are sacred. I keep saying that they're a tool — that truth requires point of view, as well; it needs to be cobbled *from* facts.

I wonder what our world would look like if refugees were asked, instead of reciting facts, to write a story that shows their truth in another way. What if those stories were then evaluated by professional editors, using the same skills they use to see if novels are "true" enough? It is a fantasy, but I decide to try it. In 2017, I join SINGA UK to launch a refugee storytelling workshop. For our first session, we sit around a big table at Libreria Bookshop in London, and we struggle for two hours. Half the class demurs. The other half doesn't speak English — why are they here? I keep thinking of a story from my cousin Pooyan's wife, a visual artist and fellow Iranian: she gave an Afghani boy pencils and asked him to draw.

He drew SpongeBob. He drew a truck. He drew a crane with spidery arms, two men hanging from it with crosses for eyes. Then, another SpongeBob.

I want to ask everyone in my class to draw a crane, the way in beginning writing workshops you are asked to describe a barn.

Maybe the new arrivals sitting around my table at Libreria are tired of crafting their one story according to other people's rules. Maybe they want to create something different now, or to finally tell their story *truly,* raw and full of dirty details, in the authentic storytelling language of their youth. Because to pass an asylum interview, you don't just need a true story. You need to tell that story the English way, or the Dutch or American way. Americans enjoy drama; they want to be moved. The Dutch want facts. The English have precedents, stories from each country deemed true that year, that month. The Dutch have something similar. Americans like the possibility of a grand success story; they adore exceptionalism and want to make all greatness American.

Iranian storytelling doesn't satisfy any of these requirements — just watch a film by Abbas Kiarostami. No narrative rules. Iranians have no problem with spoilers — the ending isn't the pleasure of a story for them. They don't start in the middle of the action (as Western writers are taught to do) or even at the beginning (where Western logic may take them); they start long before the beginning: "Let me tell you about modern Iran," they say, because that is how they are trained to begin. And those are the savvy ones; the rest begin with the creation of the universe. But you start philosophizing and you've lost your Western listener.

Iranians like symbols and metaphors. Lies aren't lies if they point somewhere. And you can signal your trauma and shame with a pointed "this isn't something for saying." Try that on a Dutch asylum officer who asks, "Why did you run?" Sometimes traumatized Iranians speak in generalities. "The government is corrupt. They're murderers. I cannot say more. Please." So, the Dutch officer decides you're lying; he won't change his mind. The English and the American will give you a few seconds more. In Iran, our literature is winding and dramatic. We bury the lede. We flourish and twist. The Dutch and Germans see these as markers of deception — in the Western world, literary critics condemn these techniques as false.

To satisfy an asylum officer takes the same narrative sophistication it takes to please book critics. At once logical and judgmental of demeanor, both are on guard for manipulation and emotional trickery. Stick to the concrete, the five senses, they say. Sound natural, human, but also dazzle with your prose. Make me cry, but a whiff of sentimentality and you're done. Stay in scene, but also give compelling evidence of internal change. Go ahead. Try it. It's not so hard, you penniless, traumatized fugitive from a ravaged village, just write a story worthy of *The New Yorker*.

How does any ordinary person reprogram the storytelling habits that they learned as children, listening on the laps of their mothers and fathers?

Everyone wants ownership of their one, formative, true story — they want to choose how it will be told. My mother despises that I write about our escape, because that is *her* story, her tilting planet. She gets to decide what it looks like, and she has settled on a hagiographic story of faith and the power of Jesus Christ. There are no muddying details revealed. Everyone is protected from embarrassment. Jesus is exalted, and that's that.

On the other hand, when I write stories that have nothing to do with our escape, stories of mothers and fathers struggling in America, she thinks that I've chosen the wrong wedge — that the moment of irrevocable change is ignored elsewhere on my arc, while I gaze at a trivial spot a few yards down. My narrative, she believes, is salvation by a parent who toiled to offer opportunities that I squandered. My stories disregard this thread, though it should consume me, and so they lack an essential element: respect from the child. Respect and thanks from the world.

Dutch asylum lawyer Marq Wijngaarden tells me of a Chinese woman from a persecuted sect. She was afraid for her life, and she stretched herself, her sense of privacy and shame, to find her most essential story. She gave detail after detail of her conversion process, all those moments of agony and delight, just as she had been taught. But the IND officer called her uncooperative, because she wouldn't give a straight answer to "Why did you leave?" She found that part obvious (*when you choose the right wedge, everything before and everything after falls into place; it becomes obvious*). Her religious conversion was the point of no return in her story, the moment when the world is irreversibly altered. It was the *undoing,* the moment to which any good writer would ascribe the greatest importance. But it was also the part that IND officer had heard most often — he was numbed to it. Wijngaarden had the case reviewed, and won, but the first rejection was unnerving: *they need to be better at hearing people.*

So, you see, poor, traumatized fugitive from a ravaged village, even if you *do* choose the right wedge, even if you do gather up the sensory details, avoid melodrama, and write that story worthy of *The New Yorker,* nothing's guaranteed — even the greatest writer can't reach a lazy, cynical reader.

VI

In Amsterdam, my first stop is Parvis Noshirrani, Kambiz's old friend. I take a train to Almere, a depressing suburb close to a refugee camp. I poke around the business park where Parvis has a Persian restaurant. I take a breath and push open the door. Parvis makes tea. All afternoon we sit in the empty eatery and talk, about exile, truth, Kambiz. Persian men come in and out. Some say hello and sit with us, reminiscing about Kambiz. A name comes up: Ahmed Pouri. Kambiz visited him once, maybe to ask for help. We drain our teas and Parvis puts on coffee. He invites me to return the next day to talk to others in the community. Before I leave, he gives me a phone number to call if I want a complete picture of asylum struggles in the Netherlands. I take the scrap of paper. It says: *Ahmed Pouri.*

Over the next few days the name keeps appearing. Undocumented immigrants and longtime Dutch citizens and asylum lawyers and aid workers keep pushing his phone number into my hand, saying: speak to Ahmed Pouri. He isn't a lawyer. No, he's not an asylum worker, either. He's a helper. He makes things happen because he can see through both lenses. He understands the asylum process, Dutch culture, many Middle Eastern cultures (especially Iranian), and most of all human laziness, sloppiness, and foolishness. That's how he gets people their papers. Ahmed Pouri is a refugee whisperer, a fixer of status troubles — his NGO is called PRIME. One afternoon, I call him. He answers on the second ring, his voice rich and warm. Later I find that, though a stranger calls him every ten or fifteen minutes, he always answers as if expecting a friend. I tell him my name. "I know you, young lady!" he says. "I read your work. You write very well."

Instantly I like him. Here is another fatherly voice to tell me I'm clever. Before I have a chance to ask him for an interview, he begins talking — he doesn't stop for a long time. He has made it his life's work to teach refugees how to be believed by the Dutch, how to tell a convincing story the *Western* way. He tells me about families and lone wanderers he's worked with, about the many suicides, about his efforts to make Iranians understand Dutch logic, about the injustices of the detention centers, about Hegel and other philosophers. He quotes Sun Tzu, that to win you must know yourself, your enemy, and the battlefield. "They know zero of the three! How can they win? How can a twenty-five-hundred-year-old foreigner understand and not an Iranian doctor?" I laugh at the presumption of Iranian superiority that all middle-aged Persians share. "The asylum process is about crafting a story that is believed so you can stop waiting and make a life," he says. "I tell refugees what to say to IND and to reporters so they don't work against themselves, so they don't make all refugees look like crazies and liars and manipulators. So that their humanity shows the European way." I find this moving and start to speak, but he continues on, "There are two things to know about your audience (your 'enemy,' to continue the Sun Tzu analogy): who he is and what he considers truth."

"Yes," I begin again, "can we set a time to — ?"

"Look, Ms. Dina, the asylum officer is cynical and overworked. He's not listening for the truth. He's looking for a single lie. Just one. An asylum lawyer stood up at a recent conference and spoke about a conversation he overhead in the IND lunchroom at Ter Apel: one asylum officer bragging to another, 'Today I had a real and true political dissident. It was hard work, but after three hours of pressing, I got a contradiction out of him and sent him packing.' He was so proud that he had found his needle in the hay, he didn't even hear himself call the man 'a real and true political dissident.'

"That is your audience," says Mr. Pouri, "Then there's their notion of truth. There's a terrible tactic in Holland. In a given year from each country, there are two or three stories that are most successful. If they only let in gays and Christians from Iran, that's the story they hear most — what choice does anyone have? After a while they say, 'How can everyone from that country be gay and Christian?' They don't think, *We're the ones who said those are the only legitimate reasons to run, when in truth there are a hundred.* So, they say, 'Some must be lying.' They lead you down a funnel with a dead end. If you're a communist in Iran your life is in greater danger than a quiet Christian. But no one gives a communist case because the Dutch don't acknowledge the gruesome things the Iranian government does to communists — they hang them for drugs or kill them in secret, and the Dutch say, 'They don't persecute communists.' If your life is in danger, the Dutch force you into a gay or Christian case. After a while, those stories grow stale, overused, and the channel closes. People hear of another."

I'm starting to wonder if Dutch calls are covered by my UK phone plan. If they're not, this trip just got really expensive. He continues on.

"They've already decided what is true. If you offer a different story, you are lying. If you confirm their preferred story too often, you are lying."

"Madness," I say. "I'd love to sit down with you and —"

"And again, I should emphasize, Miss Dina, that they are dishonest about what goes on in these countries! Many of the rejections come from things they say are impossible, that actually happen all the time in Iran. They apply the logic of a democratic nation to brutal dictatorships.

"I once helped a badly raped Kurdish girl.

Soldiers came through her village and raped her in the stable beside the horses. She kept weeping, 'I wish I could find a pill to forget the past. I wish I didn't remember.' She was losing her mind. They rejected her claim. Do you know why? Because half the village had been raped. They said, 'You are not an interesting person for the government. It was a random act, and you were in the wrong place. You don't have a credible fear that the soldiers will return for *you*.' See, your story must be individual. If she had said, 'They took me away and raped and tortured me,' that's individual; but a public pillage isn't *about* you. You're not a dissident, just an ordinary rape victim. You must say, 'The government is targeting me. I am a threat to them.' Then, you're a real refugee. But, tell me, Dina, do you know any Western country where soldiers do this? Those men went to that village to target Kurds. Surely, there is a case in that.

"I swear I want to gather these stories and make a play of them. I used to joke that if a rapist comes, it's best to ask, 'Please, sir, take me into a room alone for the rape. Please single me out.' Then you've got a hope. But group rape won't help you. You see, the criminal has to acknowledge your humanity for the IND to respect it. If the criminal treats you like a cow in a stable, the IND will too. They say, soldiers don't come back for the cows.

"I had a former communist come to me, an honest man, no case-*bazi*. He had spent ten years in Iranian jail. He was tortured in the horrifying ways of the 1980s. His body is a torture museum. He had been free and inactive for years. Every month he checked in with the authorities and got a stamp. One day he saw that the old political boys of the past were being rounded up. Two of his friends disappeared. Memories flooded back, and he ran. The IND asked, 'Did you get involved in underground work again?' He said, 'No, but I have experience with this regime. I know the signs.' The Dutch said, 'Impossible. You didn't do anything, so you're fine. Your friends must have been involved. But your fear is psychological. Not based on fact.'

"If that man understood Dutch logic, he would have said, 'Yes, I did it. The three of us started underground work again. They caught the other two, and I ran.' He'd be accepted in an hour. But he told them the facts, expecting knowledge of Iran, and he spent five years in camps. Finally Amnesty lawyers got him his papers, but he's mental now. Ten years in Iranian jail and five years in Dutch camp. He's gone. He won't have peace until he dies."

How can this be true? It seems that anyone using such logic is either so foolish that they don't realize the Islamic Republic is corrupt and fallible, or they are disingenuous and reckless with refugee lives.

Briefly I stop worrying about my phone bill and consider Mr. Pouri's mental space — it is clogged with this one global injustice, that people from the poor and war-ravaged countries of the world are routinely labeled liars and opportunists. How devastating to know something is right and to stand alone against the planet — how torturous to be a socialist or a feminist or a migrant, vilified when you're only saying, "We're all worth the same."

It wasn't like this for us. We were believed, at least by asylum people. Some asylum officer saw us and waved us through. In 1989, "I'm Christian" wasn't the most common excuse for leaving Iran. Still, I've heard Baba and others casually say that Maman brought it on herself, that she didn't have to be so reckless. She could have been happy in Iran. She *chose* to shed her skin, and she loves her Lazarus story; it's her new identity. Before coming to Amsterdam, I asked Kaweh, my resource now for legal and philosophical dilemmas, "What if a person puts themselves in the way of danger? Is their escape diminished? Will the officer say, *You did this to yourself*?"

He leaned back in his chair. This time his answer was simple and sure, no lists or legal caveats. "There is no such a thing as bad faith in life-or-death situations," he said. "This was established in 2001. If you *put* your life in danger in order to escape or be granted asylum, you're still in danger."

"So, if I come here and get rejected and I have some writing ability, so I write ten articles blasting the regime, and I sell five to *The Guardian* . . ."

"I guarantee you asylum in two weeks," he said. "Courts have accepted that prisons in Iran are so bad, just being there for a few days will breach your human rights. There's the prospect of detention, torture, rape. These are breaches of human rights. Bad faith is irrelevant in this case."

Funny, the things they let go.

"This is an area where people have the wrong instincts," says Mr. Pouri. "They want to claim innocence. It's better to claim guilt." The more dumb and reckless you were at home, the better. The same applies after you're in Europe. If you're the one poking the lion, you get pulled out first.

So, then what do they want? The story must be compelling, full of strange, but not-too-strange, details. It must not mimic other stories, but the heart of it, its motive and inciting incident, can be contrived, impure, selfish. You can posture. You *must* posture. Show that you *behaved* as a Christian or communist or gay: we don't care why. What a strange storytelling tradition. In MFA workshop, we learned that the *why* matters more than almost anything else. How can Iranians — who are trained in poetry and polemics, for whom love is a wordy mono-logue, every truth buried under layers of meaning, and all stories begin at creation — adjust to it? In Holland, they pass around Mr. Pouri's phone number.

When I put this paradox to Marq Wijn-gaarden, he says I have bad information — in Holland *all* they care about in conversion and LGBTQ cases is the process, the moti-vation. What compelled you to live this way? He is adamant that the law forbids officers from asking for any sexual facts, and cer-tainly they can't ask for any to be per-formed. They must reject any photos or videos freely offered — this is the ruling of the European Court of Justice. In fact, he says, you can gain asylum without ever hav-ing had sex with someone of the same gender, if you can give a full account of your coming-out process, and the discovery of your desires. For conversion, you must first prove your rejection of Islam. It's not enough to behave like a Christian. You must be an apostate, and a slow-cooked one.

Mr. Pouri says, "This is one of the Dutch lies. They *say* they're evolving, but the offi-cers still ask humiliating questions. If you're gay, you have to prove that you're part of the gay community. You go to clubs. You are out." The law may have adapted, but the nuances of coming out haven't sunk in for the individual asylum officers. Until they do, you can't be a quiet, bookish lesbian. Forget about being questioning, bi, celibate, heartbroken and not in the mood for new love, culturally beaten down or too afraid to act. Every gay person has to be a flamboy-ant scene-kid, out at clubs and fashion shows and on Grindr texting strangers at a nightclub. And according to Mr. Pouri, you have a better chance if you act out the cliché than if you try to convince them of a complex internal process.

It's easier to hang a case on big, showy gestures and concrete dangers than good faith or motivation. Maybe it depends much more on the individual officer's ego and biases than we'd care to admit. Some want an honest motive and a convincing intellectual process in the home country; others demand evidence of danger. Many have no respect for international standards. I remember Shrouk El-Attar, a twenty-five-year-old queer Egyptian engineering student who, during a petition to the UK parliament in March 2018, spoke of the humiliation of having to describe her sexual encounters in graphic detail to asylum officers. Whatever the official line, many gay asylum seekers have such tales. They are asked to *perform* their gayness, to prove they have acted on it.

Mr. Pouri stops midsentence to take a call. Then he rushes off. He is meeting a family of deportees about to be put on a plane. He agrees to meet me at Schiphol Airport four hours before my departure back to London.

The next day, I return to Almere. Parvis introduces me to Houshiar, a day worker for a local Iranian businessman in construction, handbags, and tailoring. "This boy has a good story," Parvis says. "He's illegal. Keeps getting rejected. You'll see." After two rejections, Houshiar has given up on asylum. He lives illegally at the camp, sneaking in and bunking with friends.

About an hour into my conversation with

Houshiar, I realize I am missing a vital chunk of the truth. There is something here that is perhaps hidden from me. We are talking about Houshiar's faith, the day he became a Christian, and his struggle to be believed. But, somehow, I sense that I have the wrong wedge. This man has a story, and I'm not hearing it.

Houshiar wears a leather jacket and skinny jeans. He is young, modern, except for all the hair gel. He shows me photos of his beautiful son, a boy styled to look like a European adult from the late nineties. Every photo is a studio shot. He shows me his unhappy wife, speaks casually of the way his family took the boy from her. He says he converted because the boy was gravely ill and, in the hospital, a Christian man prayed with him. His boy was set to die, but when he recovered, Houshiar believed.

The more he speaks, the more I crave the real story — it isn't that I don't believe the one he is offering. I just know he has a better, more fundamental one. What compelled him to drop everything and run? Though he knows the language of the convert ("I gave my heart," "I repented," "I found a flock"), nothing he says feels like enough.

He pauses and looks at me, searching my eyes. Do I believe?

The restaurant door chimes announce three new visitors, a well-dressed Iranian-Dutch couple in their early sixties and a man around Parvis's age — he is Houshiar's employer, the one who gives him odd jobs. The couple were naturalized decades ago. They have lived in Holland for thirty years, speak Dutch, and have raised their children in both cultures.

Parvis instructs his cook to make some omelets and eggplant-whey. We sit around a long table and our talk turns to Houshiar's latest asylum rejection. Why is this young man still floating?

"They said I didn't explain my apostasy from Islam well enough." Houshiar shrugs, sighs, then tells us that his mother is sick.

The employer shakes his head and drops his bread. "Listen, son, when you fall into the water, no one will save you but *you*. In that interview, 'my mom is sick, my aunt cut her hand, my sister's earring is lost,' what is that? You have to shut it out. Focus. Pretend you're in the sea."

The husband is nodding a lot. He leans in. "Look, here's a small piece of advice for you: Whatever lie you tell, you must first convince yourself. Give the story branches and leaves. You are the first who must believe."

Houshiar fidgets in his chair. "When you first leave Iran," he says, "your life is scattered, your dreams gone, your wife gone, your house gone, your mother in a coma, you haven't seen your kid in a year and a half —"

The husband has forgotten about his food. He raises both hands. "It's the best moment to tell them your feelings!" He looks at his wife, who nods.

"You can't in that moment," says Houshiar. I recall a rule: don't write a story too soon. You need distance, perspective, to shed sentimentality.

There is a bit of chatter, then Houshiar says, "I don't understand. I told them, *Islam is war.* They say, we have no problem with your Christianity. We don't believe your apostasy." But isn't conversion by definition apostasy from the former religion? I pose this to the table.

"You have to prove it!" two of them say at once. Casual converts don't present like church leaders. They're not loud and feverish with devotion, and they live in a mixed-up culture, the Iranian and the Western all jumbled together. They celebrate Christmas with saffron pudding. They make pilgrimages on Easter and Ascension. Out of habit, they mutter to Muslim prophets as they haul their tired bodies off the ground. These are *their* specific, moving contradictions — the natural flaws that bring a story to life.

This lunch has become a perverse workshop. Rejected asylum seekers are always refining their story, asking for advice; eventually they deplete it of joy and meaning, the orphan details that embed in memories. Remember, your audience is listening for contradiction, any contradiction, and life is full of those. A moving detail can get you rejected. So, forget about meaning. Meaning will hurt you. Complexity is compromising.

Wijngaarden has told me that the IND has four lines of questioning for authenticating religious conversion: knowledge of the new religion, its daily practicalities, motivation for, and process of conversion (beginning with apostasy). Some answers are no longer deemed good enough. My mother's true conversion story is this: She believed in one night. She attributes it to miracles in her body and heart. She says she found peace. There was no period of apostasy. She went from feverish devotion to feverish devotion — because that is who she is. Perhaps she had a few numb weeks in between, but that would have been uncon-

361

scious and short-lived. She was at a breaking point, ready to bolt, and the runaway mother who had denied her love suddenly offered an escape. She was primed for it. But today, stories like that are flatly rejected. You can't say "I had a dream" or "I saw a miracle." Those stories stink of deception. A logical person goes through a process: first Islam fails to satisfy some fundamental need. Injustices become unignorable, and the apostate rages privately, perhaps publicly. There is a period of falling away from faith, failing to do religious duties, then she feels a void and goes seeking. She isn't satisfied without a god. She comes into contact with a new faith, becomes interested, reads up.

For my mother, all this happened subconsciously, but it was no less real for going unexamined. She was an educated woman in sexist Iran; of course, she had years of frustrations. She had to cover her body and surrender her parental and property rights to her husband. But if you ask her, she would say, "It was a miracle," like some superstitious village woman. Today, she would be rejected because doctors from Tehran University aren't supposed to believe in miracles.

Iranians give their hearts quickly and

intensely. Educated ones indulge in magical thinking, and rural ones submit to religions based purely on instinct, sometimes with no reading or knowledge. A devout Iranian farmer isn't like the Dutch farmer with a Bible on his pillow. "They want book knowledge," says Houshiar, his voice strained, "but that's not faith! If I'm an illiterate old villager, and I decide there are things Islam hasn't given me, but I recognize good and bad in my bones and I choose Christianity, that's legitimate. Maybe I don't know all the names and dates . . ."

This class problem is, according to Marq Wijngaarden, a true flaw of the asylum process. Like the tax system and property and everything else, it's biased against the poor and the uneducated, the very people most likely to be running out of fear. A villager who has never seen the borders of the next town doesn't pick up and leave home lightly. That villager smells danger. And yet, he is the least likely to know the coded words that open the door to safety. Is his faith any less true? He lives his faith in other ways.

Self-analysis is a problem for uneducated LGBTQ refugees, too. "If you never learned how to express development, a process, a way of changing," says Wijngaarden, "you express your feelings through sexual acts. You don't speak of what you feel and how that feeling developed. The Dutch want more complexity." This is a problem, not just for the uneducated, but for trauma victims who have gaps in memory, and rape victims who are ashamed. "People from a society that has more similarities with Western society get easier asylum than those from societies that are quite different. The asylum system in general is quite unfair."

About two hours into the lunch, the wife starts casting meaningful glances at me. Her glance flits back and forth between me and Houshiar, and suddenly, I know that everyone except Houshiar is thinking the same thing. We know the missing part of Houshiar's story, the wedge, the thing he is keeping from us and from the asylum officers, and perhaps the reason he is rejected. But we can't just blurt out this question; we need to say it without violating Iranian social rules, to cloak it in a second meaning.

"Your case is important," says the husband. He speaks cautiously, choosing each word. "You can convince them, even if you're lying, that your story is true . . ." The "even if you're lying" is pointed and merciful — he wants Houshiar to know that this suggested story doesn't have to be the truth, that we don't believe it about him. The table hushes. We can't be certain, but somehow, silently, we've agreed that this is a much more vital wedge of Houshiar's story than his conversion. What strange collusion: outwardly we're telling this man to lie. Really, we're urging him to be honest with himself, to accept his truth and be at peace. Lie to them; not to yourself.

"Whatever you say," says the husband, tiptoeing closer to the point, "the guy will smile and doubt you. There was a time they would give answers fast. Back when the students were getting killed, the Dutch answered fast. Then there were some programs on television about . . . gays back home. After that every Iranian was gay. So many got papers."

I hold my breath and watch Houshiar's face. He seems unmoved. The wife and I keep glancing at each other. She touches her face. We can't just tell a closeted married Iranian man that he needs to face his sexuality. I know that it's wrong: we could traumatize him; and how can we even be sure? We're not in his mind — we only know that he is much more convincing as a gay man than as a convert, and that is probably because it's the truth. We say, "Gay is a better case," or "It's useful to be gay," when what we mean is, "It's OK. You are allowed to be *you*." We want to tell Houshiar that Iran is long behind him and he *can* have an open life here, in this hamlet of scattered countrymen. *Just tell them the fucking truth,* we want to say, but instead we say, *Just tell this more convincing lie.*

After a while, the wife speaks up. She has been watching the simmer and wants to stir the pot. "It wouldn't work, anyway," she says, goading him. "It's so easy to tell. Gay men can't hide it."

Houshiar gives her an impatient look, "Of course they can hide it."

Again, we're all silent. Houshiar, it seems, has no idea we suspect him.

"*Many* are anonymous," says Parvis. "Not the ones with hormone problems, but the gay husbands, you can't tell with them." I drop down in my seat. He thinks he's helping and carries on. "There are some thick necks; it's not obvious unless they wear an earring or shave their heads."

That these are liberal Iranians reminds me how brutal our culture is to the LGBTQ community, which remains underground in Iran. The outdated language and gender expectations are embedded in our national psyche: to be a man is to be strong and

366

macho; a woman must be chic and dainty.

"Some of them even do bodybuilding," says the husband — bless him, he is trying to be encouraging. "Of course, the second they say two words, you know they're a match without danger." My hand flies to my mouth.

"For women," his wife is quick to clarify. She's the more progressive of the pair. She explains the safety-match metaphor to me and assures the table that those men have plenty of spark for other men and that's just fine.

Houshiar looks thoughtful. "I've seen it. So many young people out of Iran give a gay case. And then every day they go to church."

"Why shouldn't they?" says Parvis. "You can be gay and Christian."

Houshiar sits up. His voice is disdainful and angry. "What does a gay person know about religion and faith?" It's the first time he's raised his voice, and a current of alarm passes between the rest of us.

"Oh, come now," says the wife. She's tearing her napkin into strips. Houshiar has been raised on this homophobia for three decades. We can't convince him in a single lunch that an accepting society exists.

"Your Christianity is nothing," says Parvis. "Prove that your life is in danger." Everyone nods; whether Houshiar is a Christian or gay, his life is indeed in danger. Now Parvis grows bolder. "Bring your pastor here and ask him, can a gay person be a Christian? Want me to call him? Let me say to him that a gay man wants to come to church. Let's see what he says."

The wife shreds another napkin. "Whatever your case," says the husband, "you must throw yourself in it, drown in it. Before you tell a story, you must first believe it yourself."

"Make it true," says Parvis. "I grew up in the Christian district. I know what Christians sound like . . . this is why none of us believe you . . ."

Houshiar rubs his palm. "But when I entered Europe, I said I was Christian. If I wasn't, I'd live at home, work for my father. Every day he begs me to come back. I could be with my son. My sister would make me tea."

"Didn't I make you tea?" says Parvis, and Houshiar tries to smile. The couple look at their plates. "Houshiar *joon,* I can see the veins in your neck. You're under stress. The simpler you approach it, the better."

For three hours, we drag this sideways conversation along. We argue. We step out

368

for smokes. We bring out more eggplant. Lunch takes another bizarre turn when Parvis telephones the pastor. Houshiar grumbles, "Leave the man alone." Parvis explains with great care, "Our friend is not gay himself, of course. He's one of the new Christians. Just wants to prove to us gays can't be Christian." Houshiar drops his face into his hands.

If Houshiar is gay, he is years from admitting it. Shame keeps many true stories hidden. What matters is that this man *presents* as gay to other Iranians under a homophobic regime. That's danger. Whether he applies with the Christian story or the gay story, the essential truth is this: his life in Iran would be entirely in the shadows, until the day he crosses paths with the wrong person and then he might be hanged. That would be his life. The truest thing is that he needs and deserves asylum.

What we assign as our story, our compelling case, will shape all our future days. The whole of the arc, from birth to death, leads to and grows out from the wedge, that cluster of days when life was forever altered. Was it conversion over a dying baby? Or an unexpected desire?

If he is gay, Houshiar must say so aloud.

369

He must articulate that he was closeted, even from himself, mired in a hypermasculine culture.

I ask Wijngaarden, "What if the process happens subconsciously?"

"Then you're screwed," he says. I like his Dutch candor.

One thing is clear: in a regime that murders religious minorities, a sudden conversion after some good luck in the hospital isn't believable. Iranians may act on miracles, and visits from the ungrateful refugee jinnis, and prophetic dreams, but as in the case of the novice writer, "it happened" isn't enough.

In an essay, "Against Epiphanies," Charles Baxter says that epiphanies are by nature deceptive. Foundational shocks happen to children. For adults, they are, at least in part, posturing. *Melodrama.* In fiction workshop, we asked, have I written this truthfully? We didn't mean, "Are my facts correct?" We meant, "Is the story believable?" Often the facts are the least believable, and it is fiction's job to fix them in service of the truth. A fact, given disproportionate context and attention, can lie about a life, or a day, or a marriage, a war, a childhood. A fiction can be true, when it throws a light on the unseen, those unclaimed spectacles

370

that occur again and again but that shame and trauma keep hidden from view.

A truthful short story about my mother's conversion wouldn't rely on miracles as an explanation. It would show her sadness, her ache for a mother's love, her painful marriage, her longing to have faith. But, even Baxter would agree, that the *character* can chalk it all up to miracle, and that would only deepen our understanding of her. From her vantage point, she sees a miracle — fiction allows for that nuance. And yet, the asylum officer, who appropriates the rules of good storytelling, fails to realize, when sitting across from a petitioning refugee, that you are speaking to a *character* in the story, not the *author.* If an Iranian character says, "It was a miracle," she is using cultural shorthand, labeling a long process that her upbringing hasn't given her the tools to unpack.

If Houshiar manages to evade detention long enough, perhaps he could try again in some years. Wijngaarden says that in past years, if a refugee didn't declare themselves LGBTQ on arrival, they wouldn't be believed in subsequent attempts, because it was assumed they were coached. But a recent court decision in Luxembourg established that coming out can take years. And sometimes people need time in a free country to come to terms with their sexual orientation. They may resist because of shame, trauma, and fear. This understanding has changed Dutch jurisprudence — a bit. In practice, much still depends on what each asylum officer finds credible. For that, the refugee must take control of the story and behave as the storyteller, not just a character. As ever, the same timeless good advice applies. It is repeated by lawyers and former refugees and writers and book critics, each in their own way. *It will be truer after you believe. After you do the long, slow work of believing.*

VII

In Amsterdam, I visit my mother's childhood friend Forough and her son, Pooyan, a philosopher. Forough is Baba's cousin. She introduced my parents to each other. She's an activist and a scholar, progressive, feminist, well-read. Shortly after our escape, when life in Iran became unbearable for communists and intellectuals, she picked up toddler Pooyan and ran. The story goes that she went straight to the university in Amsterdam, locking Pooyan in a small philosophy library until he was old enough for school.

During my final days of marriage, I befriended them and took solace in the notion that I come from a gifted, liberal family. Forough and Pooyan were unpretentious. They worked tirelessly. They were always learning. Meanwhile, after a decade, I was realizing that I couldn't care less about the shiny life I had built. I wanted to live and to think and to be useful. *I'm worth more than this,* I thought. When I found Forough and Pooyan, I allowed myself to believe that maybe my value doesn't come from Philip or Princeton or a mastery of English — my love of words goes back centuries.

Pooyan and his wife host dinner at their home. I'm eager to talk about my mother. Did she tell any lies? Did it all happen as I remember?

I tell them about Houshiar, and my mother's reaction when I told her his story. "He won't say he's gay," she said, "because it goes against something more important to him than asylum."

Pooyan nods. "Everyone chooses something that's most essential to their identity," he says. "We're willing to lie *around* it, but not *about* it."

We can lie in service of our formative story, but not in opposition to it. Even the most open-minded struggle to accept a point of view that goes against their center of identity. "It's like recent critiques of Cartesian foundationalism. Scholars argue that you have a set of certainties that determine the place from which you head out. Those certainties cannot be touched. They form your worldview. Changing those means radically changing how you think. For example, my worldview is partly based on Darwinism. That functions as certainty. To change that means to restructure my entire web, and that would cost too much. I'd be a different person. The core of the web cannot be touched. The further out from the core, the easier to change a thought without unraveling the whole thing."

The core of the web is existential.

Pooyan tells me that the IND has approached him, asking if he and a colleague can help them understand and verify conversion among Iranians. They need sincerity tutors. The problem, says Pooyan, is that sincerity is culturally determined. The Dutch concept of belief is a Calvinist one. They believe that true faith comes from within: the invisible church of the heart. It comes from reading the Bible in vernacular. It comes from internalizing doctrine. But plenty of clever unbelievers take Bible lessons. And plenty of poor farmers hear about

Jesus on the radio and in one afternoon give their heart to this concept. "A Protestant believer isn't the same as a sincere Orthodox Jew," says Pooyan. "If you ask them if they believe, the Jew might answer, 'On Saturdays I hold Shabbat.' For a protestant that's weird. Belief is in your heart. For the Orthodox Jew, ritual is far more important."

Pooyan wants to explain to the IND that some Iranian believers may stop going to Dutch churches because they are accustomed to dramatic, intense underground congregations. Dutch churches disappoint them. "They say, in those hidden churches, our faith was deeper. We felt it more."

I ask Forough for more about Maman's story. She demurs. Her friendship with my mother is too complicated for one dinner. But she points out another lie. She says my first novel struck her as untrue. It was too far from the life I knew. I pushed my protagonist into false choices. Did I know her? Did I first believe? "Why didn't you write *your* story, Dina *joon*?"

As I ride the tram home, I think of honesty and my writing life. What is my story? Am I, like Houshiar, loudly defending a wedge that fails to represent my life? A decade ago, I thought my story was a refugee girl who toils and makes good, who wears coral dresses, holds safe passports, earns the good diplomas, doesn't take shit from men, and is loved and respected by Americans. I want to tell Forough that it is a struggle to be honest. You can only continue talking, crafting, weaving closer to the core of the web. A decade ago, I was at Harvard Business School, the biggest lie. Last month, I came across an old Word file called "Memoirs of a lucky girl." It was horrifying: stories from my first year in Oklahoma paired with scenes from Harvard. It was supposed to show how far I had come. All I see now is two threads about extreme discomfort — a girl forever in the wrong setting.

Readers always find the lie, even if everything around it is true. It's easy, like picking the stone out of a pot of cherry rice: you either see it or it cracks your teeth. It's reassuring to know that my work has been a gradual unmasking, that I've shed my cloaks on the road. Maybe truth is only a direction to aim for. "In talking about the past," says William Maxwell, "We lie with every breath we draw." As I fall asleep, I make a decision: I won't reach out to the Armenian, or any of Maman's doubters. I believe her story.

In the morning, I walk around Amsterdam,

visiting my old haunts. I drink a cappuccino at the Koffie Salon. Two for Joy is gone. Amsterdam was a waiting place for me, a hesitation before setting off on a long road. The heavy sensation of those days returns, and I don't know where to put it. I don't have the right muscles anymore. I scratch at my neck and keep walking. It's tulip season; the cracks of the city are bursting with flowers; the air is saturated with the smell of food for tourists: pancakes with sugar and *stroopwafels*. I take a detour past the flat I bought and renovated with Philip. Months ago, he made a point of telling me he sold it. His name is still on the door. Maybe it's a corporate rental now — it's high design and sterile.

Sam texts photos of new blossoms in our garden. In case you're feeling nostalgic for your old life. I text back: The opposite. It's dead here.

Today is April 6, 2018, the seventh anniversary of the day Kambiz lit a final match. The confusion and quiet frenzy of that day returns. The passersby go about their day, eating ice cream, riding bikes. I make my way toward Dam Square — maybe there is a memorial — and toward the offices of Frank van Haren, the asylum lawyer quoted in the stories about Kambiz.

At dinner last night, Pooyan's wife showed me her drawing of Kambiz and her diary from the days after his death. The drawing is captioned, "almost like he wasn't flesh and bone." Those words echo in my mind as I circle Dam Square; it really does seem like he was never here. There is no memorial. As I approach the place where Kambiz set himself alight, I hear Farsi. Two men are talking on the steps. I sit beside them and listen. They speak about death but don't mention Kambiz. It's as likely that their presence is a coincidence as it is a tribute.

I listen for ten minutes. They talk about the sensation of death, the pain of passing. They talk about how best to live. "Life is like a film," says one man. "You can choose not to focus on any one thing, just float above it. Or you could zoom in somewhere, and keep your focus there. If there's pain, you'll feel it more. If there's joy, you'll feel that more too. But if you stay high above everything, I guess you could avoid every sharp feeling."

"If you want to live, you have no choice but to zoom in," says the other man. "Each time, you breathe in and let yourself go. Then you're in it. You've dropped down from the god view. Your film-director view."

It is all apropos of nothing, but I stay on

that step for a while and listen to them circle in on a crude philosophy. When one speaks of listening for the music of life, I decide it is beautiful enough to get up and go.

On my final day, I arrive at Schiphol Airport four hours early to meet the refugee whisperer. I choose a café. Here and there I see professional men approaching, and I lift my head. Still, I miss his arrival. He appears beside me like a phantom and shakes my hand. He is dressed like one of the vagrants with whom he spends most of his life — I'm grateful; I look shabby too, dressed in the same clothes I wore on my inbound flight. There is something fundamentally honest about his choices. He eats with refugees, protests with them, with groups like Refugees on the Street or We Are Here. Sometimes he squats with them in open tents or empty buildings, squalid places like the "refugee garage," an abandoned parking lot outside Amsterdam full of rejected refugees who cannot return home and are forced into destitution once the Dutch have washed their hands of them.

I see now that Mr. Pouri's monologues are mellow and smiley. He doesn't gesticulate or pace frantically as I had imagined when we spoke on the phone. He is warm.

His *ch*'s and *j*'s are soft, almost *z*'s — this detail, too, didn't carry by phone. In 2002, a few years after he began giving all his time to refugees, he tells me, his wife and children left him for America.

During our talk, his phone rings again and again. He tells me his own displacement story. He was a communist, and, in the 1980s, the Islamic Republic killed or jailed all of his friends. "One day I realized, if I die, nothing will change. I had to go. So, I climbed the mountains to Turkey."

He says he's been vilified by the Dutch who refuse to believe that he doesn't take money from vulnerable refugees. He works one day a week for a lawyer and earns enough. Why shouldn't he spend his free days on work he believes in? Is the world so cynical? No one who works eighteen hours a day does it for money — those are obsession hours. "I want to say that this government isn't friendly to refugees. It sends them back into danger."

Yesterday, Frank van Haren told me a bit more about this man, whose role baffles me. "Ahmed Pouri is a volunteer," he said. "Not a lawyer, but close to a lawyer. He is a good man. He keeps fighting, but he's not nuanced. The bad guy is always the government. The good guy is the poor foreigner." I know that I'm in for many stories, so I prepare to listen. Ahmed Pouri doesn't even pause for his coffee. The stories pour out of him.

"In twenty-four years the most shocking thing I've seen is the way they turn people into plants," he says. He tells story after story of raped women finding their way to PRIME, his NGO. One young woman became homeless and was taken in by a stranger who kept her locked in a room for three years. She was raped every night, by many. She never spoke up, for fear of being tossed into detention. She escaped and found Mr. Pouri but was too ashamed to go public. "She had no personality left."

Another woman was sleeping in Central Station when, at around 1 a.m., a policeman came to her and said, "It's cold here. You can sleep at my house." There she was raped for an entire night by three men. Pouri told her, "If you have the guts to say this on television, we'll make them pay." But the woman didn't want to be forever associated with that shameful moment — it wasn't her story, and she didn't want to brand herself.

"These things happen because they put you on the street," says Mr. Pouri, "until you agree to dig your own grave and lie in it. They take away your dignity until you agree to help them kick you out. You see, the human rights standard is *bed, bath, bread.* But they keep those things from refugees until they help with their own deportation. The Iranian embassy won't issue you a passport unless *you* request it. If you refuse to request a passport, the IND can't return you to Iran. So, the Dutch say you can't eat or stay at the camps, unless you go to the embassy (of the nation that tried to kill you!) and ask for a passport. If you say no, you're on the streets. From there, you could end up in detention for eighteen months at a time."

He tells me about a client who lived for twenty-six years in the Netherlands, eleven of those in detention. They kept catching him for minor infractions (sleeping in stations, squatting) and putting him into detention, sometimes for the maximum time, sometimes less. "Who would spend eleven years in jail if they could go back? At some point, is it so hard to believe that home isn't an option?" Even by strict Dutch logic, he has proved his case by his choices, because that eleventh year in Dutch jail is not preferable to requesting a passport home. It just isn't — unless home wants to kill you. But by that time, he was a schizophrenic. "What right do you have to make a man crazy?" says Mr. Pouri. "Why should he come here looking for help and return mad? People kill themselves in detention and in the camps. In detention, they look in every hole in your body. It's crushing humiliation, and it retraumatizes all the rape victims. There's a rape victim screaming and four guards pour onto her, their hands everywhere. They have no sense of how a traumatized person behaves when touched. And for Iranian culture, you know this, there is nothing worse. And let me ask, why not use airport scanners? Because they want to humiliate; the law is designed to crush people from Eastern cultures," he takes a breath. "Imagine a life spent between the streets, the camps, and jail, not because you're a criminal or have no skills, but just because no country wants you!"

In all these years, I've never met a more passionate advocate for the displaced. Several times Mr. Pouri's voice breaks. He tears up. We are at the epicenter of his own story. Despite my suspicious nature, I believe every word from this man.

I ask him who calls him all the time — his phone never stops ringing. Everyone, he says, from lawyers to refugees to activists, police, professors, allies (later Frank van

Haren, Forough, and Pooyan confirm this). They call him for bridge jumpers and hunger strikers. Hardly anyone else will defend them. And the Dutch don't know what to say. A man stands on a wall and the police say, "Don't you care about your girlfriend? Why do you want to die?" Pouri knows that the man has said goodbye to such concerns for a while now. Another is on a bridge; he has asked the authorities to phone Pouri. He wouldn't ask this if he wanted to die, but Pouri doesn't let him off so easily. "You climbed up there, dragged everyone out of bed. Now you need demands. People have faces to save. If you come down for nothing, you'll be in jail for wasting everyone's time."

Hunger strikers are a special case, because the authorities don't like to have their arms twisted. "If it's more than thirty days, I know they're telling the truth. A person who can last thirty days is telling the truth. The first week is very hard. Most people stop then. After a week, you can go for three weeks. But by the fourth week, you feel death coming. A man called me from jail. He said, 'I want to use my claws and eat the dirt of these walls. My stomach hurts so much.' In detention they put food in front of you every day. To refuse it for that long, you must believe you'll die at home. The people who continue, they have something to say, some true reason.

"Showing someone the truth of your past is so complicated, Miss Dina," he says. Memories are full of inconsistencies. I can see why he despairs of this particular battle-field: memories. It's like fighting on clouds. The Dutch, all they listen for is inconsistency: is the time or location you gave at the start of the interview different from the end? If you fumble and give two answers, this is proof of dishonesty, not human error.

And human frailty afflicts both sides of the table. Officers can become power mad and vindictive. A woman and her lawyer, one of the idealists who work extra hours for nothing, have prepared a perfect case: her infant son is Dutch through his father. The law says he is entitled to his mother. Her case is routine. The officer asks at the start, as an aside, "Where is your old expired passport? Did you leave it at home?" She says yes. She doesn't know where that old thing is stashed. Hours later, he asks, again casually, "So your old passport, it's at the embassy?" She nods. It doesn't matter. It's long gone. He says, "You are lying," and rejects her claim.

Her lawyer says, "What does it have to do

385

with you? It's an expired passport from the country she's denouncing. Pay attention to the relevant documents!" She says, "Here's the birth certificate, the child's Dutch passport, the passport of the Dutch father. I can get a 'yes' from a judge in five minutes if you want to waste more money. Why not end this now?"

"Because it's my decision," the officer says. "Here, I decide."

Often people come to Mr. Pouri frustrated with Dutch logic, their strategic ignorance of the ways of brutal nations. No matter what happens, the Dutch say, "He was given his democratic rights." Three Kurdish boys were sent back to Turkey and killed. Both governments called the killings suicide, even after one family showed proof that the barrel of the gun was longer than the boy's arm, that the casing was found twenty meters away. "We asked the Turkish," repeated the Dutch. "They say it was a suicide."

And then there is the problem of what people say on arrival day, before they speak to lawyers or Mr. Pouri. As in Houshiar's case, LGBTQ Iranians take a long time to believe that gayness isn't shameful. They're embarrassed. The same is true for rape victims. On day one, they stumble onto a half-baked story and they're stuck with it. Once Mr. Pouri was called to speak to a man who had refused to tell IND that he was raped in Iranian jail. He was religious, humiliated, desperate to forget. He kept saying, "My body is dirty. I'm dirty. I hate my body." He was sweating and crying as he spoke. He wept while Mr. Pouri tried to calm him. "Son, do you know that you are a champion? Do you understand? You survived all that torture. You survived and didn't give up any of your friends. Be proud of yourself! Your body withstood all that — don't insult it! Don't say stupid things. Rape is just a torture. Many of my friends have survived torture."

The man wouldn't be comforted, and so Mr. Pouri brought in an old communist friend who was tortured after the Iranian revolution. He wasn't poetic or emotional, like Pouri. He spoke in the language of brothers at war. He said, as fact, "All that matters is that you didn't give up your friend."

As he finishes this story, Mr. Pouri shakes his head. "When you finally bring the IND the truth in the second case, after you've worked through the trauma and self-hate, the Dutch say, 'You went off and learned the system. You've been coached. You're lying.' They don't think, maybe you had some therapy. A raped Iranian man isn't like a raped Dutch man. They will never understand this. And so, what happens? These victims of atrocities stick to that first generic story they told, they stick to the bullshit about becoming a Christian after their child's miraculous healing."

Before saying goodbye, I ask Mr. Pouri for his most splendid memory. He takes no time in answering. It is Zeinab, another Turkish Kurd. She was raped in a room across from her husband, who was also raped. When he discovered that she too was violated, he tried to kill her. She ran away, spent three winter nights in a phone booth with two toddlers. Finally, she found Mr. Pouri. The case took years, with several rejections. One day, she arrived at the office as scheduled, to receive news from Mr. Pouri. He said, "Zeinab, you got a negative again. What did you do in that interview?"

Her shoulders dropped. "I don't know what else to do," she muttered.

"Don't look so glum," he said, giving her a sad smile. "Go get us some sweets from across the street." She frowned and stared at him like he was crazy. "To celebrate, because, I lied. You got your papers."

He expected her to laugh at the joke, but

she didn't. She dropped onto the ground and wept for thirty minutes. As the minutes passed, one by one, the workers broke into tears. I imagine that Mr. Pouri was the first one.

"Her life was changing. And, do you know what, her story started to come out involuntarily. She sat there and named all of the houses she had passed through. All of the rapes. She listed every night she had run out with the children to escape a rapist. She named the men." Here Mr. Pouri stops, his voice breaking. He wipes his eyes and apologizes, but I'm crying too. We're a couple of silly, idealistic Iranians on a hopeless mission, crying in an airport café, while a family glances over from the next table.

"After thirty minutes," he says, "she got up from the ground, her misfortunes forgotten. She left them on that floor. She said, 'Ahmed, I always thought that if you got me an answer, I'd dance for an hour on this table. And here I am crying.' It was the true, honest response of her body. There was no pretense. No awareness of her audience." Sometimes the truth requires drama to show itself fully. "It was the pure, and beautiful, and honest response of the human. She didn't let them turn her into a plant. So, I took a photo. I thought, *I won't ask. If I ask, I'll lose the true moment."*

VIII

For centuries, the civilized world has respected "the right of asylum." It is an ancient juridical concept recognizing the right of the imperiled to sanctuary. Historically, whatever criticisms arise, every Western government has respected and understood this principle — until now. In the new century, this simple, foundational belief is in question among the world's freest, most comfortable populations. When they do internalize the obligation to make room, they do so grudgingly, or with arguments about the supplication and usefulness of immigrants. Most, still, call them liars, opportunists, a scourge. It is heartbreaking how many innocents run from their beloved villages or shanties or farms and whisper along the way, *We only have to reach Europe. They will take us. The civilized world is kind; it has the Geneva Convention, a court of human rights. After meals, there is food to throw away.* "They sell you the birds of the sky!" says Mr. Pouri.

Refugees will spend the rest of their lives battling to be believed. Not because they are liars but because they're forced to make their facts fit narrow conceptions of truth.

An officer digging for a single inconsistency does not act in good faith. This is not how honest people listen for truth.

"I've been sleeping in phone booths with my children for a month." *Your clothes are clean. Where do you wash them?*

"A powerful Basiji vows to kill me." *It sounds like a personal matter.*

"I'm a lesbian from Ethiopia. I will be killed." How do you have sex with another woman? Describe it to me.

How is one to present the truth to such a listener? When he accepts only one danger, and there are hundreds. When he has no empathy for the daily threat of unchecked violence; when the soldiers, who may not have been targeting you specifically, shattered your psyche, nonetheless. How do you make your *true* story the "right" kind of true? If your listener already has far greater lies embedded into their worldview, then the only way to sneak the truth into their mind is covertly, like sneaking medicine into a child's food. Perhaps this is why Christ spoke in parables.

Truth is hard work — it is rigor. You can lie with sloppy facts. And you can tell the truth with well-crafted fiction. It is all a question of motive: whatever your technique, do you wish for the listener to come closer or farther from understanding a place, a situation? If after hearing your story, they could drop into your past and live it for themselves, would they say, "I understand now," or would they feel tricked?

Stories lie when they're dead, when they reveal nothing new about the world. When they're heartless or mindless or a deflection from more important stories. When characters are one-dimensional or flat, they lie. Language lies when it obfuscates, or distracts from the way things are.

George Orwell warned that the most common way we lie isn't with stories but with words, which we twist to suit our purposes. When we rely on clichés, for instance, we try to pass off shallow ideas as considered ones.

One of my business school classmates died. His friend shared the news via email. In minutes, replies appeared: "Words cannot describe," said one. "Beyond devastating," said another. *We sincerely feel. Our sincerest grief. Our deepest condolences.* I was struck by the hyperbole: "beyond devastating" from one who hasn't chosen to see the deceased in a decade is untrue. Devastating is the end of a spectrum: what is beyond it? What do you say if your own child dies?

The language of grief is raw. Grieving people don't use prefabricated phrases. They succumb to the five senses, to surprising images. My classmates weren't sad. They were "replying all." This is how our public figures speak to us. This is the language of "thoughts and prayers," and, as recent experience shows, tired, empty sentiments lead to inaction. Lying happens in the most benign well-meaning moments.

Originality is the privilege of the educated. And yet, when the refugee refuses to be original or specific, her story fails; she is sent away. If, in her terror and shame, her memory alters or embellishes, collapsing ten years of suffering into a year, or changing a lost hand to a lost arm, it is because she knows that if you were transported to her home, you'd see hangings, shootings, beheadings. You'd say, "Get the hell out."

When you lift your babies into a dinghy, you show your truth. Shame, trauma, and fear may strike you mute, but that act is enough. "No one leaves home, unless home is the mouth of a shark," writes poet Warsan Shire.

And here is the biggest lie in the refugee crisis. It isn't the faulty individual stories. It is the language of disaster often used to describe incoming refugees — *deluge* or *flood* or *swarm.* These words are lies.

Many news outlets report total asylum *requests* as a proxy for asylum seekers. "Sometimes, this includes second requests," says Mr. Pouri. Another source of double-counting error is the Dublin Regulation, which limits asylum applications to one European country; many who enter the Netherlands have already registered in another European country. When they are sent back there, Dutch entry data aren't adjusted. "You can't just count each time someone enters the door. If the true number is a fraction of what some of the news claims, then this is fear mongering with a motive."

UNHCR data show 68 million displaced people in the world. Of these, 40 million are internally displaced, 25 million are refugees, and 3 million are asylum seekers. But, these numbers don't specify that *most* refugees go to neighboring countries. Only a few million try for Europe, and yet, everyone thinks that Syria and Afghanistan and Iraq are emptying into the West. In 2017, the twenty-eight European Union countries had 650,000 first-time asylum seekers. That's 1,270 per million people in the population, or one refugee per thousand natives. Europe turned away more than half of those. The other half became EU refugees — adding one refugee per roughly two thousand in population for that year. Put another way, you'd need to go to four massive weddings or two graduations or a small concert to encounter a single new refugee.

That is not a deluge. Looking down from high above, an honest image isn't a flood or swarm. It's a small stream, or a thin, dying herd, finding its way onto a vast, fertile land. The world isn't pouring into Europe. What few broken and wretched lives the richest nations take in, they should do so graciously, as the chief consumers of the world's bounty. In many cases, the pursuit of that bounty is the very thing that has impoverished and war-ravaged the East. Maybe we should just pay our dues. Maybe we shouldn't lose our minds if we see four Muslims walking down the street, *one time.*

Nativist fury, not an exile's pleas for rescue, is the irrational spectacle, the unearned reaction, in today's refugee narrative.

And yet, here is the dilemma at the heart of asylum storytelling: With each passing day, the refugee behaves less like an honest petitioner. Like the lover kept waiting, his desire overwhelms him. He becomes intense, unattractive. What irony for the asylum seeker to know that every hour in limbo makes his story less believable ("I can't tell . . . he's hysterical!") and salvation less likely. He grows frantic, a risk to a new country. Meanwhile, the actual hysteria, the insidious nativist rhetoric shouted down from safe perches, doesn't sound like a lie at all — it sounds clever, rational, calm.

Waiting *compels* melodrama. So, if in desperation the exile decides to take a breath, learn the rules (according to those who cringe at Eastern manifestations of sorrow), and make a true thing appear true, is that a lie?

This question never fails to plunge me in icy shame, transporting me to my high school remaking, the admissions committees who, thinking they had found passion and talent, fell for the symptoms of my disproportion.

The last thing Mr. Pouri tells me is that, after a few months, all the refugees forget his phone number. They fall out of touch. They never return to thank him. "They think Europe is paradise. That if they can only be free of Iran or Iraq or Turkey, life will be heaven. Soon they realize that it's not." Once the new life begins, bringing its own complications, people get mired in the everyday. They forget the rapture they once felt. Calming is a part of assimilation, after all. Great joys and dramas pass quickly into the air.

I say goodbye to Mr. Pouri an hour before my flight. He offers to walk me to the gate. As I'm packing up my things, he reaches into his briefcase and pulls out a box of mixed nuts. "I knew I'd take up your time to prepare for flying, so I brought you this for your journey."

I'm starving, and unsure what to say. The nuts throw me off my game; he doesn't seem to notice. "Thank you, Agha Pouri," I say in Farsi.

At the gate, he says goodbye, pats me on the back. A guard stares at us. In our functional clothes, we look very much the refugees we once were.

I'm grateful for all that he's told me. On the plane, I remind myself to keep in touch, even as the months pass and that feeling wanes.

When I grow up, I want to be like Agha Pouri. Why did his family leave him? Maybe I don't know the whole story. Of course, I don't.

I spend the flight remembering Baba, his pockets full of sour cherries, whom I left behind thirty years ago, in a third-floor office in Isfahan.

■ ■ ■ ■

PART FOUR:
ASSIMILATION

■ ■ ■ ■

(on shame, past selves,
and chameleon life)

I

In the Edmond Public Library, one early nineties afternoon in the stacks, I came upon the solution to this puzzling universe we now inhabited — *Harvard.* It became the great project of my young life. I had found my future home, a place with no stepsisters eating their feelings, no stepfathers bursting with unspent fury, a place without tube-topped grandmothers watching and judging, without blond boys with names like Chad and Brad and Tanner and Taylor shouting that you belong in your druggie apartment complex. Instead, this new place would be full of strange girls who count everything, who maybe have a raw spot on their neck, or maybe their arms shoot out in front of them sometimes, or maybe they don't have these quirks but they love stories and puzzles and math problems, funny girls like I was in Iran, girls who would one day change the world. The criteria were daunting. Everyone with a hope of getting in had stellar grades and test scores. They were all athletic and brave. Most were nationally recognized for something. It would be hard, but not impossible. Soon I would be twelve, and this was my great advantage — no one my age was planning yet, but they soon would. I only had a handful of years to learn to do something, anything, better than every other kid in the country.

I considered swimming and tennis. I had learned to swim in the brain-melting heat of Dubai, so I had stamina, and tennis was my mother's girlhood sport, her pastime before the revolution. I signed up for a beginning lesson at the YMCA. I showed up with an old racket and blue street shorts down to my knees and glanced around. "Am I in the wrong class?" I asked the instructor, a boy my age, when the class filled with six-year-olds. "Nope," he said, undaunted. "Let's do this!" In our suburb, it seemed, people chose their sports early. There were too many wealthy girls in Oklahoma with more passion for tennis than I had, more money, more time and muscle. I would never even win a local title. I ruled out swimming for the same reason, though I found a low-hanging fruit: I could be an American Red

Cross lifeguard just by passing a series of timed tests.

I chose Tae Kwon Do, not because of my stepfather and his third-degree black belt, but over his loud objections that it wasn't a sport for women. I chose it precisely because it was deeply unattractive to other girls. It wasn't sexy or elegant. All the glory came from bloodying or being bloodied. You could really fuck up your face.

I convinced my mother that it was ideal — it would teach me self-defense. I would have to share sweaty helmets and practice strangleholds on geriatric hobbyists for months before being allowed to practice on serious athletes, but when I walked into that studio, I knew I was right. There were almost no girls my age. The male-to-female ratio was roughly three to one. And further improving my odds, championships at the local, state, and national levels were handed out by gender, belt, age, and weight categories. I could win a national championship against skinny green-belt girls; I could starve myself into their weight category, make myself a block of muscle competing with anorexics. If this was the way one gained admission to a top university in the United States, strange as it might seem, I could adapt.

I began practicing Tae Kwon Do for an hour a day, three times a week. Soon, I was at the studio every weekday, then every day, then four or five hours a day. I stopped eating fats. Then fats and sugar. Soon, I was surviving on water-packed tuna, pita bread, mustard, baked potatoes, watery fruit, and gallons of water. In a year, I was one long block of muscle and had stopped menstruating. My thighs no longer touched. I never relaxed my abs. Highly literal as I was in my new language, I thought bouncing a coin off my abs was a real thing — I made it a goal. I woke from frequent nightmares, and my first waking instinct was to tighten my abs. Each time I performed drills on the kicking bag, pivoting on the thick carpet until the balls of my feet bled, I thought, I am a refugee girl with brains and muscles, and I've landed in a country where every road is open to me. There may be stronger, better people who hate Iranians or women, but I'm deaf to them. I have a green card tucked away with Maman's treasures, in a spot I can check. I have everything. I won't be a pussy about bloody feet.

Some nights I failed to lift my own spirits. I would wake up and cry in Maman's arms. "I'll never get into Harvard. I'll die ordinary and forgotten."

"You won't!" said Maman. "You're already not ordinary."

"I'm not Harvard-worthy," I'd weep. "Look, my knees are a mess."

Maman snorted. "Oh god, Dina *joon,*" she said in English. "You're crazy but very proudable! You get in. Please eat something."

I won many trophies and medals, including a state title in both forms and sparring — every medal was stamped with two men fighting, just like the wrestling medal I had found in the empty closet. I displayed them proudly: those girls who had teased me were cheerleaders now, a sport founded on the notion that women should stand aside and cheer on men instead of sweating and bleeding for their own success. Girls like that would get into Oklahoma State and they'd throw parties to celebrate. I felt sad for their wasted potential. What happens, I wondered, if the next Marie Curie is born into a pretty Oklahoma body? She'd take a science class or two where the teacher would keep calling on Chad or Brad, she'd stamp out her frustrations on the tennis court, and she'd die the wife of some middle manager — America, I was learning, was no feminist paradise.

And yet, Oklahoma gave me some of my

greatest joys.

In 1994, when I was fifteen, we became American citizens. I was relieved. The following Fourth of July, we attended a citizenship ceremony on the football field of a local college campus. Dozens of new citizens from the last year would be sworn in with us. It was a bittersweet day, the stadium filled with cheering locals, a line of men, women, and children winding around and around the field toward a microphone at the end zone, where each of us would be named and sworn in. I stared in wonder at the others in line: I didn't realize there were this many other brown and yellow people in Oklahoma. Yes, there were a handful of black people, a few Jews here or there. But this many Indians? This many Sri Lankans and Pakistanis and Chinese and Bangladeshis and Iranians and Afghans? Where had they been hiding? (Not that I had looked.)

Halfway through the ceremony, an elderly Indian man was led to the microphone, where he introduced himself and swore allegiance to the United States. When he was finished, he raised his fists and thrashed the sky. "I AM AMERICAN!" he shouted into the microphone. "FINALLY, I AM AMERICAN!" The crowd erupted, joining his celebration. As he stepped away, he wobbled and collapsed from the effort, but someone caught him. He turned back and smiled to the crowd to show he was OK, that this fit of joy hadn't killed him, then walked away.

That's my favorite day as an American, my first one as a citizen, still unsurpassed. No one was putting on a face that day. No one felt obliged or humbled, imagining their truer home. That old man was heaving with love. The people in the stands were roaring with it. It's a complicated memory for me now. I refuse to deny the simple and vast beauty of it, though I know that they cheered not the old man himself, but his spasm of gratitude, an avowal of transformation into someone new, into them.

I loved winning at a male sport. I was still angry about so many things — *hijab,* the Islamic Republic, the fat old church men who made high school football players feel like gods while they shamed women who dared to want too much. Try as I did, I couldn't reconcile Christianity with what every instinct told me I deserved; I couldn't believe that God wanted humility and submission from me, and greatness from some boy who could hardly add. Now and then, I had a small triumph. One fall, at sixteen, I spent a Saturday in an advanced

407

Red Cross Lifeguarding course. After years of intensive Tae Kwon Do, my legs were skinny and iron hard, like golf clubs. That morning, twenty teenage lifeguards entered the pool for an endurance test, treading water without arms for ten minutes. It was an easy test: most of the kids in the class were on swim teams. We yawned through it. But, when the whistle blew and the test was done, only half the group left the water. The rest smiled and treaded on. Everyone cheered — a challenge! At the thirty-minute mark, it was down to a handful of boys, me, and one other girl. "Let's get the ladies out and see who's got this thing!" someone shouted. The girl and I glanced at each other. She mouthed, *Keep going?* and I nodded. When she dragged herself out at around fifty minutes, the boys hooted. Someone slapped her butt. I decided I would die in this water before I let those boys outlast me. I closed my eyes and conjured up the moral police and our leering associate pastor and the Oklahoma parishioners who talked casually of protecting their daughters from the corruption of college. And when I opened my eyes, eighty-seven minutes had passed, a whistle was blowing, and the last boy was lifting himself out. The class stood dripping at the edge of the pool, clapping as if it had been a friendly game. I treaded water for another minute as a *Fuck you, bro.* Then I got out, accepting somebody's extended arm, and I collapsed on the tiles.

I lay there for a while watching the inside of my eyelids change from reds to blues. "Well, that was weird and intense," a far-off voice muttered.

How else was a person supposed to live, I wondered? How do you find any happiness without goals? Without a place to go? Maybe it was just me — home was already far away; I couldn't be stuck in this nothing land.

Six months before nationals, I pinched a spinal nerve. I signed up for the tournament anyway. I stopped practicing but swam every day. At night, my mother held my feet in her lap as I strengthened my core. I barely ate. My lips turned blue. When I returned to the studio, the pain was bearable. To protect my back, I made a rule: every second in sports gear, my stomach muscles must be flexed. I'm not going to Harvard in a wheelchair.

At the weigh-ins for the nationals in San Antonio, I stripped down to my underwear. I hadn't drunk water for a day. I had shaved my body and barely avoided laxatives. I made it into the lower weight class by .01 pound. If I hadn't, I would've closed my eyes and stripped down to nothing. I would've run to the bathroom and expelled what bile remained. I would've stood naked before a crowd of men and shaved my head and eyebrows.

Daniel had signed up, too. For a thirteen-year-old boy, winning the nationals was a much tougher prospect — every rich boy in Oklahoma did martial arts. And he had nothing at stake. He ate normal foods, practiced an hour or two a day, had friendships and hobbies. At nationals, he completed his fights and waited around with his friends.

Daniel and I weren't close, and moments of sibling kindness were rare. But when I stumbled away from my last fight, having just beaten a fast, angry girl by a single point to secure the gold medal, Daniel rushed to my side with an ice cream bar — Dove, the most expensive kind. He had spent his own money and, though it looked like poison, I ate it for his sake. Iranians show love with gifts of food, and over the years I've received many such offerings — maybe one or two others felt as true as Daniel's Dove bar.

I spent the next hour in the bathroom

enduring the violent protests of a body that hadn't digested fat, sugar, or dairy for over a year. I managed to make it to the winner's block and then went back home. Having accomplished my goal, I quit Tae Kwon Do and returned to eating normally. My coach was dumbstruck — had I lost my passion for the sport?

"What passion?" I said. "I'm not an athlete. This was about Harvard."

I was beginning to worry my mother — if one day my lips were a little bluer than usual, she'd go bananas. "Mom! Who cares about my lips?" I said. I had begun calling her *Mom* a year into our American lives. It felt fine.

One sticky Oklahoma Saturday, she suggested that we treat ourselves to pedicures or pastries or something. I had just unlocked the front door. An armful of books in mismatched sizes threatened to spill to the floor. *How can I go for pastries?* I thought. How would going for pastries help get me out of here? Would a single pedicure and fancy coffee guarantee me pedicures and fancy coffees weekly, or even monthly, for the rest of my life? Or at least a significant enough portion of my life so that I might say later on, *In this era, I went for pedicures*

411

and coffees? Because here was something I knew: when a life is obliterated, all its joys taken away, what makes memories stick is repetition. If an experience isn't part of an established-enough pattern to survive the dulling of memories over decades, what's the use of it? You don't become refined because you drank a good Merlot *that one time* or traveled to Europe *one summer back in the day.* A flaky pastry or an expert massage would be lost on me now — it would be a waste — I hadn't earned it, or kept it, or made a slow study of its quality. The key is to have a wide range of these good things . . . *regularly.*

So maybe after college, I could be the sort of person who spends a year learning what makes an oyster good, and then a year stomping French grapes, and then a year getting Thai massages. But if I spend my time now "treating myself" to useless, one-off versions of those things whose quality I can't even assess, making small, imprecise memories doomed to the abyss, am I not wasting my life? Wasn't I lucky to have been taken along in my mother's escape? How could I, after being granted that, ignore my own flight now? It would be ungrateful and un-American and wrong. I might as well just find the nearest alley and go smoke some midafternoon crack.

I called it "my great project," but only in the privacy of my mind, because it wasn't just about college, and I didn't want to hurt my mother any more than I already had. I didn't want her to know that it was her fate I wanted to escape. Our flight was still so fresh, and the thought that I too could lose everything I had worked for, my entire identity as a smart, capable girl, and be looked down on by ordinary people was like waking to the lid of a coffin sliding shut, like catching a glimpse of a boulder rolling atop it as the light slivers out. I needed a way to protect myself from that fate — my brilliant Maman, all her squandered years of study. My great project was about trans- forming, becoming someone unrelated to Iran, my family, my dramatic circumstances. It was about proving my worth in every sphere: body, mind, spirit. It was about sit- ting on a perch from which I could judge Oklahoma the way it had judged my mother.

Now and then, I would glimpse her in mo- ments of quiet rage. She had failed the Medical Licensing Exam (USMLE) twice. Both times, her score was exactly the same, a statistical improbability, even if she hadn't studied sixteen hours a day the second time. I'd hear her say that the tests were classist and rigged against foreign doctors, that the facilitators were racist and xenophobic and all kinds of other things. She tried to tell them that they had made a clerical error, but no one would believe her because of her accent — oh, how the wit dulls with a few wrong words. Later I would see that my mother's broken English was far more beautiful than my perfect one. She had a strong voice, writers would say. "I got no wave" is so much more evocative than "my phone isn't getting reception." "Here is all over poops," is leagues more succinct and indignant than "There's too much shit on this street." This is my mother's razor tongue. But back then, I thought she was just making excuses — if only she had studied as hard as I did.

"I have too much work to go for a treat," I told my mom.

By then my mother and I were already what we would become: two people forever separated by the circumstances of our child-hoods: hers, a strict Iranian upbringing in the home of modern but austere Tehrani intellectuals; mine, those unstable refugee years in Dubai and Rome followed by asylum in the United States, where I was a lesser citizen among Americans who had seen nothing of the world.

If I was unkind toward Oklahoma, my view of Iran was worse. Once the backdrop of every warm childhood memory, I now considered it inferior — shedding its taint was part of repaying my debt to the West. Iran was a shameful, confused part of my past, a jumble of contradictions I could solve only by murdering the wild village girl and becoming the best kind of American: elegant and iron hard, a woman without need.

"What if you don't get into Harvard?" my mother's friend, an Indian American psychologist, asked once. "Can you be happy somewhere else?"

"I doubt it," I said. We were sitting in our living room. She wore a sari and perfume and arranged herself in irritatingly restful poses. My feet were bloody from drills. I wore my martial arts bottoms atop my lifeguard swimsuit. My hair smelled like chlorine and my nails were chewed raw.

Though I could easily see that she was underestimating and judging me, that she wasn't one of the people who could ever come to understand, it felt important that I didn't waste her time. I respected professional people — my parents were doctors. Or, rather, Maman *had* been in Iran. I was sure that what she needed was within my reach. I could get it for her, if only I could understand Americans enough, be successful enough in their eyes. This country was a meritocracy; it was fair — I would redeem us.

But here was this barefoot doctor with her russet toes on the couch, a fellow foreigner but so much more settled, eyeing the black ink smudge on the blade of my hand, plotting to advise me to "take it easy" or "make some friends." Her disapproval didn't frighten me — it meant I was doing things right. If my life was grueling, it was a kind of grueling that hadn't been imposed by politics or war; it was fair and rational and would bear fruit. It wasn't senseless as it had been when I lost my family and my *baba*'s village and our beautiful house and Baba along with it. In Iran, I had been a devourer of joy, boisterous daughter to a known pleasure-seeker.

Now I hated small indulgences. To veer from whatever toil you've chosen, just to wallow in the act of existing, breathing, eating, being rubbed down and groomed, like a fattening pig . . . it was *that* disgusting to me.

Waste was impossible, the height of entitlement and the first sign of impending catastrophe. It made my chest close in on itself. Nothing in the present mattered to me, only the future. All one-off things, therefore, whether pleasurable or sad or even physically torturous, didn't count. If something was finished or would soon be finished, it was irrelevant; I could look past it. And, so, I was invincible to everything but patterns: unending poverty, intellectual hunger, body fat, drudgery. The worst thing was to be wrongly categorized, as a worthless immigrant or a mediocre student or just a nameless Oklahoman working in a pharmacy or even my own doctor's office, ordinary and forever left there, to rot.

So, then, how could I take it easy with so much at stake?

The doctor leaned her head into her hand and stared at me. She spoke carefully. "Don't you think it's a little intense?" she said. "Focusing all your energy on just one thing?" I was done explaining. She was a waster of good fortune, a woman with brains and opportunities but small dreams.

But she pressed on. "Do you have a boyfriend?"

"I don't have time for that," I said. "And I don't plan to stay here."

"But you want to have a boyfriend someday?"

"At Harvard. I'll have one that goes there."

She laughed, because I had allowed a teasing quality to enter my voice. She said, "OK, fair enough. Tell me what you want to do then."

"I'm going to be an international corporate lawyer," I said. "On average, international lawyers earn 20 percent more for every language they speak. Did you know that? I'm studying French, and maybe Farsi will count, though it's not that important a language." She scoffed. Realizing I had been too much again, I added, "Because of the regime."

She must have known, on some level, that I was performing for her. "But what about fun?" The doctor shifted on the couch and eyed my sports gear. "Such pressure."

I shrugged. "I'll have fun when I've set up my life," I said.

"Forget about Harvard for now," she said. I could see in her expression that we were now just tolerating each other. She thought I was arrogant. I thought she was ungrateful, that she had failed to earn her place in America. "Let's talk about home."

Isn't that what we had been doing? Talking about Harvard was talking about home, my hope of one day having one that was suited to a strange, intense girl like me. Just because I didn't yet have it, this woman thought that I had no claim to the good feelings it gave me. Well, I'd show her the wonders I'd one day claim. No, actually I wouldn't show her, because I would be gone from Oklahoma and I wouldn't come back, or think of it, or any of the people in it. But, for now, she wanted to hear about Iran, so I told her about the Khomeini mural in my schoolyard.

"Who can survive like this?" she muttered near the end of our session, leaning back on our couch, her terracotta feet pulled beneath her haunches as she fondled her hairline with an idle finger.

For years I toiled. My school only offered three Advanced Placement classes, and though the counselor assured me that no one from Oklahoma was ever accepted to those universities, she agreed to help. I enrolled in a fourth AP class via satellite television, a fifth at a neighboring high school (to which I drove between classes), a sixth course alone after school with the French teacher, and a seventh, BC Calculus, at a table with different textbooks and three other overachieving misfits, in the corner of an easier course, AB Calculus — our teacher was a wizard of classroom management. Sometimes I felt like a fraud, trying for something that wasn't meant for me. The movies were clear: Harvard was for pretty white boys with money. Even my counselor didn't believe. But of the many things Tae Kwon Do taught me, the most vital was this: the body adjusts, just as the mind adjusts. "Habits take three weeks to form," said my instructor. "The suffering ends there." Every habit becomes easy with time. Every identity and practice and profession, no matter how grueling, is open to a person willing to survive for three weeks — it takes three weeks of hard work to begin transforming into anything you are pretending to be. And if you look and behave like it, it doesn't occur to anyone to call you a fraud.

I volunteered at the food bank, bagging crunchy peanut butter for the poor. I organized a citywide tutoring program that brought high schoolers from wealthy areas to middle school kids in poor neighborhoods. I worked several jobs. I hardly slept. On quiet Saturdays, I watched *Rudy,* a movie about a boy with zero chance of playing football for Notre Dame, who nevertheless does. People called me a robot, but they thought my ambition worthy of a nod in the halls. As we grew older, Oklahomans became accustomed to us; we made friends. Daniel, the darkest skinned of us, was ironically the most American and beloved. He played football, befriended cheerleaders, drove around town with white boys in Jeeps. "Just chill," he'd say to my OCD, when I surveyed the ground behind me for a beat too long, or checked the locks one too many times. We mellowed in our Iranian-ness, and the end of the Gulf War renewed the feelings of gratitude and American exceptionalism already in the air. We no longer frightened them.

We assimilated. We followed the rules. No family of four logged fewer hours of sleep — a typical midnight found Maman reading health policy textbooks, me doing calculus, Daniel writing poems, Rahim taking out an engine or marinating bulgogi. I began to imagine that one day I would grow into a person whose past didn't define her every step. That one day I would have time to care for my body, to mend my bloody feet, to let the calluses on my fingers heal. Maybe one day someone would love me.

At eighteen, I got into Princeton but not Harvard. I found that I didn't care. Princeton was the same, and was featured in as many glossy films. I had no loyalty to Harvard; and in fact, my loyalty was transferred instantly and forever by the simple fact that a great institution had said, *We want you.*

We had our choice of American students, and you, Dina Nayeri, are one worth having. How I craved to be claimed. If I couldn't have a country, I would have something equally indestructible. Princeton would be my home. Academia would be my home. I asked a surgeon to cut me a European nose — I begged Baba for the money. I dyed my hair chestnut in the bathtub. Sometimes as a reward, I ate secret spoonfuls of cream.

Recently a London friend told me about her aunt, who took a newly arrived Syrian boy into her home. She spoke of his allegiance to sell-by dates, to instructions on boxes. How strange that he should be so militant about written rules, when most would eat a ham a day past its date if their nose told them it's good. In the early days, you don't trust your own five senses, your intuition. You grasp at any instruction, and you hold on tight. After you learn, you are more versatile, able to make choices — but not yet.

It takes years even to *want* your agency back.

In my early twenties, I had news from Isfahan that Baba's wife had given birth to a daughter. "You have a half sister!" Baba said on the phone.

"No, I don't," I said, desperate to hang up.

"Yes," he said, hurt, "you do."

"Congratulations," I said, fuming. "But I'm the product of a mother with a PhD who busted her ass for decades. This girl's mother sits around the *manghal* getting high, so let's not throw around the word 'sister,' please."

"What a thing to say to your *baba.*" He cleared his throat.

"You have to get your baby ready for life, OK? You have to promise to get her English classes from an early age. Baba, are you listening?"

"OK, Dina *joon.*" He sounded tired. Iranian music I had long forgotten came on in the background. Now I wanted him to be quiet so I could hear. He told me a few more things about my half sister, about my cousins, aunts, and uncles — who had married, who was sick, who was well again.

At a pause, I said again, "If you don't get her English classes before she's ten, her life will be hard. English is everything — not just the stuff people say, but what they don't say. The world turns on English subtext."

"OK," he said. "It's not so easy here. People will ask questions, and good tutors are rare. And I think she'll be a simpler person than you."

"I'm the simplest person there is," I said. "That's how I can be sure."

He never enrolled her in English. Why would he? He trusted his own instincts, his own five senses, his language. He was home.

II

Spring 2017. Minoo phones me as I'm preparing a class on James Baldwin's "Sonny's Blues" and drafting an email to a parent who's wondering why, given hefty tuitions, I'm not teaching her child more Hemingway or Twain. Her primary concern, "How will she get by at cocktail parties?" Minoo, a newly arrived refugee, is living in a council flat the size of a shipping crate, with her sick husband and preadolescent son and daughter. She tells me that she thinks her son is good enough for an Arsenal boys' team. Can I do something for him? I'm confused. Then I remember that new refugees believe all settled Westerners have access to each other, that I belong to a secret network including the head coach of Arsenal. Minoo is my age, from Isfahan. A woman at her church asked that I befriend her, and for a year, I've consistently failed at that. I try to listen, to advise her. She stares wide-eyed and numb. I suggest ways to kick-start her new life, to smooth the way for herself and family. It's hard making suggestions. Do the concessions I'm asking of her amount to self-harm?

"Can you do something for him?" she asks. "Speak to someone?"

"Is he good?" I ask. "Is he already part of a team?"

"Yes, he's the best. He plays at school."

I write a Facebook post asking if anyone knows anyone. They don't. I watch videos of the boy keeping the ball in the air with his feet. I don't know how to judge its impressiveness. I call his coach. I ask him what the family should do for their son. "Look," he says, "the processes are in place. Recruiters come. The top kids get seen." I know this. The family is already in England, a country that takes its soccer seriously. Now they need to sweat. That's the rule. "He should just keep playing. Keep getting stronger."

I tell Minoo — I give her a long, thrilling pep talk about the road ahead, the toil and the sacrifice, the glorious final scene when her son doesn't get into Arsenal, but has worked hard enough to get into Oxford! How about that? My heart is beating — I love this story. She is disappointed.

We meet for coffee at a café in Camden.

Her eyes are puffy, her thin body weighed down. She drags herself. It's always a struggle to pay; she insists on buying my coffee though they're living off fumes. I have to pretend that I'm sensitive to the subtle differences in foam and that I have to be the one to order while she watches our purses. I return with two cappuccinos and a cookie. "You look tired," I say. "You need some sugar."

"We can't keep living like this," she says. The council has put the family of four, including a very ill husband, in a studio apartment so small you can touch the bathroom door and the kitchen table from the bed (which the four have shared for nearly a year). It's a coffin. Her husband is growing sicker. The children can't be in the flat after school, to do homework or to play, because it's stifling and unhealthy. I try to relate — Sam and I are temporarily living with his parents outside London with our baby. Everything is in flux. "In a year, we'll both be in our own homes," I tell her. "We'll have dinner parties with *ghorme sabzi* and we'll say, 'Remember the days when we were homeless and miserable and we couldn't tell the flat white from the cappuccino because the new Gail's barista was so perfectly useless?'" She laughs. "My Farsi is a mess," I say.

"It's not so bad," she says. "They say I have to practice English."

"We'll speak English then," I say. She smiles through her misery.

The next day in the private high school, one of my students arrives early to class. She's arranging a brunch for her friends. She sighs loudly and slams her laptop shut. "If we don't reserve today, we'll end up at Nando's!"

"What's Nando's?" I ask. It sounds familiar.

"A terrible restaurant chain," she says. Now I remember. Kaweh spoke of it. *If your kids are begging for Nando's . . .* I tell my student about Kaweh, the asylum lawyer, and about living off thirty-five dollars a week. She says, "Actually, to be honest, I secretly like Nando's."

Months pass. My real estate chain closes, and Sam, Elena, and I move into a flat in London. The council keeps sending Minoo letters, putting off hope of new housing. Her husband's condition worsens. Her children grow restless. I'm leaving soon for Greece, to visit two refugee camps. Maman Moti appears, with her manic devotion to a strange man, her neighbors with the radiation machine pointed through the planks of

427

her floor.

We decide to have a birthday party for Elena. I invite Minoo and her family. I ask Maman Moti if she'll come and speak to Minoo about becoming British: the initial struggle of transforming, the slow falling into place.

"I don't want anything to do with refugees," says Maman Moti, her lips tightening. She is adamant on this point — she repeats it fearfully. "I got away from that life. I'm not going to chase Iranians here."

She clears her throat and adjusts herself at my kitchen table. She wrings her hands. She wants to help me, but breaking her rule pains her. The English pride she's cultivating is ever at odds with latent immigrant self-loathing. I try another way. "You can be an example to this poor girl."

She looks me over and nods. "Of course, dear. I'll talk to her."

Maman Moti's philosophy is full-on assimilation. "You don't wear an Eskimo coat in the Sahara," she says. "In England, it's best to be English." For this, she considers herself progressive, modern. Once in reply to an obvious phishing scam email, she wrote a message that began, "Dear Microsoft, thank you for your kind letter." She takes great care with etiquette. "How society sees you makes your personality," she says.

She seems concerned about our obligations to Minoo. "But, darling, I don't have advice. This girl *must* leave the past in the past."

"I know, Maman Moti," I say, "I just want her to see how far you've come, that your life is easy now. I want her to see that it's possible."

Maman Moti nods gravely. At the party, she sits in a corner as she is served. To be fair, she's the oldest person in the room. No one expects her to mingle or blend. She speaks with Minoo for a while — they both look deeply uncomfortable. And yet in my imagination, they are two ends of the same story. Don't they each crave a word from the other side?

"I'm finished with that life," Maman Moti reminds us, afterward. "I told her to learn English immediately, no excuses, no sadness."

"Good," I say. I'm unsatisfied. I had imagined tears and hugs and grandmotherly wisdom. "What about the culture? What did you tell her?"

"To leave it behind! Don't go looking for other Iranians. Befriend the English. Learn English ways. I like Iranian food, but I also like tea in the afternoon with nice tea biscuits. I like cakes by Gü. Do you know Gü?"

What is she babbling about? "Gü is nice," she sighs. "I told her to keep her eyes on Jesus. Keep her eyes on the Lord, and all will be well." Her faith saddens me — all she wants is to succumb to someone. How can her response to exile be capitulation?

She adds, about her talk with Minoo, "I explained that the East rejected the Lord and so, he rejected them. Now the West accepts him and they have all the prosperity. We follow our Lord to prosperity."

A few months after Elena's birthday party, Mom visits from the States. I invite Maman Moti to lunch. She brings Gü. It's delicious. Maman is weirdly deferential to her, using formal Farsi pronouns, serving Maman Moti as if she's her mother's personal handmaid and not a woman with a doctorate. *Wow,* I think, t*his retired housewife really has her shit figured out.* She hasn't just assimilated to England: she could teach negotiations at Harvard Business School. Just withhold until you're worshipped. Funny she doesn't follow this rule with her English friends, on whom she dotes.

I decide to invite Minoo again, for a kebab cookout in the garden. I ask Maman if she can speak to her. "They're a family of exiled

Christians!" I say. "They're exactly like us. It would be unchristian not to."

When they arrive, Mom begins to grill them almost right away. Which church did you attend? Who was your pastor? Did you know so-and-so? When did you become born-again? How do you like your church here? She is making a point of using certain code words: flock, congregation, believers, born-again. I am appalled and embarrassed. But I know what Maman is doing. Their presence is bringing out her survival instinct. After thirty years, she lives in a universe where frauds have to be rooted out.

Minoo's husband answers evasively. He pretends to recognize a name or an address — the reasons seem clear to me. She is being pushy. Or maybe he's afraid of sharing information with strangers. Or maybe, as Pooyan says, he finds Christians in the West disappointing — maybe *we're* not devout enough for *him.* I definitely am not. Minoo helps in the kitchen. She's attentive and quick. When she smiles I notice a drop in the white of her eye, like a lodged tear. It's always been there; I'm sure I've seen it. She marvels at my uselessness in the kitchen. "Do you do *any* housework?"

I explain that Sam and I have a reverse-gender arrangement. I make the money. I

do as much around the house as her husband would — more.

"That makes no sense, Dina *joon,*" she
says. I fume.

That night, Maman wants to talk.
"They're not Christians," she says.

"How —" I begin, then change tack. "So,
what? They're refugees."

"Dina!" she says, frantic. "You don't know
their secrets. Didn't you see? They're afraid
of their shadow. You have a baby girl. Are
you insane?"

Oh my god — my pulse quickens. To what
dangers have I exposed my baby girl? How
do I fix it? Maybe if I make some calls I can
get my hands on their papers. Wait . . . *No.
No, this is in my head.* In *our* heads. In our
insane, rattled heads. I shake it off. "Of
course, they're scared!" I shout at her.
"They live in a three-by-three hole for a
year, then come out *one time* and you're
suspicious because they're not socially
perfect? They agree too much? They say
what we want to hear? They're just afraid of
us because we're settled and intimidating!
Don't you remember how scared we were?"

"Yes, that's right," she says, calmer now.
"But we were *never* afraid of our story. The
truth is the truth, and it has to be told. And
when did I say they have to be socially

perfect? We were having a nice talk about home, and you were so uncomfortable and making everyone else uncomfortable with your behavior — you should have seen yourself."

I fill a water glass with white wine. I feel the urge to abuse Sam, but he's doing the dishes alone and I'm not that much of a hobgoblin yet. I wish I had one of my old kick bags from Tae Kwon Do. I take my wine to bed and spend ten minutes remembering the way a double kick-pad claps against a roundhouse, stinging the top of your foot. It's not the singular sound of home — I haven't decided what that is yet — but one of them.

For a brief period early on, I translated words and customs for an unwilling Maman. I was only ten and, within months, I understood our new country in ways she couldn't fathom. Over time, she accepted some of my wild claims as American basics but, back then, she glared as if I was culpable in the West's sins. Some things I couldn't make her accept:

All church youth groups have a costume party for Halloween. They are not secret pagans. We don't have to move to an underground church.

433

Ice-skating is a tough sport. People don't practice for eighteen hours a day just so they can hold each other by the crotch on television.

If a boy with longish hair knocks on our door, it's because I have no friends. He isn't selling drugs. "Student Council" isn't the name of his gang. There's zero chance he'll talk to me tomorrow.

It was dispiriting, this period after (and before) Maman and I spoke the same language, when we were unmoored from each other, and I was a child drifting in a lonely world. I didn't forgive her for it until I was twenty-eight, when I moved to a French village and understood what it meant to burn with shame as a cheesemonger or a grocery clerk snorts as if you're stupid, oblivious to the name or reputation of your illustrious university.

After I met Minoo, I tried to explain what would soon happen to her daughter. "She will become English!" I said. "And you shouldn't be frightened. She'll do so much good with her fluency. She'll be able to slip in and out of every party, from Norooz dinner at grandma's to Easter dinner with the queen, like a beautiful little chameleon with her gorgeous dark hair and clever eyes." She squinted at the unknown word. "Never

434

mind," I said, because I didn't want to say "lizard." "She'll be happy, and English."

"Yes," said Minoo sadly, "but what about me?" I didn't feel sorry for her then; I thought only of her daughter, of how Minoo would drag the girl back as she struggled to fit in. I thought of Maman's refusal to let me shave my legs, wear shorts or skirts. Growing up was a constant fight with Maman, who saw every adolescent alteration as surrender to the hedonistic West: her child becoming a loose American teenager. Maybe I was meant to help Minoo's daughter. As for Minoo's transformation, I knew too little of that. I thought, *I'll introduce her to Maman and Maman Moti.*

It wasn't a mistake. The morning after the awkward cookout, Mom and I spoke again. We had both had a sleepless night. I made a pot of coffee. She said, "Minoo is a sweet girl. Of course, we'll help. Of course, you should befriend her." The instinct to cut all ties from the old life is so strong — my mother, brave as she is, is still nervous around new arrivals, still afraid of being hunted down by the past. As is *her* mother. As am I.

Later we talked about perspective in people's stories, what is true, and what is imagined, and whose memory is most reliable. "Last night I was thinking," she said. "The gospels are four versions of the same story. And they are all somehow true." It was two long, narrow roads, finally crossing.

In the early summer the Camden Council sends Minoo another noncommittal letter. She asks if I can do anything. I join her for a visit to her caseworker. I bring Sam's brother (called Daniel, like my brother), a barrister. After months of refusing to let me see her home, always meeting me in cafés and parks and subway stops, Minoo relents, and we visit. There's nowhere to look — her husband sits beside their children on the bed. A callus part of me wants him to reach out and touch the bathroom door, the kitchen table, so I can confirm this for my rant to the council bureaucrats. Minoo serves fruit and tea. We stare at a pile of grim papers.

At the meeting, a young caseworker explains the process. Minoo can apply for medical disability points for her husband, and she can use those points toward a suitable home in Camden. Otherwise, she can get in line for subsidized private housing. It's a labyrinth. After an hour, I think I understand it. I ask if the two processes can begin simultaneously, so that she doesn't have to wait twice if the request for points is rejected. The caseworker says yes. I translate as she takes Minoo through a series of humiliating forms. No Iranian would continue being my friend after I've witnessed and taken part in this abjection. When we leave, I ask about the timeline and next steps. The caseworker says, ever cheerfully, that the application will be processed within days and the medical points resolved.

When we don't hear from the council in several weeks, I call again. I can't reach the worker, though she sends annoyed emails hinting that my involvement isn't welcome. When I reach her by phone, she says Minoo's file is missing key medical statements. "You never mentioned those," I say.

"Maybe not in the meeting with you, but Minoo knew." She didn't.

"But I triple-checked every step with you. I asked many times. I made a list." We chase up the forms. Then they say that it would help to have a letter attesting to the worsening of the husband's condition in the flat. We jump through hoop after hoop until the request is rejected. We discover that the two processes were indeed *not* simultaneous — the caseworker claims never to have said that it was. The wait begins again at day one, with Minoo's small children still sharing a bed with a sick man, and Camden Council officials claiming, straight-faced, that this is acceptable to them.

"They made my neighbor wait four years," Minoo tells me, her voice breaking. "Then her kids grew and they said she was no longer eligible."

Minoo falls into a depression. A friend at Amnesty International tells me that Minoo's situation is enviable compared with some others. She reminds me of the twenty-eight-day rule: asylum seekers have four weeks after acceptance to find a home, a bank account, and a job, or they face the streets. At least Minoo's family has the one bed, the roof, the sink. She's farther along the long road to respectable Britishness.

Minoo and I drift apart. I try to adjust to the way she communicates. Again, I fail. Iranian pride has only two textures: marble hard or crumbling. It's never a malleable, habitable thing. Her situation makes hers worse. She responds in two-word texts, even to open questions. Then, randomly, she says she misses me very much. She can't calibrate. I realize that I'm her only friend. She is trying to behave as she thinks British friends do — cool, unmoved. I recoil. Then I text again. We meet in parks, and she always shows up at the wrong end of the park, then suddenly forgets how to read a map. She turns off the data on her phone, so she doesn't receive my texts or Whats-App messages, and she won't place a call. Even if she's lost, she waits for me to ring her. I understand why. I've seen her finances — it still makes me angry. Where is her savvy? Her agency and drive? Did she leave it in Iran? Because this is a chance to start again. "So, start already!" I want to scream. I tell her that it's enviable to live in central London, that she should be spending her days in libraries, reading, studying English, visiting museums. She shrugs listlessly, and I get it, I get it, I get it. But.

Maybe this is my role. I'm not very good at friendship. I'm intense and impatient with other people's needs. But there are things only I am allowed to say — because I understand Iranian doublespeak, and I was a refugee once. No British person would ever tell Minoo to stop the damn moping. But I can say that. I can say, "OK, saving phone minutes is legit, but avoiding the library is laziness. You have a bus pass. You have Google Maps. Stop crippling yourself with sorrow." I try to say it. But she's so sad. How does anyone communicate with her? I start pummeling myself with jokes instead. I joke about my itchy brain, my

439

post-baby tummy, my gray hairs, the men who dumped me, my bad cooking (I'm a good cook, but Minoo is undoubtedly better), my failures as a daughter. Is this how people help the depressed? I've become a circus clown, a jester.

That night, reading Edward Said's *Orientalism,* I stumble on a passage that soothes me. One day, years from now, I will show it to Minoo's daughter. "The more one is able to leave one's cultural home, the more easily is one able to judge it, and the whole world as well, with the spiritual detachment and generosity necessary for true vision. The more easily, too, does one assess oneself and alien cultures with the same combination of intimacy and distance." Maybe I'm not detached enough from home to relate to Minoo. Or maybe she just needs a professional. We visit the National Gallery, and I walk her children through the Tudor rooms, telling stories of Henry VIII and his wives, the rivalry of Elizabeth and Mary, Queen of Scots. "Who is the winner, do you think?" I ask them. "England's most glorious queen or the one who mothered every king and queen since?" The children love the scandals. Minoo follows glumly. "How do you know all this?" she mutters. "Books, Minoo *joon,*" I say, pointedly. She looks away.

"Books," I whisper to her daughter, winking. She giggles.

What a clever girl she is. She describes school lunches. "The meat is orange!" She tells me that when children tease her, she goes away and thinks, then writes down what she will say next time. Her brother is popular because of soccer (as mine was, for football). He's beginning to understand that he can outwit poverty, that displaying shame is an undoing. When the children ask if he has an Xbox, he smirks and says, "Xbox? I play with two magnets at night." They think it's hilarious. Sport is making him confident. Good going, kid. I learned that trick at twenty-three.

I find that I love the children, though Minoo exhausts me.

In the evening, Maman Moti texts. *How are the roses?* Last time she visited, she brought a rose bush for our garden. Now if I'm silent for too long, she asks after them — this saves her pride. She has planted a piece of herself in our garden, rooting herself to us since her home frightens her.

When I began volunteering with refugees in London, an aid worker warned me that I might be frustrated. "New arrivals have so many needs. Everything is hard at first. They drag their feet. You need to be patient in ways you wouldn't be with a friend." I like this woman — she is frank and empathic. She understands shame, and she handles people's dignity with care. I promise her that I'll try. I'm not a patient human, but I've been a terrified foreigner. There was a time when I wore the same outfit every day, aching for my school uniform, when I refused to shape a pile of wet papier-mâché.

Sometimes Minoo appears in my nightmares — I see her accepting a dossier from a cleric; in the dream, she is sent by the Islamic Republic to find me. I wake up whispering, "It's in your head, you madwoman." On those mornings, I can't separate the anger from the guilt, and I lash out at Sam. I do insane things like count all the shirts I bought in Amsterdam, or find that lipstick from my thirtieth birthday. I have to locate it because the itch, the metal bar, need tending. Am I the right person for this? Look at me, trying to soothe myself by counting my possessions. It's gross, and unsubtle. I'm a caricature of myself. Should former refugees have a hand in assimilating the newly arrived? Maybe my grandmother has it right. I'll fuck Minoo up.

On a drive through the Cotswolds last year, I saw a poster, sponsored by UKIP, the United Kingdom Independence Party, demanding *Integration, not multiculturalism.* To crave transformation from each other — to want others to change into us — seems a natural survival instinct of the ego. That sign reeked of the ego's fear of extinction. But in forcing assimilation, are we asking for performance? We want to see that newcomers are happy, grateful, that they're *trying.* But real gratitude doesn't present itself loudly, in lofty gestures. And learning to posture is a much quicker process than transforming — to quell nativist fears we grill burgers and attend church, listen to Coldplay, buy old polo shirts. What if one day we learn to like those things? Which is a truer moment of change?

Whether born into safety or danger, sometimes people need rescue. They need to be let off the hook for that — after rescue, they need balance, work and rest, love, home. They need a chance to figure themselves out. The painful work of forging a new face must be slow, starting within.

In his *Confessions,* Saint Augustine asks God for freedom from physical desire, but *not yet.* "For I was afraid lest You should hear me soon, and soon deliver me from the disease of concupiscence, which I desired to have satisfied rather than extinguished." He both craves and resents the

443

transformation. He fights against it. And he knows it will take time. He *wants* it to take time, so that he can come to terms with his desire, to satisfy it one way or another, and perhaps because he realizes that a quick transformation won't be real or lasting.

In asylum interviews, no one believes an instant conversion. And yet, the moment the refugee is welcomed in, he is expected to make just such a quick transformation, to shed his past, to walk through the gates clean, unencumbered by a past self. Can a person's heart and mind change in an instant? Can the habits of his hands, the words on his tongue? My mother's did, though her psyche had been preparing for it for years. In *The Varieties of Religious Experience,* William James famously describes the conversion of a fourteen-year-old boy, when, for only a second, Christ appears in his room, arms extended, bidding him to follow. To James, such experiences are as authentic as slow apostasy. More than that, they are the psyche's way to redemption — James's theory doesn't reject the notion that my mother's subconscious had been preparing for years. It embraces that. Her soul was looking for redemption, and she found it.

In *The Varieties of Religious Experience,* James says that psychology can't give an answer to why there has to be a moment when a mind's "center of energy" shifts, or why it comes when it comes. "All we know is that there are dead feelings, dead ideas, and cold beliefs, and there are hot and live ones; and when one grows hot and alive within us, everything has to re-crystallize about it." I am reminded of Baxter's irreversible axis-tilt, the wedge that is our truest story. What is my truest story? The day I fumed at the *pasdars* berating my mother? When I saw Khanom Yadolai transform into an old woman and understood the purpose of *hijab*? The day I read about Harvard in the college entrance book? The day I got a letter from Princeton that said "Yes!"? Maybe I *am* religious. But those moments weren't my conversions. Since adolescence, my every transformation has been incremental, orbiting my intellectual life but leaving it intact — it is the core of my web; the one unchangeable thing. College, becoming a writer, they weren't remakings. So maybe my conversion happened much earlier, that first morning on the blacktop when I decided to look away from Khomeini's beard and look for my own name on a list on the wall. "Is nothing sacred to you?" my ex-husband asked after I wrote about our divorce. I felt an instant of panic, then calm.

An answer fell easily from my mouth, "Writing is sacred. Books are sacred." *My point of view is sacred.*

"A mind is a system of ideas . . . which mutually check or reinforce one another," writes James. "The collection of ideas alters by subtraction or by addition in the course of experience, and the tendencies alter as the organism gets more aged . . . But a new perception, a sudden emotional shock, or an occasion which lays bare the organic alteration, will make the whole fabric fall together; and then the centre of gravity sinks into an attitude more stable, for the new ideas that reach the centre in the rearrangement seem now to be locked there, and the new structure remains permanent." This description of religious conversion sounds an awful lot like the core of the web being blasted away. Like Pooyan, I don't believe that adults can do away with their core; it's too fundamental. A refugee's sudden conversion from Islam to Christianity can be honest and powerful and life-changing, but I take that to mean that she had never made Islam a foundation for her identity, or that Islam had slowly lost that position. Either way, at the time of conversion, instantaneous as it was, the center of her identity was safe elsewhere. Over time, that center may, or may not, shift toward the new religion, and merge with it. Again, I don't think that happens in a day; though (and this is vital for immigration officers to understand) awareness, commitment, and euphoria might.

Accepting that conversion can only be an outcome of a psychological process, not a disruption of the self, James's description sounds more like assimilation: never sudden, never an epiphany, even if it is attached to a dramatic moment. It is always a long time coming, an answer to a search.

It sounds like *my* assimilation — my devotion to an academy, offering myself up for a grade, these weren't new. Toiling slowly remade me, but the basic nugget of my identity was unchanged from year to year. That the psyche enables conversion, that the soul prepares for redemption, *over years,* this makes me question the notion that conversion remakes the soul into some "new structure." You can't prepare for annihilation — preparation implies that something, some tiny thing, will survive it.

Early in my teenage years, Baba got a visa to visit us in Oklahoma — it was surreal, the most jarring thing that could happen to a teen in the midst of an American remaking. I was embarrassed by his loud, marrow-sucking ways: his big, red mustache and enormous ice creams and tangerine shorts. The way he took us to a Japanese grill and ordered a bottle of sake for himself. When I kept blushing and turning away, Baba joked that next time he would stop in Dallas or New York to have the Iranian washed off him. After a few weeks with us, Baba succumbed to the church's proselytizing and allowed himself to be baptized. I didn't object, but I was appalled by the way everyone was playing along. He hated religion. Didn't they see that he was faking? And for the worst reason, to avoid social discomfort!

And yet, maybe, that is where cultural change begins. We fake new habits, we commit to the task, until the habits come without forethought. Maman's first prayer to Jesus can't have sounded all that natural. My first American spelling test was a mess of backward letters. But we were already the thing we were pretending to be, because we were devoted.

I believe in slow baking. I also know that the flavor is decided long before the baking is done, when the batter is mixed and poured. Transformation is decided in an instant, *and* it takes years. Augustine's prayer to be remade slowly, to have a while longer with his desire but ultimately to change, moves me. It is wise, humble, and self-aware.

A sign says *Integration, not multiculturalism!* It might as well say *don't stop time*! Refugees will assimilate just as surely as time will pass. Some will live for three decades as if they're in the home country, then call it a done deed when they enjoy their first bite of Marmite or peanut butter. Others will be indistinguishable from their hosts in a year or two. Most will become chameleons, able to go back and forth. But whatever their place on the spectrum, assimilation begins in unseen places. To enforce it is to demand performance. There are things we crave from each other whose value we diminish by asking for them: love, gratitude, understanding. To have these things, we must first offer something of ourselves. In refugee communities, volunteers often ask each other, "What can I do to make it easier for them?" They offer their homes, run errands, set up language tables, soccer games, meals. Again and again, I've met neighbors like these. The question, though, isn't one of generosity but of shame, dignity, and belonging. Permission for the stranger to show his true face. In every small interaction, one ego shines, while the other fades. To the native-born who want to open their arms, I would say: let yourself fade away, ever briefly. Don't shine in your good deeds, because people keep their dignity quite near the core of their identity. Show your humblest face (at first). See what happens to the question of assimilation in a year, in two years. No one wants to transform. And yet no one can avoid it — we alter with every breath. Other people transform us with their love, their kindness, and also with their indifference. We change by being seen or unseen. We badly want to show ourselves to each other. Those who have suffered stumble in the attempt. In trying to connect without succumbing to harm, they behave clumsily, their words tense, cautious, sometimes hurtful.

Minoo's caseworker leaves her job. It turns out she never even put Minoo's family on the list for subsidized private housing. I rage — I call Sam's brother, Daniel, the human rights lawyer. "It's time for the lawyer treatment," I say. I write to the council, demanding a meeting. They delay, for a translator. *I am the translator she has chosen,* I write. *I am taking careful note of all your actions from here on out.* They find a translator.

Her Persian is bad. She's a Kurd from the evictions unit that they've dragged in. I end up doing most of the translation; she jumps in now and then. Sam's brother is fabulously intimidating. We discover that the humiliating questionnaire has to be repeated. Minoo bursts into tears, her chin dimpling, shoulders shaking. She hides her face in her hands.

Halfway through the interview, we find out that the Kurdish woman is an expert in London housing. Feeling underused, she begins advising us on neighborhoods where Minoo's family may have a shot of getting a house. Minoo sniffles. We describe Enfield and Haringey, assuring her that there are safe boroughs outside central London. Afterward, I get the translator's number. "Should we call her to hang out?" I ask Minoo. "She's Persian."

Minoo wipes her face and says, "Maybe." She heads for the subway.

One day over coffee, Minoo opens up to me. She tells me about the family's first nights in a London hostel. Mice dashed brazenly about as the children pulled their feet onto the shared bed and screamed. Then they all held each other and collapsed into laughter. "With us it was cockroaches in Dubai," I say. Minoo and I chuckle into our coffees, like real friends. I think I would've liked the version of Minoo who lived in Isfahan. She says, "I used to work all the time. I was like you, with day care and a job. But, did you know sometimes in Iranian day care they sedate the children? They give them cold medicine with sleep aids. You can't do anything about it. You can't prove it." She sighs, sips her coffee. "When we were crouching from the mice, my son said, 'I like it here because you can be my mom.' So, the mouse room is actually a sweet memory for me." I remember my brother looking worriedly at Maman. *But who will do your man things?*

"You'll tell each other that story," I say, "when you have a big house and he's a doctor and famous soccer player."

"Yes!" she says. "God willing."

The next day, the man from the council visits Minoo at the hostel building and compels her, without me or Daniel present, to add a ground-floor restriction to her housing request. She loses the next available flat, which is on the second floor. When we complain, they write to Minoo and Daniel that they won't communicate with me anymore, having discovered that I'm a writer, a thing I've told them in every call and meeting. They are certain I'm writing a book about Minoo, a thing they have no way of knowing and isn't true (yet). They demand a medical examination, to decide if

Minoo's husband can use stairs. The family's assurances aren't enough, as if they don't suffer daily alongside him, as if they aren't the ones on whose shoulders he will lean. Barred from communication, I dictate emails for Minoo to send the council. They ignore all pleas on behalf of the children, who have grown into adolescence in a tiny room, in one bed, with their parents. On our next call, Minoo's voice is barely above a whisper.

III

On March 8, 2018, International Women's Day, I walked into parliament with several hundred women from forty organizations, mostly undocumented immigrants and asylum seekers from sub-Saharan Africa, to lobby for safety, dignity, and liberty. "Shut down Yarl's Wood!" we cried, protesting the infamous detention center where many are held for weeks or months with no purpose. Eventually most Yarl's Wood inmates are released back into English society, though not exactly, because when you are barred from work, you become a part of a separate underground society.

How do you assimilate if you're in quarantine?

Lawyer and activist Dr. Shola Mos-

Shogbamimu, who chaired the parliament lobby, teaches a class on intersectional feminism in the headquarters of the advocacy group Women for Refugee Women. Last spring, I attended a prep session for the parliament lobby. Her students, most in their forties and fifties, sat around a long table in their worn cardigans and bright mismatched jackets, having taken care with their hair, with their accessories. I was hypnotized by the rainbow of purses, all big and bright and fat with necessities. The women in Shola's class have left everything behind, sometimes even their children. Some are trafficked, raped, prostituted, many undocumented, vagrant, without hope or family or welcome. Some have endured female genital mutilation. Some have been going from basement to basement, couch to couch for two decades, the asylum rejections piling as their years slip away.

In class, their excitement, their questions and casual skepticism betrayed the fact that these women had only recently found their voices, their own power. Their enthusiasm was childlike, and yet they were hardened by years of rejection and indifference. Most had been in detention centers at one time or another. But here they were making political campaign plans, pounding the table, sipping weak tea from paper cups as a handful of children ran around the room, amusing themselves. "Train us, don't detain us!" one said, her accent thick and melodic, a hard emphasis on the rhyme. Though the ladies were prone to bouts of elation, no one laughed at that. "Yes!" they said. Others chimed in. "I have a brain," said one woman. "Why can't I use it here? I am being wasted." Others wanted to ask MPs about the cruelties at Yarl's Wood detention center, or the use of the National Health Service (NHS) to root out undocumented immigrants. "If I am sick, treat me! Don't try to find my status. My status is that I'm sick." Most wanted freedom, a status so they could begin living.

Shola's class is a marvel: it's not about surviving in a foreign land, or about perfecting English, or how to write a résumé. It's about the rights and obligations of women: *We must learn!* It's about the suffragettes and their modern counterparts in the Me Too and Time's Up movements. Shola is preparing her students to speak out with their stories, and to make a case for themselves to lawmakers. They have no freedom to build a life and a vocation, and most are left to stagnate and grow old without roots. They are abandoned. Many use this word, along with another, "I am a slave here," they say, well aware of the weight of that word.

Without the liberty to work, the confidence to report violence and exploitation without fear of one's own smaller crimes, a dark economy springs up. To stateless women, those without refuge or protection, it assigns three uses: household work, sex, and childcare. Once branded "illegal," most women find their way into these kinds of work, sometimes for cash, sometimes for food and a place to sleep. It always begins with childcare, then they are expected to perform the other two duties.

"It seems that going from home to home, not having any place, is my curse," says one of the women. "I turn up. I feel like an imposition. All I wanted my entire life is to have the dignity of my own home." Instead, she has spent twenty years being passed from home to home as free childcare. People offer her a place to sleep on the floor, often on a mattress that she has to procure herself from charity organizations, in exchange for taking full-time care of the children free of charge. If the authorities come, she has to identify herself as the child's official caregiver, so that the parents don't get in trouble. This, of course, poses a problem for her because she can be arrested, detained, and deported — she is working for room and board, a clear violation of the rules. She has no choice, and the families know this. Their excuse is that they, too, are poor Africans (though legal residents) who can't afford childcare, and they are helping someone. If there are houseguests, she is asked to leave for the night. Sometimes the men visit her in the night. She cannot report them. And when the kids are old enough for school, the families say, "We've done enough for you. You must leave."

When you have no rights, everyone has power over you.

Shola's mantra is "educate yourself." In class, she shouts, points, paces. She teaches with her whole body, takes no back talk or negativity, offers courage to skeptics. Inspiring and energetic as her activist heroines, she shines in her belief in these twenty-first-century suffragettes. Today's fight isn't for *every* woman, Shola knows. It is for the rootless, the powerless.

On March 8, many women told their stories; many begged, "Set us free." From Yarl's Wood. From the torture of detainment after having been beaten and raped in our home countries. But mostly from statelessness, from those who would exploit us.

"Isn't the ability to say 'no' a basic dignity?" one woman asked in a poem. "Am I nonhuman?"

When women are powerless, the first thing the world exploits from them is what men perceive as the assets of their gender: sex, motherhood, homemaking. My mother hid this part of the larger refugee story from me, so I could grow up believing in myself, so I could think being a refugee is a series of open doors, to the United States, then college, then everywhere.

Like Shola, mother to this roomful of castaway mothers, mine taught me that these labors men want to extract from us are female joys belonging only to us. And that they are most certainly not the entirety of our worth.

After everything, exile has made my mother fearless. If home is gone, why fear smaller losses? In her fifties, she packed up her life and joined the Peace Corps in northern Thailand. When she became interested in organic farms, she moved to one, as an intern. She can silence her Iranian pride if an education is calling. I hear echoes of feminists like Shola in her actions. *Educate yourself!* My mother has guided my assimilation, not to America, but to myself. If I were to write a model refugee narrative, it

458

wouldn't be the Good Immigrant, but the exile who, having endured many changes, now fears no risk. It is the immigrant who kept her agency, who has no shame, who believes in herself. The Good Immigrant would become The Capable Immigrant. Capable differs from good, because the choice to act isn't taken for granted. And from whose point of view is "good" defined, anyway?

This, I know, is my own immigrant faith. In high school, I read Emerson's "Self-Reliance," enraptured. I read it, not as instruction, but as permission. "Life only avails, not the having lived," Emerson writes. "Power ceases in the instant of repose; it resides in the moment of transition from a past to a new state, in the shooting of a gulf, in the darting to an aim. This one fact turns all riches to poverty, all reputation to shame, confounds the saint with the rogue, shoves Jesus and Judas equally aside." Astonishing — all that matters to Emerson is the state of transition, the toiling, the wanting, all the parts of myself I found ugliest. *Darting to an aim.*

And yet, changing identity is a wallowing, self-loathing business. I know this, not because I've been a refugee, but because I've been a new mother. I've never been more wretched and unpalatable than in those first days of motherhood when my brain ached from the change, when every flavor seemed new and people watched me for mistakes. I was instructed to take classes, to learn a new language, a new culture, and rules. I lost my strength, my personal power. I kept making schedules, to-do lists, goals. Every breath was impossible, and yet it happened. The body knows how to change. That doesn't stop it from resisting. The former me, the one who wasn't a mother, fought annihilation, though she had no chance.

For weeks, I sat in cafés with my new baby, staring into space, unable to write, knowing that people found me useless.

I travel to Berlin, where a friend introduces me to a group of refugees from Syria and Afghanistan. I meet a writer who tells me that in Syria, he had ninety minutes of electricity every six hours. He would sleep and smoke and think during the dark hours, then, when the lights came on, he would plug in his laptop and write, continuing as long as his battery lasted. He can't imagine anyone would want his stories now, because the writers in the West have had all the hours of the day to practice their craft. How will he compete? "When I arrived, I made that assumption too," I tell him. "But a life of plenty doesn't translate to discipline. It's full of distractions. Let those other writers have their unlimited TV. You keep writing."

He laughs. It's not always so easy as that. The wounded mind rebels.

Displacement isn't mental illness, but it makes visible the daily, hourly, work of staying sane — work that is unconscious in the rooted life. Suddenly, it takes effort to hold on to reason. And, like breathing, the work doesn't store up. If you stop, its rewards are gone, like vapor.

Another Syrian refugee tells me quick joys come easy in Berlin. "If you're young, you look healthy and strong, full of potential. People are happy for you, and you want to preserve that good faith." He tells me that the fitful black nights are easy to hide. Sometimes, he wakes to memories of the day in Sicily when, without a word, border control sprayed him with chemicals, gave him an injection. He pauses. "I lost the human inside me."

One young man traveled on foot across the world to be with his mother, and when he found her in an English hospital, they wouldn't let him care for her. "I wanted to lotion my mother's legs. They said no. Did they think I was a danger to her? If I didn't

461

die that day, I'll never die."

It's not so easy to seize back your power. Memories of home mix so toxically with shame, it's hard to hold both in the mind at the same time. And yet they always appear together. How can one be self-reliant, in the Emersonian way, never reposing, always transitioning, taking control of the change in oneself, if one is taught to hate the very self that is supposed to do all this work? What if that self is no longer part of a desired class? What if every sign points to its inferiority? Years ago, Philip and I traveled to Istanbul. While touring Topkapi Palace, we saw a family from Iran. My life then contained so little of Iran that I couldn't resist greeting them in Farsi as we passed. Their daughter, a young woman in her early twenties, stopped short. She returned the greeting shyly, then turned back, eying us now and again. An hour later, we crossed paths in another room. She whispered to her family. Then she walked over to me and said, "Are you Iranian?" I nodded, and as explanation for my bad accent, said that I had finished growing up in the United States. I asked her what city she came from. I thought, now we'd reminisce about home or complain about Turkish food. But she glanced behind her, then said, rather formally, in Farsi, "Can you please tell me how you got that man to marry you?"

IV

Iowa was like a foreign country. Miles and miles of emptiness with no car, I was trapped inside a circle of four or five blocks. I ate the same hummus sandwich every day. Watched the same TV shows, blindly, deafly. Skipped dinner. Went to workshop. Grew thin. Sometimes I forgot to shower. Sometimes I stared at the same spot on the wall for three hours, motionless. The television blared; I pretended to engage. I drank carafes of coffee and tea, pairing three cups with one vanilla wafer. It was fall 2011 and I was living alone for the first time in a decade. I missed my friend. It was another assimilation: to singleness, to life as a writer, to myself.

My only joy, the only time I savored food and felt briefly human, was when I cooked for my classmates — dishes of eggplant and lamb and butternut squash and pomegranate that took hours and saturated the air in my friends' houses. By April I would move into a house, with roommates and a fireplace. I would buy the first bed of my own, having gone from my childhood beds to the ones in dorms to the ones I shared with Philip. In the new house, I inhabited the kitchen. Even when I wasn't cooking I sat at the counter, in the same chair, waiting for someone to come down and talk.

I was marooned. I craved the domestic and yet I was mired in so much errancy and strangeness that I sank to the ground, lying with my face on the wooden floor slats for hours. Maybe I was hoping to take root again.

The craving to build a home is a tricky thing: when you have it, it's like a heavy woolen coat in summer. Without it you're naked, skinless. I cooked so much in that wild, hopeless season. I was delirious. I shed fat and tears, wrote garbage, and made food, watching rapturously as others ate and drank and grew full and satisfied. Fullness was alien.

One night, my roommate hosted Passover, and something about the ritual hinted of home — here was a table of strangers reciting text that meant nothing to them; they did it to connect with their friend. How miraculous! And haven't my American neighbors always been curious about me? Maybe it isn't their fault that all we felt comfortable offering were the dramatic escape stories, that we didn't show them pomegranate stews and photos of the duck ponds and rivers and mountain hikes. Maybe if we had shown ourselves, they would have loved what they saw. But we were afraid, like Minoo. We couldn't manage it.

I lay awake for many dark nights, thinking of where I had gone wrong. I spent my marriage feeling guilty: I wanted too much, I made everything political, I didn't appreciate the life Philip provided for us, I didn't have babies. And yet I couldn't shake the notion that I lived and breathed the sexist, racist fumes of a society that I had chosen because I thought they were "America's best." At Princeton and later at Harvard, I was surrounded by right-wing Christian ideology. As a woman, I was expected to be just a bit humbler, quieter, more patient. Both my mother and Philip's wrung their hands at the notion that I should displease him. And I went to bed each night thinking they were right. I needed to kill the selfish beast inside. And yet, I wanted to know, why were *his* ambitions laudable and mine unimportant, despite my better grades and more rigorous academic history? Why were my views second-class? Why did I have to learn French and Philip never learned Farsi? Why did my mother ask me not to hang my diplomas, which outnumbered Philip's? Why did she say that it was boastful to hang my MBA from Harvard Business School beside (and level with) the one he earned in France?

I had been fooling myself. My biggest sin was denying that all those afternoons by the river in Ardestoon, the hikes at dawn, the Thirty-Three Arches, the sour cherries and the music and the henna-scented grandmothers with their stories, these had made me. In Iowa, safe in another stellar academic home, I needed to undo the excesses of my assimilation. I was done with my immigrant inferiority complex. Now, if I wanted to excel, I'd do it right — honestly, as myself, an Iranian girl who has inherited math and literature and sport and whatever savvy I have from thousands of years of Iranian excellence — not from America.

I needed Iranian friends, and American ones who knew me.

I learned that the University of Iowa had a good medical program, and engineering schools that attracted foreign students, including Iranians. I decided to look. I sat in a café called Java House, where I often wrote, and I listened until I heard the familiar music of spoken Farsi. Then I got up to say hello, an act that felt much like asking to sit at a fifth-grade lunch table.

"Do you go to school here?" I used the word for "primary school."

My accent in Farsi had deteriorated so much that I was a curiosity: a foreigner who spoke their mother tongue. They were a mix of graduate students — engineers, scientists, doctors, their wives from Tehran and Shiraz and elsewhere. They invited me to sit, so I fetched my coffee and laptop and joined them at their table. They peppered their talk with slang that they were happy to explain, along with a year or location. "This one is very Rashti," or "People started saying this in the mid nineties."

A young woman sat up when I mentioned that I would divorce soon. The table shifted a little, as they glanced at each other, leaned forward: they knew that, as an American, divorce wouldn't devastate my life, but a woman owning up to it so gleefully was absurd. I wasn't gleeful; I wanted to perform my Americanness, and I wanted to show disdain for sexist Iranian ways. "It was a good first marriage," I said. "Maybe my next will be an Iranian Javad." I giggled at my own joke. I had recently learned the word from an American-born Iranian friend who visited me sometimes from Chicago. A Javad is the Tehrani equivalent of a Jersey girl or Chav, the kind of Iranian who, in an attempt to display American culture, covers himself in gold chains and listens to Farsi rap produced in LA or Paris and is generally embarrassing to our people. Javad men are slick-haired and smooth-talking, bathed in cologne. The women take the Jackie O. look too far — Bumpits and massive sunglasses with pushed-back scarves, pounds of makeup, streaky highlights. Some wear dainty nose-job plasters long after their noses have healed, or if they never had the operation at all.

They didn't laugh. Why didn't they laugh? Had I offended? None were that kind of Iranian. Maybe I was being too much again — why did being around Iranians turn me into a fanged and skinless monster, striking and retreating and afraid of my own footfalls? Our phones beeped in unison. A security warning from Iowa City Police that a menacing person had been reported following an undergraduate and was still at large. "These alarms are madness," said an engineering student with dark cropped hair who had, until now, been silent, her gaze always down. "In Chicago," she said, "*maybe* they bother to call the news if there's a corpse in the river. Here, some guy looks at an undergrad and we all have to

468

wake up so we can know about it."

She said a Farsi word I hadn't heard in decades: *corpse.* I felt giddy for every resurrected word. I repeated it, turning it over in my mouth.

One of the men laughed. "They forget they have Iranians here."

"It's true!" one said. "Eight years in war, and it's not even voluntary: if there's an alarm, you grab your children and run to the neighbor's. How many Iowans did you wake up the first night there was an alarm?"

Chairs tipped back in laughter. "There has to be a report somewhere of the Iranians running into the street in their underwear, random children tucked under each arm, because they got a text with the word 'alert.' "

"And then the next alarm: *Middle Eastern agitator taking children into basements.*" I choked on my coffee. I hadn't laughed so much in years.

"Just turn off your ringer," said the quiet female engineer. "No text in this country is ever important, anyway." I noted her sadness.

I told a story of Baba visiting Oklahoma when I was fourteen, how he had asked me to lotion his mane of red back hair at a waterpark. They hooted and slapped the table.

I found that this was the intersection in our severed cultures: shame about our Iranian antics, and those of our families.

I invited the whole crew of Iranians to dinner. I told my roommates that I was planning to cook a huge Persian meal. I researched music and found an album called *Pomegranates: Persian Pop, Funk, Folk and Psych of the '60s and '70s.* I moved the dining table and set up a *sofreh* on the living room floor using blankets and many decorative pillows. For two days, I sweated eggplants and fried them, roasted walnut, stewed lamb, chopped cucumbers.

I was delirious with excitement, and my roommates were eager to join in, helping set up the *sofreh,* asking if they had done it correctly. Though it satisfied my private needs, I had created a caricature of an Iranian dinner and I hadn't bothered to tell my guests; I had only said I would serve Persian food. My new friends arrived thinking they were attending a normal Iowa City dinner party. "What is this music?" said a tall, athletic man named Rohan. "I haven't heard this since I was a kid."

"It used to play in my dentist's office," one of the women giggled.

"My *baba* is a dentist! Is that why I like it? Oh god, I thought this was hip vintage

470

music. Is it *waiting room music*?" Maybe it wasn't so embarrassing to be laughed at by this group — their teasing felt kind, as if they found my efforts charming.

Around the *sofreh* a young woman said, "You know, usually this is done on a very thick Persian carpet, not on a wooden floor." She tucked a pillow under her haunches. "The boys could just move the table back."

"Oh, but it's so nice," said one of my roommates. I took a breath and started bringing out the sauces and salads and rice to whistles and cheers.

"What is this?" said the oldest guest, a visiting scholar from Tehran, lifting a forkful of kale. "It's like lettuce made love to a piece of fabric."

We ate and drank and talked about the origins of the songs. I thought, as we ate dessert, I'm going to remember this night for a long time.

I was seeing a man from Chicago, an American-born Persian with an accent like mine and a Columbia degree. His relationship with East, West, nomadism, and exile was familiar and comforting. We were cynical and cruel and insecure in precisely the same ways.

"Know something weird?" I said, one

471

night when we were talking about home. "The Iranians got uncomfortable when I talked about Javads. They sort of cringed." I had assumed it was acceptable to joke about Javads, as it is hipsters, because it crosses economic class (the worst offenders are rich). To be a Javad, I thought, is to have overshot the unsavory goal of seeming American, just as hipsters have overshot seeming artsy and poor.

"They cringe because they're exactly one step above Javads," he said.

His naked arrogance fascinated me. I had never heard an Iranian in America speak this way, as if he's the best person in the room (or of his own kind). Still, I was confused. Because if a Javad was a point on a spectrum of Westernness (someone who fakes it from afar), then he ought to say they were "one step further along." But my friend always chose his words carefully. He *did* mean that the Iranians in Iowa were one step closer to authentic Westernization. And he also meant *above*.

I thought about that conversation for a long time, and I decided that I couldn't judge him, because I thought exactly the same way — for us to do American right was an accomplishment, whereas if an American ever did Iranian right, that was magnanimity of the highest order. As he spoke, I breathed out, relieved once again for having escaped Ardestoon, for not being a village girl. I wanted to hurt him for reminding me of my lowly roots. My grief in those days included a lot of self-loathing and shame.

Later I would think that this man, who dropped in and out of my life, was the platonic chameleon. He traveled the world, blending in city and village, mansion and hut, always belonging. He could hang with Javads if he wanted to, and yet he knew himself to be free of labels. I wanted to be him. But I wasn't born here. I had sweated for years under mandatory *hijab*. I had shouted into an Islamic Republic bullhorn. I had seen my mother berated by *pasdars*. He didn't do any of that. He didn't wake up to those first confusing refugee mornings when everything is frighteningly foreign, when no food satisfies, and no one quite relates to your stories, and you keep replaying your social gaffes and coming no closer to understanding what you did wrong. One day, he played me a Persian rap, recorded in LA, with the lyric, "She preens in front of the *Gashte-Ershad*." I shuddered at the image, then listened to the song on repeat for a day.

One day, as one of the newly arrived Iranian men drove me home, I played him the song. He grew tense. "Don't American rappers write about their police?" he asked. I saw a piece of paper in his cup holder, symptoms for body dysmorphic disorder on a local clinic's stationery. He glanced at me with nervous eyes, but I didn't tell him that I understood his shame about his body, his craving for perfection, that it happens to so many displaced people, in just the same way. I thought of the Indian doctor who had stared at me in wonder; *who can survive like this?*

"Why do you have so much shame about Iran?" I asked. He gripped the wheel, his eyes angry. After that, I remembered that assimilation is a long, slow process, at once imperceptible and unseemly, and though I may not be as clean and settled as my American-born friend, I couldn't indulge in new exile theater. Plunging a hand into another's remaking is a serious business; I had taken it far too lightly. I drifted away from the Iranians.

Years later, on a Greek highway between camps, Paul from Refugee Support told me that one of the biggest social issues at the camps is volunteers becoming romantically involved with refugees. An idealistic volunteer falls for an Iranian or Syrian man who seems strong despite his situation. She loses herself in the high of it, maybe even dreaming that she *can* save her new lover. After a few weeks, when she becomes his only hope for a life, when triggers abound and the logistics become a nightmarish tangle, she feels beset by so much need and abandons him, calling it "an experience for us both." He is devastated. It wasn't just about a passport for him; this capable, carefree woman represented life without psychological shackles. She was freedom and agency and the possibility of fitting in.

But should the volunteer have stayed away? Was I right to pull away from my Iranian friends in Iowa? Now, as I try to navigate London's refugee support system, all those English men and women wanting to help, I try to make sense of these stories. People ask, how can I help? Get involved? Give them space? I want to say, be patient. Give them many chances.

New immigrants are lonely and cautious. And refugees arrive traumatized. Every last one, even the happiest, is broken in places. They won't always behave deservingly. Many suffer from shame, notions of inferiority. They are prone to embracing the very racism and classism that most harms them.

They want to believe that the systems are fair, that they can earn their way into the good graces of the well-placed white man.

They need friendship, not salvation. They need the dignity of becoming an essential part of a society. They have been so often on the receiving end of charity that when faced with someone else's need, their generosity and skill shines. Now and then, they will fall short, their wounds will open, they will have too many needs. You might misstep and cause harm. That is better than drawing a thick line around them. In life, people disappoint each other. Messes are made. The only way to avoid pain is to distance yourself, to look down at them from the rescuer's perch. But that denies them what they most urgently need: to be useful. To belong to a place.

This, I believe, is the way to help the displaced. It is what we owe each other, to love, to bring in outsiders. Again and again, I've failed at it.

A few months ago, Sam's mother's Bulgarian housecleaner showed us photos of her daughter's wedding back home. I was sitting at the kitchen table writing. Sam's mother had been thawing a tart. When the photos came out, she poured three coffees and we huddled over her phone, gushing. In one shot, sisters and cousins lined up in purple chiffon dresses. Sam's mother said, "Who made those beautiful dresses?" She wanted to flatter, implying they had hired an expensive tailor. I thought, a villager from the East routinely makes her own clothes. She would take pride in buying off racks. I said, "Those look like Selfridges!" Sam's mother gave me a funny look. The housecleaner gave *her* a funny look. We shot back our coffees and returned to our work. I'm not sure who got it more wrong.

Hours later as the housecleaner was leaving, we had both rethought our compliments and started in on the physical beauty and youth of the daughter. She pulled out her phone again and showed us videos of the dancing. Now we had hit on something universal. *Look at her dance! What a figure she has! May she have many happy years with him.*

I tell this story to a counselor specializing in refugees. She laughs. "You were trying too hard to say the exact *right* thing. She can tell when you're lying about what impresses you. You were honestly impressed with the dancing, right? It's easy — just be you. Let them be them. That's it."

I'm grateful for these translators and way-makers. Kind people like Paul Hutchings and Ahmed Pouri and Dr. Shola Mos-Shogbamimu. They know that assimilation isn't policy, to be advocated on road signs and measured by statisticians. It is personal, between two people, two families. It's much like marrying into a family and gritting your teeth at their customs, the way your new father-in-law sits at the head of the table, waiting to be served, or the way your new aunt swipes a careless finger across a dirty plate. Assimilation is coming to understand that when your own grandmother plunges a dinner spoon into her boot, it will stain you.

Assimilation is grappling with a language, the sting of shame until you learn. It is knowing not only the meaning of words, but how to use them, how to ask questions, how to make a joke, what gives offense. *How society sees you makes your personality,* my grandmother says.

But there is help, waves of kindness spilling through the cracks of the day. People are generous, longing to plunge in with their fellow men.

Sam told me a story about walking with a friend and seeing a dog jump into a pile of another dog's shit. He rolled in it, eyes delirious. "He wants to lose himself in another dog's scent," said the friend. It's what we all want, to lose ourselves in each other. That means embracing our foulness. I never stop marveling at the closeness of beauty and decay.

Like most, I recoil from small, everyday scenes of human frailty. I think, "Is this too hard? Am I naive? Should I protect myself?"

Once on a London train, a man in prayer clothes patted my hand, almost lovingly. This felt somehow solicited.

Once on another London train, in front of a crowd of tired commuters, an Afghan man slapped me hard across the bridge of the nose, causing it to swell for a week. My first thought was Tourette's, because I know the compulsions of the mind. My second thought was my hair, my face. Was this old-world sexism from home? That, too, was a devil I knew. His nephew began begging for forgiveness before he had returned his hand to its humble position, crossed across his groin. The nephew touched my face as if in mutual sorrow. All day long, I obsessed over that man, his foreignness, the itch in his brain. I thought of the discomfort on the faces of the commuters, and the danger it posed for these two men. They shifted on their heels, every eye on them. I remembered soon after we arrived, I hated crowds. I wanted to disappear from them. So often in those years, we arrived in musty new homes — the hostel in Dubai or the apartment in Oklahoma. You could only smell them for one day, but, after that, you still worried. Had the smell gone? Had it become a part of you? You looked for it in the eyes of passersby. In crowds, you didn't dare move.

On sealed trains, all are vulnerable, the wait heightening our senses.

To assimilate is to please other people's senses. It is submission, but also a powerful act of love, unity, brotherhood. It is a complicated and misunderstood metamorphosis. So often, we ask refugees to perform an open mimicry of our culture. This we call assimilation. It is theater. In return, we try to show our good faith by displaying enjoyment of palatable segments of their culture: sushi and curry, bubble tea and baklava. But assimilation isn't like tourism. You don't get to dabble for a day. Refugees resign themselves to deep-tissue change from the day their feet touch new soil, when the shape and sound of it is still unimaginable. They commit to changing their senses, to making a practice of their new culture — it happens only by repetition. As a teenager, when I thought it useless to treat myself to a single fancy coffee, valuing only what came regularly, this was assimilation instinct. I didn't want to play the outsider to yet another life. I wanted to alter my senses, so that I could trust them again.

While assimilation isn't scalable (and shouldn't be framed that way), it also can't be done alone. We need each other to make a community — the immigrant can't transform by sheer will. My grandmother sitting alone in a park, writing her stories for a man who doesn't care, this isn't assimilation but capitulation. She is offering her power, the wealth of our scattered family and the source of its division, letter by letter, story by story, to an unimpressed white man who doesn't want her. It is abjection, shame.

A lasting, progressive kind of assimilation requires reciprocation. It is mutual and humble and *intertwined* with multiculturalism, never at odds with it. It is about allowing newcomers to affect you on your native soil, to change *you*. It is about understanding that, for centuries, the white native-born (and, more brazenly, white colonizers) have blithely chosen what habits and sensations from other people's homes are worth keeping. The Western palate holds so much unearned attention and value. What it finds unpalatable, what fails to spark its curiosity, is often lost.

481

And yet, refugees, like most outsiders, won't help themselves be seen. We have an instinct to self-sanitize, to hide our moral struggles, for the benefit of the powerful. In a 1963 essay, "Writing About Jews," Philip Roth responded to Jewish readers claiming that his pungent characters fuel anti-Semitism. Publish in Israel, they suggested, keep it private. "This is not fighting anti-Semitism, but submitting to it," said Roth. "All the tolerance of persecution that has seeped into the Jewish character — the adaptability, the patience, the resignation, the silence, the self-denial, must be squeezed out." Fight hatred, but "not by putting on a good face . . . not by pretending that Jews have existences less in need of, less deserving of, honest attention than the lives of their neighbors; not by making Jews invisible." To publish in Israel is to imply that "there is nothing in our lives we need to tell the Gentiles about, unless it has to do with how well we manage. Beyond that, it's none of their business. We are important to no one but ourselves."

Our shame has helped create a cynical, sedated world wherein being a fully realized human is the privilege of whites, Christians, and the native-born. Insiders never question their most basic impulses; they just *are,* an inevitable ingredient in the air others breathe. The rest of us tiptoe and dance for their good opinion, filtering every smell and sound through a second skin. It is hardened instinct, but those with power can help break it.

Curiosity is a powerful corrective tool. It returns people to their natural state, however briefly. You need no expertise to aim for curiosity. To care is enough. If you love a person, a family, you don't want them to change into you. You want them to be *them*. You want to know about their tics and foibles, the home they left behind and all its strange flavors, their childhood songs, their bad habits, the music of their every celebration.

When I was a teenager, I attended a church retreat called Chrysalis (it was billed as "a transformation," and I was drawn to that) wherein the staff orchestrated a number of surprises for each attendee. One such gesture was to gather encouraging letters from friends, teachers, and family to give to each attendee on the final afternoon. It was a program tradition, designed to stir up emotions. As I entered the room where white paper bags full of letters were awaiting each girl, a pastor called to me. "I hear you have a very special letter in there," he said, "from Isfahan?"

"What?" I said, "Are you serious?" I ran into the room. Had this tiny local organization managed to get a letter from Baba? I sat in a row of girls, unpacking my paper bag. I leafed through the letters, fingers shaking, each one a burst of pride and joy — I was loved. Glancing back, I saw the preacher watching me from a bench. His eager smile was gone. He sat swaying, arms on knees, hands folded. A woman was whispering in his ear.

I returned to my letters. A few minutes later, I glanced back again. The two adults were still watching me. Finally, the woman got up and walked over to my bench. "Honey," she whispered. "I thought I should tell you before you reach the bottom of that pile. The pastor made a terrible mistake. We weren't able to get that letter. I'm so sorry."

I wish I had held back the tears; the pastor misread them. He hurried over to apologize. I was too young and inarticulate to explain that it didn't matter. Yes, I had wanted that letter, but Baba had disappointed me before, and there would be other letters. I was moved by the image of the pastor on the bench, wringing his hands. After years of daily calibrations — one day I belonged to someone or someplace, the next day I didn't

— I knew I could eventually earn my place in America, but I never expected to register in the emotional calculus of an American adult. I didn't have that kind of power. Was his swaying for *my* sake? Now, years later, I remember how much he cared, how the possibility of hurting me affected him. How, as an insecure teenager, I marveled at that and thought better of myself. Here was someone who wasn't pretending to want me around. What a thing, to be loved by a stranger, to have a stranger bother to meddle in your life.

We are constantly assimilating to each other, all of us, because we want to love and be loved. We find redemption and kinship in the superficial, these small nothings that contain our shared joy — dancing brides, letters from fathers, a first taste of kale. These small moments remake us in each other's image. It is a kindness to realize that the toiling, fast-succumbing immigrant is gesturing peace, and to relieve him from the obligation of keeping it up. He makes a show of conversion and gratitude because he wants his neighbor to trust him, to know that he is adaptable. Change is coming, but it will take years — in that time, his neighbors, too, will seem altered. Time softens everyone's contours. Though, to have your edges smoothed, I suppose, you must first allow yourself to be touched.

Once in a Mexican restaurant in Iowa City, I saw two newly arrived Iranian men staring into a bowl of guacamole, as if waiting for the green paste to identify itself. One said, "What is this?" The other, a doctor, whispered with perfect sincerity, "Don't touch it. It tastes like Nivea Creme." His friend laughed, and they both ate — there was never any question of it. They had suffered for their place in this new country. Every taste and smell made them shiver with curiosity, and they couldn't trust their senses to know what's good. I thought, to assimilate is exactly this, played out over years. You eat the Nivea Creme again and again, not because it will change but because you know one day your tongue will.

■ ■ ■ ■

PART FIVE:
CULTURAL
REPATRIATION

■ ■ ■ ■

(on being claimed, gratitude,
and the return home)

In 2009, my younger brother, Daniel, and I were traveling together in Texas. In the airport security line, an officer waved us through while choosing the old white woman behind us for a random check. I breathed a sigh of relief, since the "born in Tehran" in our American passports always got us a pat-down, at least. As we passed, Daniel said to the officer in a jokey American tone, "I don't feel safe on this flight." The officer looked up. I thought, *What the hell is happening right now?* This was the Daniel who, as a toddler, watched airport security disembowel his toy sheep, the person whose dark face and unpronounceable first name still on his passport routinely invite second and third glances from border control. What was he doing rousing the attention of a white officer? Was he tired of freedom? He smiled at the officer and said, "You're checking *her*? Isn't the random

489

checking for guys like me?"

I snorted, but I was also terrified. The guard laughed and waved us through. We walked onto the plane without trouble but, for a solid ten minutes, I wanted to pull down the oxygen mask and crouch in a corner sucking in good air. Brown men don't taunt the police. He knew this.

For years I tried to untangle that memory. It pained me to know that my brother lived, for a part of each day, in a menacing universe of white male aggression, every gesture an assessment of belonging or otherness, a place to which I'd never have access. How maddening that he should need to nod to the officer's beliefs, to make him laugh. To say, "Hey, I may be dark and foreign, but I get you. I'm not scary. I love God and America and pumpkin pie." Maybe the officer had eyed him and he wanted to respond by displaying his American accent. Regardless, I doubt he'd make that joke today. He was young and idealistic, and, even though it was post-9/11, airport security wasn't as fraught for Iranians as it is in Trump's America.

Daniel is a good immigrant — hardworking and talented and grateful, the kind who makes America better. He thanks his new country with his every move. And yes, the

United States and England and Holland and Germany would be better if all immigrants were like him. I wonder, though, how many are just keeping their mouths shut and their ideas trapped in for fear of seeming defiant to the mediocre white man scrutinizing their papers.

A few years ago, my brother told me that he couldn't trust me. I think he may have been the first to compare me to a chameleon. He said I had a creepy ability to choose a person I wanted to be, then transform into that person so accurately that the overall effect was something sinister. And while, as a child, my obsessions and compulsions and tics were charming, they aren't so palatable when wielded by an intelligent adult with motives.

"Do you ever make a choice that goes *against* your desires?" he said.

He's right. Each time we uprooted we had the option of crafting ourselves anew. I've always taken it. Should I have not?

I don't think Daniel needs me to be a Christian, or to be consistently one person year after year without changing or adapting. Daniel has read Emerson too. "A foolish consistency," wrote Emerson, "is the hobgoblin of little minds." I don't think he even cares if my primary ethical tool is my own desires (which it isn't). But I think he feels instinctively that my lighter skin, my range of hair colors, and my sculpted nose have given me access to white privilege. Chameleon isn't a casual metaphor to him. It is an accusation, because not everyone can go back and forth.

In our early days in America, he didn't blame me — there was a crack in the wall that kept us both out of the nicer rooms; I had found a way to peek in, but I was still just an Iranian kid with slightly lighter skin than her brother, still a kid who was mocked and excluded and made to feel like nothing. Daniel, though, like Minoo's son, had found a kind of acceptance from football. We had our struggles, but I was still on his team.

And later, as a college student, when I began to transform, it was a novelty. We joked about Philip's Waspy ways. Sometimes in cafés if I heard someone mention Oklahoma, I would say, "Oh, I'm from there!" and I'd have an entire conversation without anyone saying, "Where are you really from, though?" or "Where did you live before that?" (Mexico, they assumed). But, as a grown adult capable of slipping back and forth, ruthlessly choosing a face each morning, plucking the best of both identities — Iranian for college applications and essays and Norooz parties, unthreatening white girl in airports and taxi stands and dating sites — the sheer possibility appalls him.

It appalls me too, not just my own too-frequent taste of white privilege but his lack of access to it, and the fact that it exists at all. I can't change my natural instinct to care for myself and for my family, or to live my life and share my stories, whatever they may reveal about the world. I am human, and selfish. I feel no shame at displaying my Iranian face in my writings or in my private life, at remembering aloud how I once lived, and what I lost, and how I've been altered. The shame comes afterward, when I am waved into a waiting taxi while a darker person waits across the street. It has taken decades to see that Western society, this institution to which I aspired, is badly broken and that I benefit from its faults in ways that I didn't as a child and that my brother still doesn't.

But I can try to fix it. I'd like to try to fix it.

Though we often discuss this back-and-forth between cultures, my immigrant friends and I don't talk much of a physical return. When we *have* discussed it, the conversation has devolved into fights — we fight about who can go back, who *should* go back, and who is more Iranian. Who can go back is, of course, fraught. The refugees among us would never risk it. Communists and apostates and others who have spent any time in jail would rather stay safe than to reminisce. For those who can return, there's cultural and economic hand-wringing. Let's face it, most of them go back with wallets full of hefty Western currencies; they eat, drink, ski, swim, and tour. They try to taste home, and fail, then return unsatisfied, leaving their countrymen, the ones who looked after them, who cooked and cleaned for them, more miserable and desperate for a life abroad.

Among Iranians, the people who can easily go back are the ones who left before or around the time of the revolution. I admit that it angers me to hear Iranians describe their hardships if they left before 1979 and were able to take their money with them, or if they left before they were four years old and started their education in the West. To me, it matters whether you lived with cockroaches as you fled. It matters whether school meant sweaty gray scarves and billowing black chadors, screaming *dictées* and bloody-fisted murals. It matters if you had to chant "Death to America."

I'm being possessive, I know. History belongs to everyone. I guard my story jealously precisely because I can't go back. All that's left is a series of scenes and the many orphan details stuck in my memory. In my family, the story is our currency. My stories grate on my mother partly because she sees me the way I see those baby refugees, the ones who arrived at one or two. She got her PhD in Iran, a degree that became useless in her new country. She spent her adulthood not understanding jokes, feeling always mocked, straining to remember words. I don't get to complain to *her* about exile.

My mother would say that a return isn't worth thinking about — it would be foolish, wasteful, and deeply ungrateful. And thinking about it hypothetically doesn't change what you should do with your days. You must keep living. This is what I learned from her at Hotel Barba. You can't fall into the waiting space. You must find work, some small gear you can turn — you must make *something* happen.

"You are a girl from Iran," my mother says every time life deals me a blow. "A refugee girl who should have grown trapped under the scarf, running from bombs, but instead spent her life reading good books in other people's best universities. You don't cry at hardship. You adapt!" Such logic is a habit for refugee mothers. They expect their children to adapt quickly and contribute heftily to *other* people's communities. Though nothing is theirs, they are free and toughened by displacement. Why shouldn't they spend their lives showing their mothers what miracles they can perform?

In his 1988 essay "Spelling Our Proper Name," Chinua Achebe talks about African American writer James Baldwin, who, as a tormented child and young man, judged Africa for its "lack of achievement" and compared himself harshly to Swiss peasants whose ancestors were marginally related to the likes of Dante, Shakespeare, and Rembrandt. Their legacy of achievement would forever give them a leg up, and Baldwin's young instinct told him to blame his ancestors, who had failed to measure up, though he had been deprived of their stories by the very Western education that he so revered.

Achebe recoiled at the notion that achievement should be any kind of gauge of our human obligations to one another. In conversations about the refugee crisis, educated people continue to make the barbaric argument that open doors will benefit the host nation. The time for this outdated colonialist argument has run out; migrants don't derive their value from their benefit to the Western-born, and civilized people don't ask for résumés from the edge of the grave. Achebe said, in 1988, "I do not see that it is necessary for any people to prove to another that they built cathedrals or pyramids before they can be entitled to peace and safety. Flowing from that, it is not necessary for black people to invent a great fictitious past in order to justify their human existence and dignity today. What they must do is recover what belongs to them — their story — and tell it themselves."

Achebe describes meeting James Baldwin at a 1983 conference. He recalls Baldwin addressing him in this way, "My brother, whom I met yesterday — who I have not seen in four hundred years; it was never intended that we should meet." Achebe is struck by the word "intended," which echoes a warning Baldwin gave to his nephew: "It was intended that you should perish in the ghetto." Contained in that word, "intended," Achebe argues, is the realization that the white conquerors benefit from keeping the two brothers apart, from hiding their legacies from history, and from sowing bitterness in the hearts of African Americans by propagating the idea that

Africans achieved little before the Europeans came along. This, I would add, justifies the hoarding of modern African American talents and achievements for the West, and deprives Africa of the stellar work of its descendants. To keep the African and the African American separate, to make one look down at the other ("They're just one step above Javad"), is the way to continue claiming people of color as their own, by annexing their best work as a byproduct of Western education and creativity.

In a recent monologue to his audience, television host Trevor Noah read an angry response from the French ambassador to the joke "Africa won the World Cup." The letter accused Noah of denying the winning players' French-ness, and went on repeatedly to claim them, their talents, training, and education, for France. "Why can't they be both?" said Noah. "In order to be French you have to erase everything that is African? Why?"

Because if they turned their attention homeward, they would stop being indebted to France, they would no longer belong to the West. After my 2017 *Guardian* Long Read about how refugees are expected to behave toward their adopted countrymen, a reader wrote to me, reminding me that the direction of gratitude posturing isn't always from newcomers toward native-born. In formerly colonized countries, it is the darker native-born who must still bow and thank the children of their past colonizers. Another reader, a man in his seventies, wrote to me that, despite a lifetime of displacement and dramatic fits and starts, he never felt removed from his own identity. He found he could be at home anywhere. Though he was an exile, he never felt like one. He felt like a traveler with his roots firmly intact. Is it a surprise that the direction of his exile was Eastward?

It *is* a question of racial dominance. If whiteness is to be linked to education, culture, the creation of great cities, the brightest people of color cannot have their attention on home. They must belong to white culture.

Noah points out in his segment that France recently gave citizenship to an African man who saved a baby. Suddenly, he belonged to France. If he had committed a crime, he would, of course, still be African. "The first order of business for Africans and their relatives, African Americans," says Achebe, "is to defeat the intention Baldwin speaks about. They must work together to uncover their story, whose truth

499

has been buried so deeply in mischief and prejudice that a whole army of archeologists will now be needed to unearth it. We must be that army on both sides of the Atlantic."

Maybe the West wants the same for me — I have been an investment. It would be a shame if I offer no return on that investment. But even if I were to swim against the tide of Western intention, and connect to my native country somehow, would Iran want anything to do with me? I sound like a foreigner. I act like one. Home is never the same, for anyone, not just refugees. You go back and find that you've grown, and so has your country. Home is gone; it lives in the mind. Time exiles us all from our childhood.

Once, on a dark day, a friend quoted the late Jim Harrison to me, an echo of a warning from Rilke: *Beware, o wanderer, the road is walking too.*

By the time I was thirty, I had given that hungry immigrant girl everything she wanted. Left without goals, I felt hollowed out, without identity. Slowly I filled the void with Iranian things, all that I had ignored or put away in the quest to become American. Now firmly entrenched in my borrowed Western identity, I could afford to add a few Iranian flourishes. I cooked and cooked, trying every recipe I knew. I invited dozens of people over to taste these Persian feasts. I discovered Persian music of many eras, the art, the movies, the poetry. Before long, I was plunging back into my old life, digging for photos and videos, trying to remember. All this led, inevitably, to writing about home.

For my parents, this was a betrayal. For so many Iranians who left in their adulthood, my decade of work to shed my skin makes me ineligible to romanticize Iran. Memory is a tricky thing, and my mother prefers her own. And yet, the past, however far gone, is the business of writers; writing allows me to live in an unchanged past. In my memory, home is just the same, not a dish or a book misplaced. It's there, though returning to it may be considered a tic, an illness of the mind. Maybe it is a writer's disease, the choice to live in the waiting space forever. The refugee can leave it behind, with time, with effort. Maybe my grandmother and I share this disease because we're both writers. Wherever her letters and poems ended up, however indifferent their recipient, they were written. They existed.

My grandmother wants nothing to do with Iran. She will never return. She is English now. Those letters, though, are brimming with Iran. She puts her longing to return on the page, though she may not be aware of it. But to be united with her "other self," the person she would be if she had stayed in Iran, that would be unthinkable, an existential threat. I imagine that if she heard Baldwin lament the loss of access to his African brother, she would say that it's better for everyone to stay away.

I have spent a lot of imagination on the question of who I would be, had I stayed. What if I hadn't gotten on that plane? If I honestly wanted to know, I could: I have a half sister, now sixteen and raised in Iran.

One day in late summer, Baba phones. "Dina *joon,*" he says, "I want you to do something for your sister."

My defenses engage and I stand to pace. "What does she need?"

"She wants to go to university in England," he says. "She's smart and there's no future for her here."

"What do you want me to do?" I ask. "Why no future?"

Baba tells me that my half sister knows a girl who got a visa for a school trip and, on a stopover in Amsterdam, ripped up her passport and gave herself up as an unaccompanied minor. He says she is learning English now, that she has a place in school, that she is happy. He is convinced that if his daughter does something similar, if she becomes a refugee before she turns eighteen, the government will care for her, give her healthcare and protection. Didn't we, after all, do the same thirty years ago? Didn't we blow through a tourist visa? "You have to help your sister," he says.

"Are you crazy? How can I sponsor her if you just told me that plan?" I shout into my phone, which is already drenched in sweat. "Have you fully lost your mind? Do you know what people go through when they try that?"

He doesn't sound surprised by my reaction. "Her friend —"

"Without a passport, they'll decide her age themselves. She could end up on the streets. The bureaucrats don't care! They're paid to create mazes that will destroy your soul." I am pacing, shouting, waving my hands. Sam peeks into the room and watches me. He knows I'm on the phone with Iran.

"Yes, but we have family who could . . ." His voice is softening. Maybe he's realizing the ridiculousness of this plan. I can see that she's worked on him for weeks, months. Maybe he was reluctant at first. Maybe he still is. But who can say no to their pleading

503

children?

"Baba, did you for a second think that if she really wanted to go to university here, she would just apply?" Already I'm looking up admissions pages of British universities on my computer, looking for the section on international applicants. I find many, even one specifically for Iranians.

"Yes, but her English isn't good enough," he says. "She wouldn't pass."

Now I'm livid, because our conversation years ago is still fresh for me. I've thought about it now and then over the past decade; especially after I became a mother, I wondered, did my half sister ever learn English? "Did I not tell you to put her in English classes?"

"Yes, but, what's done is done. She's smart. She gets all twenties, like you did. Shouldn't she have the same opportunities as you?" Now I think to Katsikas, quiet Naser whose mother asked me to take him, to drop him off at a camp. How can Baba be so naive? How can he fail to realize that Iran is a good place for a Muslim girl with a family and money and a quiet village to run to on Fridays? Refugees escape because their lives are in danger. Even the ones we call "economic migrants," those so-called opportunists, they run from brutal, impoverished lives. This girl may be my own sister, but she'll have to prove her commitment to me. Because there is no native as judgmental of rule breakers as a former refugee.

"If she's so committed, then I'll help her pass the exams and fill out her application and come to the UK through the proper channels. Baba *joon,* the refugee crisis isn't about privileged daughters of Iranian dentists. To this day I feel like I'm taking someone else's place, and Maman almost got killed, remember? There are places for girls like her at the universities, if they're willing to work." Now I'm standing by a plant in my living room, picking off the leaves. Sam gestures for me to stop. I step away. "Do you know what I would've said if I were in her shoes? I would say, 'Great! I have a year to perfect my English and get into university.' If she's resisting that option, it's because her studies aren't the real priority. Do you think she couldn't get into the most mediocre British university if she tried? Because they all have loads of money, and the lowest bar, academically, is low, Baba *joon.* It's easier than the Konkour, by a lot. And, sister or not, I refuse to let you turn this girl into a refugee. Do you know what will happen? England won't be all freedom and parties and *hijab* burning.

They'll tell her that she's lying and she's actually twenty, and she'll end up on the streets or raped in a camp. Is that what you want?"

Baba is silent.

I'm panting. "Do you want me to send you links to the universities? Or I can talk to her about exam prep and how to plan for the next year. I know all about university admissions. I can edit essays —"

"She doesn't need you to do much once she's claimed asylum. You'd just vouch for her until she is settled into school . . . Isn't your work all about helping refugees?" Sam brings me a glass of water. I gulp it down noisily.

"I won't let you turn her into an unaccompanied minor when she has family and a home and food and a good education. Tell her to study. If she wants to apply to English programs, I'm here. The universities are here. Baba *joon,* she's not some poor villager born into an unlucky situation. Tell her to study. Other refugees, *all* they wish for is access to books and a good education." The memory of Shola's women emboldens me. "Education is everything. English is vital. Pay for a class. Force her to go. Then maybe she can come for a college visit and stay with me."

506

For two hours, I pace my flat. Has everyone gone mad? Have I gone mad? Am I a hypocrite? Am I appraising my half sister, who is a stranger to me but also another self, with the same casual mistrust that shades my mother and grandmother's view of new arrivals? Why do her motives infuriate me? It isn't only that I want her to work hard, or that I want to save her the torture of living as an undocumented migrant. I'm angry with her because her idea is unresearched and half-baked. Because she has a good life and resources that many migrants lack. She has the one thing I didn't: *Baba.* And she has Ardestoon's fruit orchards and Maman Masi's henna hands. She was born into a relatively modern family, and when she marries, she will (or can) marry a man who will want her to have a PhD, and a job. She is learning math and science and great Iranian literature. She is beloved, and well fed. Slowly, the Iranian women who surround her, the lawyers and activists and writers and artists and doctors back home, are asserting their identity. They are casting off the mandatory *hijab* and claiming their place in Iranian society. She can join them — or she can study quietly for a while and set off for the West. That she wants to hop down from a safe perch and breeze on into

England, right past the tortured dissidents and the starving babies, past the mothers clutching their children in boats, past Farzaneh and Majid, past Taraa and Vaild and Naser who still haunts me, past Darius, whose feet will probably never touch British or American soil, this is what angers me.

Maybe I am a hypocrite. I believe in open borders, but Europe is no paradise. The notion that the rest of the world is without beauty or joy, that everyone is clamoring to break down Europe's doors, is nonsense. For many, the West would be unequivocally worse — my mother lost her degree and worked in factories; if Iran had been safe she would never have left her home. I have no doubt that, without a university to claim my sister as its own, she would wither here. Unaccompanied minors aren't waved into the country. They are questioned, doubted. The ones without family or friends are left to sleep on park benches. They suffer, though they're so young. Each night, they fall asleep conjuring a mother's soft lap, her singular smell. They are cold, hungry. They don't savor freedom; they crave their families.

And, yes, I am selfish. I don't want to go backward. I don't want to witness the ugliness of assimilation again. I don't want to see my family ashamed, hiding tics, posturing gratitude as they carry out an endless search for home and identity. I wish I could give my half sister a tour of my inner world, the place I spend most of my time. It is a wreck. Though I've lived in the West for three decades, despite my degrees and passports and fluent English, I still carry my backpack everywhere I go. Though I have no reason to do so, I sigh in relief when my credit card goes through for a coffee. I hold my breath when checking my bank balance, for fear of a coup or a bank crash. The awe and wonder of ordinary things leaves me sometimes crippled for an hour, or a day. I marvel that I get my mail, that a bulb turns on when I tell it, that someone sells me food, that someone cuts my hair, that my days aren't apocalyptic. Now and then, without warning, I stumble into a scene that I saw on television thirty years ago, two boys wandering into a post-bomb rubble, looking for the bodies of their parents.

For a moment as I speak to Baba, I fantasize about forcing my indulged little sister to endure what Kaweh did, the long days in the library, the nonstop English radio, all that rigor — I will sit beside her and I will force the learning into her mind, and I will make her a doctor or a lawyer. I will remake her in my own image, or in the image of someone I admire, like Kaweh. But what if she rebels? What if my family isn't strong and resolute like Kaweh's, and the only explanation for my own hard work is that I arrived at the right age, and had the right influences? I don't want my half sister to think that she's coming to paradise and end up doing nothing but illegal childcare, vulnerable to every human wickedness.

All day after the call with Baba, I think of Ahmed Pouri in the airport. Would he find a way for her? Would he advise her to stay?

I don't *want* to turn back. I don't want to meet my sister, the version of me that was raised in Iran, and to face the truth that everything I hold most sacred and dear about myself was given to me by the West. I don't want to believe that I am the generic product of Eurocentric, colonialist thinking, that there is no going back, because America has remade me into its image. I don't want to believe that I come from an idle, ordinary people or that I am not an inevitable version of myself. I don't want to watch the Swiss peasant and find my history meager in comparison. I want to believe in my own agency and power. And so, whether or not I accept, as Baldwin eventually did, that it was never intended for me to look backward, that my disdain and judgment were installed there for the benefit of others, that my talents are routinely siphoned away from my own family, I turn away willingly, afraid to peek into another universe and see my own altered face.

Though I can't return, the suffering of today's refugees erodes my sense of home, acceptance, and belonging. I turn over orphan images; can I trust my memories? Each time I deposit the richest details into my fiction, I leave their wrung-out casings for my own story. And worse, I am not who I think — I am leagues worse. How did I evolve? Vladimir Nabokov writes, in *Speak, Memory:* "Neither in environment nor in heredity can I find the exact instrument that fashioned me, the anonymous roller that pressed upon my life a certain intricate watermark whose unique design becomes visible when the lamp of art is made to shine through life's foolscap."

Writing, then, is a repatriation for me, my way toward home.

Every week, I receive emails from strangers sharing stories and ideas. I love that they trust me in this way. Many, whether hostile or kind, end with a reminder that gratitude is healthy, as if to say, *Why not try it?*

How did I fail, again, to make myself understood? Every day, in the casual talk of migrants, I hear echoes of people I have known, stories I've heard, going back to Hotel Barba. "We count every second," they say, about the waiting. "If they open the door, we will repay the kindness." Everyone is jostling to show the West what a good investment, a good neighbor, he'd be. That fever doesn't just disappear as soon as the migrant is settled. Gratitude is a fact of a refugee's inner life; it doesn't need to be compelled. Every day after rescue pulses with thanks. My gratitude is personal and vast and it steers my every footfall. But it is mine. I no longer need to offer it as appeasement to citizens who had nothing to do with my rescue. Still, I know that new refugees will succumb to the instinct to bow for years, decades. It's a part of a journey toward home, wherever that is.

Westward travelers crave to repay, to prove our worth, to build homes and to abandon them and begin again. So many doors have opened to us, it's impossible to accept that there is no obligation, that we've arrived in a place we can relax and stretch out, that all the honest work to prove our worth, to assuage the helplessness, to rub out our previous identities, was for nothing. Is it possible ever to repay this imagined debt? What if we allow ourselves to relax and our children grow comfortable and entitled, demanding gratitude from the next batch knocking at the gates?

Have I demanded some kind of posturing from my own half sister?

In every generation, someone has to stay vigilant. Someone has to toil and compel others to do the same. But how to toil without bowing?

And when do the exile years finally end? My fear is that they never will; being marooned again is at once a refugee's nightmare and craving. It's a strange affliction that we immigrants share. The longing to return begins almost the instant the refugee has settled into their host country. The dream of return fuels the desire to live, and until then, to wander. We settle and take root only in each other, planting ourselves like roses at each other's houses. I like that this is an option, that maybe finding my way back home isn't an obligation, or even a possibility, for happiness.

Becoming a mother to a dark little girl with a mischievous smile in the age of Brexit and Trump terrifies me — whatever her gifts, she's going to get herself into trouble in this hateful world slowly coalescing around us. I fear the inevitable generational divide. It happened to me when I saw my mother struggle in Oklahoma, when she complained of racism and bias and lack of respect or true welcome. I thought she wasn't working hard enough. Slowly I became American, and that element that parents and children recognize in each other was no longer so easy for either of us to see.

One day, there will be an event like this, a breaking. I may look back and find that my daughter and I are foreigners, that we've drifted across different oceans. She will have chosen a country. I may have returned to Iran, or to any one of the other places where I've tried to make a home.

For now, somehow, without thinking, a village has sprung up inside my little flat. Mothers and neighbors and friends drop in. A stubborn grandmother sits at my table, being served tea and Gü. An Iran-born aunt arrives with gardening books and a loud infectious laugh. A cousin plays guitar. Elena sings and fakes Farsi words. Sam builds a shed. Home happened, just like that. It seems that I've grown roots. How did I miss *that*?

Outside our doors, things aren't as frightening as I expected in 2016. The English are kind. England might open its doors wider still. Kaweh might become an MP. Best of all, Elena is here. She has helped me connect with the child I once was, a hoarder of joy, an eccentric girl with an itchy brain.

My daughter is my repatriation. She is my taste of home. I can grow with her, carry her with me wherever I go. She will probably be free to return to her birthplace her entire life, though that doesn't mean that she will never be a stranger here, or elsewhere. Her future is a foreign place, as are all futures. But every refugee once set off into the dark, unsure of which way the road would turn — Elena, too, will make her own way.

We drift from the safe places of our childhood. There is no going back. Like stories, villages and cities are always growing or fading or melding into each other. We are all immigrants from the past, and home lives inside the memory, where we lock it up and pretend it is unchanged.

AUTHOR'S NOTE

I have tried to re-create events, locales, and conversations from my memories and interviews with others. I have changed the names of some individuals and places, as well as altered identifying characteristics and details such as physical properties, occupations, and places of residence. In general, if I have not provided a last name in the text, the first name is changed to protect the individual. Examples are Darius, Taraa, Farzaneh, Majid, Valid, Minoo, and all the children. My family, for obvious reasons, is an exception to this rule.

In recounting the escape stories of others, I have dramatized, putting as much as I could in scene. I have only written about events that were carefully recounted to me. Afterward, I researched the time and place, the context around each story, and brought the stories to life using sensory details that I found and imagined. Any mistakes are my own.

I have kept my language true to particular times and places. For example, though I use the word "undocumented" now, I didn't in the 1980s. Our word then was "illegal." Even now, in the casual talk of refugees and lawyers, the word I hear is "illegal." Sanitizing language has its dangers. I tried not to do that, even with my own thoughts. For example, I don't use the word "pussy" now to describe weakness. But I did at sixteen.

Regarding the story of Kambiz Roustayi, the scenes before his arrival in Europe are imagined using what little he told his friends and supporters. Scenes from later in his life, after he had met the people I interviewed, are their accounts of his years in Holland.

The line of poetry from the parliament petition in March 2018 is quoted from a public reading. The poet's name is withheld since she may not be documented.

In the portions of this book about my own life, my accounts are true according to my memory and perspective.

ACKNOWLEDGMENTS

Many thanks to Jamie Byng, who believed in this book when it was just an idea. And to Jonathan Lee, with whom I've wanted to work for years. Thank you, my brilliant editor Simon Thorogood, who understood and protected my vision (sometimes from myself), and my amazing American editor, Megha Majumdar, who challenged me always to improve. Thank you to my UK agent Georgina Capel and her team, and, most of all, to my faithful and wise agent Kathleen Anderson, who has had my back for so many years.

To the refugee support community in London, you've been so generous. Thank you for opening your doors to me and for sharing your wisdom and stories. To the impossibly kind Paul Hutchings of Refugee Support and his cofounder John Sloan, and Jon Slack of SINGA UK, Anneke Elwes of HostNation, and Dr. Shola Mos-Shogbamimu, Natasha Walter, and all the brave and hard-working ladies at Women for Refugee Women: I'm proud to know you. To Steve Crawshaw of Human Rights Watch and Freedom from Torture, Melissa Fleming of UNHCR, Eduard Nazarski and Annemarie Busser of Amnesty International Netherlands, and Anneke Van Woudenberg of RAID, and to asylum lawyers Kaweh Beheshtizadeh, Marq Wijngaarden, and Frank van Haren, and human rights lawyer Daniel Leader: thank you for smoothing so many paths. Parvis Noshirrani, thank you for telling me Kambiz's story and for that extraordinary lunch that you conjured. Ahmed Pouri, thank you for giving your life to the refugees in the Netherlands, for sharing your stories with me, and for the nuts. Thank you, cousins Pooyan Tamimi Arab, Sara Emami, and Forough Tamimi for the talks, and Kate Wiedmann Punwani for offering me a beautiful place to sleep in Amsterdam. Ros Ereira of Solidarity with Refugees (c/o Amnesty International), who spends her days thinking of ways to mend the hidden wounds of the displaced — going so far as to petition television shows like *Coronation Street* to introduce refugee storylines, in an effort to normalize their struggles for the British — you jump-started

520

my research with your generosity, opening your Rolodex and introducing me to what seemed like every refugee helper in London. You are a star! Thank you to Ariane Simard who introduced me to her incredible refugee writing workshop for Bard College Berlin. And to my friend, journalist Jen Percy, who, before I left for Greece, reminded me that sometimes the search is the story. My thanks to Iowa City, UNESCO City of Literature for recognizing this work with funding and support through the Paul Engle Prize.

Finally, to my family around the world, especially my parents. To my partner, Samuel Leader, who ran our lives as I traveled and wrote. And to all of the asylum seekers, refugees, and otherwise displaced people in these pages who entrusted me with their stories. Thank you.

ABOUT THE AUTHOR

Dina Nayeri was born in Iran during the revolution and arrived in the United States when she was ten years old. She is the winner of the UNESCO City of Literature Paul Engle Prize and a National Endowment for the Arts literature grant, as well as a finalist for the Rome Prize and a *Granta* New Voices pick. Nayeri is the author of two novels — *Refuge* and *A Teaspoon of Earth and Sea* — and her work has been translated into fourteen languages and published in *The New York Times, The Guardian, The Wall Street Journal, Granta, The Best American Short Stories, The O. Henry Prize Stories*, and many other publications. *The Ungrateful Refugee* is her first book of nonfiction. A graduate of Princeton, Harvard, and the Iowa Writers' Workshop, she lives in London and in Paris, where she is currently a Fellow at the Columbia Institute for Ideas and Imagination.